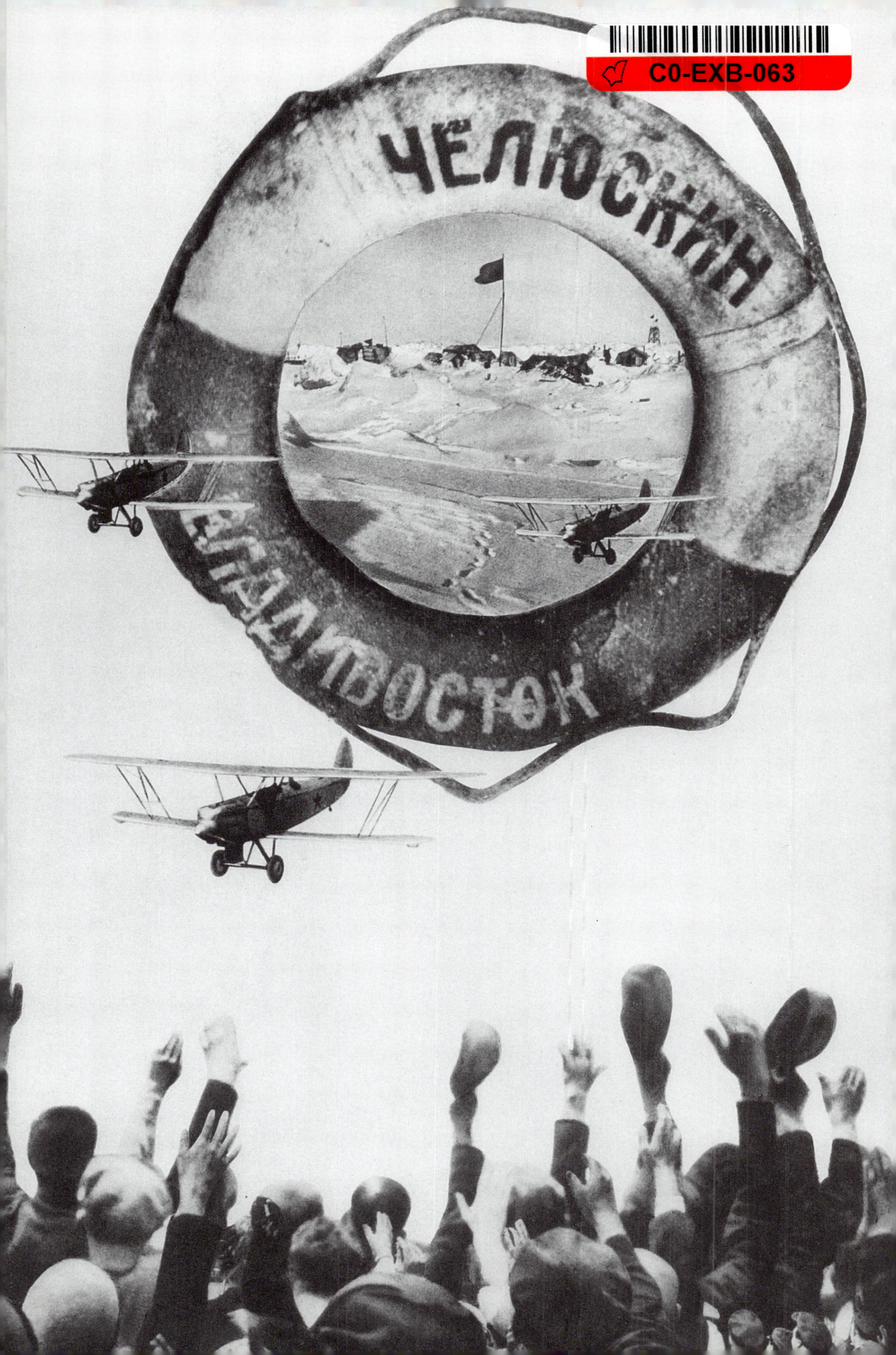
ЧЕЛЮСКИН

Ru

ssian

Modernism

Ru

Published by the Getty Research Institute for the History of Art and the Humanities

ssian Modernism

The Collections of the Getty Research Institute for the History of Art and the Humanities, 1

Introduction by Jean-Louis Cohen
Compiled and annotated by
David Woodruff and Ljiljana Grubišić

Bibliographies & Dossiers

The Getty Research Institute Publications and Exhibitions Program
Julia Bloomfield, JoAnne C. Paradise, Thomas F. Reese, Salvatore Settis, *Editors*

Bibliographies & Dossiers

Russian Modernism:
The Collections of the Getty Research Institute
for the History of Art and the Humanities, 1
Lynne Kostman, *Managing Editor*
Diane Mark-Walker, *Manuscript Editor*

Published by The Getty Research Institute
for the History of Art and the Humanities,
Santa Monica, CA 90401-1455
 Published 1997
Printed in the United States of America.

03 02 01 00 99 98 97 7 6 5 4 3 2 1

Jean-Louis Cohen's Introduction was translated by Christian Hubert.
Frontispiece: Photomontage including a life preserver with the words *Cheliuskin* and *Vladivostok*. From *SSSR na stroike*, no. 12 (1935), French edition. See no. 752.

Library of Congress Cataloging-in-Publication Data
Russian Modernism: collections of the Getty Research Institute
for the History of Art and the Humanities / introduction by
Jean-Louis Cohen; compiled and annotated by David Woodruff
and Ljiljana Grubišić.
p. cm. — (Bibliographies & dossiers)
Includes bibliographical references and index.
ISBN 0-89236-385-1
1. Russia — Civilization — 1801–1917 — Bibliography.
2. Soviet Union — Civilization — Bibliography. 3. Modernism
(Aesthetics) — Bibliography.
I. Cohen, Jean-Louis. II. Woodruff, David, 1940– .
III. Grubišić, Ljiljana. IV. Series.
Z2508.R87 1997
[DK260]
016.947'07 — dc20 96-34896
CIP

Contents

Notes to the Reader

Nearly all bibliographies demand a unique format tailored to the particular collection represented, and this bibliography is no exception. Following is a brief explanation of the types of materials included and how the individual entries have been arranged.

The present volume covers Russian Modernist periodicals, monographs, and ephemera in the collection of the Getty Research Institute for the History of Art and the Humanities; it does not include the Research Institute's complete holdings in the area of Russian art and literature. (Comprehensive information about the Research Institute's ever-growing collection of Russian materials can be accessed through an on-line database available to researchers and visitors.) In addition to Russian works of Modernist art and literature, the bibliography includes Russian translations of foreign authors, foreign translations of Russian authors, and non-Russian periodicals designed by prominent Russian artists. A few children's books related to the avant-garde movements in Russia are also listed. Although the Research Institute's holdings were assembled with a primary interest in works that are of art-historical relevance, items whose value is chiefly literary are also present either because of their noteworthy typography and layout or because they came as part of purchased collections.

The main entries in this bibliography are ordered according to letter-by-letter alphabetization. The Library of Congress system of Russian transliteration was employed with the exception of the names of well-known individuals, the spelling of which has been established in North American publishing usage. Diacritical marks have been omitted except for the apostrophe, which is used to convey the soft sign, and the quotation mark, which is used to convey the hard sign. Wherever possible, standardized first and last names of individuals are used, not nicknames or variants that may appear on the piece itself. For nearly all entries a transliterated title is given, followed by the Cyrillic title and its English translation. The subtitles of periodicals are mentioned only if they add substantive information about the nature of the publication or if they are essential to identifying it. The facts of publication are included whenever known, as are the number of pages and a work's dimensions. (The standard library cataloging practice is followed here, in which only the height measurement is provided except in those cases where the width exceeds the height.) Often there were several publishers of a particular periodical during the course of its existence. Where this is known, the publisher of the first issue is listed and the statement "publisher varies" appears in the annotation. In the case of monographs, the number of plates is provided and, where a book is divided into distinct sections, a series of numbers in the first part of the entry describes the number of pages in each section. In all entries, brackets around information such as an author's name or the date of publication indicate that it is verified but does not appear printed on the piece itself. If the number of pages or leaves is not listed, the reader may assume that the work is not paginated.

The annotations of the periodical entries provide information about the key people associated with the publication, whether it was the organ of an institution, the history of that institution, the subject areas the periodical covered, how many issues were published, and whether it was a continuation of another periodical or was later continued under another name itself. Often the editor of a periodical changed frequently, and readers should not assume that the editor listed, generally the most prominent or important editor, was the only editor involved. Likewise, only the most important contributors of articles and illustrations, particularly those whose names are main entries elsewhere in the bibliography, are listed. Artworks mentioned in the annotations should be assumed to be reproductions unless otherwise indicated. When a periodical is known to have altered its frequency of publication—for example, from a monthly to a quarterly—the annotation includes the phrase "irregularly published." If the Research Institute owns a complete run of a given title, no information about the Research Institute's holdings is provided. In other cases the statement "scattered issues" appears. The Research Institute's collection in this area continues to grow at a rapid rate, and readers who inquire directly may well learn that complete runs of such periodicals have been assembled at the Research Institute since the publication of this bibliography.

Insofar as such could be ascertained, the annotations of the monograph entries provide information about the designers of the book's various components, its artistic and literary contributors, the subject matter, significant dedications and inscriptions, the materials and printing techniques in cases where such are unusual, the copy number, and the size of the edition. As in the case of periodicals, not all of the contributors to miscellanies and other collective works are necessarily listed. For a monograph whose cover bears the imprinted initials of its artist, the annotation reads "cover signed *artist's initials,*" followed by the artist's name if such could be determined. Any remarks on the condition of the Research Institute's copy of an item are provided at the end of the annotation.

Introduction

Jean-Louis Cohen

In his contribution to the *Gutenberg Jahrbuch* of 1927, El Lissitzky claimed that ten years after the October Revolution, the "book" had become the "most monumental work of art" in the USSR.[1] In so doing, he underscored both the desire to make the publications of the New Russia reach a broader audience and the effort of the avant-garde movements to "reconstruct" books and periodicals. In the course of some twenty years, the entire realm of publications in Russia was affected by the conjunction of unprecedented changes in the political sphere—as a result of the revolutions of 1905 and 1917—and especially by an extraordinary explosion of new artistic strategies.

The Russian production of printed matter during this period was situated at the intersection of public life and literary and artistic activity, and the documents that form the collection of Russian and Soviet material at the Getty Research Institute for the History of Art and the Humanities reflect this convergence. The collection attests to the importance that the Research Institute places on the material evidence of the intellectual exchanges that define twentieth-century art and also highlights the significance of publications as a specific type of production—one that is a worthy object of study within many disciplines. Even the most cursory glance at this collection—from the woodcuts of the Primitivists to the "words in freedom" of the Futurist poems to the propaganda photomontages—cannot help but draw the viewer into an intense and contradictory universe in which the emergence, affirmation, and crisis of the various avant-garde movements are evident.

In order to appreciate the usefulness of the Getty Research Institute's collection and to understand its specific characteristics, one must recall the conditions under which researchers have hitherto had to work. Before 1991, the difficulty in gaining access to sources and archives in the Soviet Union was aggravated by the weakness and incoherence of all but a few Western collections.[2] More recently, these collections, both public and private, have been expanded greatly and have been the focus of scholarly examination,[3] while Russian resources have become more accessible. The Getty Research Institute's holdings, although relatively limited in quantity, must be seen in this context. The originality of the collection lies not in its California location—unquestionably outside the theater of Russian and European history—but in its documentary and scholarly ambitions.

The aim of the Getty Research Institute's collection of Russian Modernist materials is not to compete with the great bibliographic or museological holdings that already exist in older or larger institutions but to allow researchers a direct glimpse of certain extremely fragile documents. The fact that many were printed surreptitiously in no way detracts from their historical importance. Either impossible to find or accessible only through photographs or copies, a number of these publications originally were intended to reach a rather rarefied circle, in some cases an intimate one. Yet others were meant to reach a very large audience, especially after the Revolution of 1917. Over time many of these works have acquired the status of museum pieces. They have become collectibles and objects of speculation in the art market.[4] These developments have introduced new risks and problems for institutions providing access to this material—a situation that is all the more regrettable because reproductions are not adequate for scholarly study. The original dimensions, the papers and inks, and the very construction of these printed works carry significant information that is irretrievably lost or blurred in the process of reproduction, no matter how technically sophisticated.

The Getty Research Institute's collection is not the result of a premeditated plan but is rather an accumulation of different types of holdings, each with its own specific history, complemented by strategic purchases. At the core of the collection are several hundred books and periodicals acquired by the Parisian collector Marc Martin-Malburet, procured for the most part from among the *bukinisty* (secondhand or antiquarian booksellers) of Moscow and Leningrad, often at a ridiculously low price, or, on occasion, from the families of the artists. Thus a copy of *Faktura* (Texture), written by Vladimir Markov and published in 1914, bears Ivan Puni's signature. Other individual works and collections acquired by the Getty Research Institute from artists' families, collectors, and galleries reflect the interest with which certain European intellectuals regarded the Russian scene. This is the case, for example, with the issues of the Constructivist journal *Sovremennaia arkhitektura* (Contemporary architecture) that were part of the Prague critic Karel Teige's library and were acquired by the Getty Research Institute. Building on this composite foundation, the breadth and structure of the collection is sure to be transformed in the coming years.

There is no doubt that the Getty Research Institute's collection covers only an infinitesimal part of the vast printed production of the intellectual and cultural movements that held the Russian stage during the three decades following the Revolution of 1905. Nevertheless, it gathers together coherent groups of the essential published works of authors as important as Velimir Khlebnikov, Aleksei Kruchenykh, and Vladimir Mayakovsky. The almost comprehensive sets of Kazimir Malevich's publications and the works designed by Aleksandr Rodchenko or Lissitzky contain extremely important samples of the production of those artists. An archive, purchased in 1995, composed of 126 letters written by El Lissitzky to his wife, Es (Sophie Küppers), together with a variety of biographical materials certainly represents the largest holding of documents on this artist west of Moscow. The Getty Research Institute's Russian Modernist holdings are less complete when it comes to other graphic designers such as Gustav Klutsis, whose work has only recently begun to receive the attention of scholars,[5] and Solomon Telingater, but the collection as a whole nonetheless affords a fairly representative sample of the period's new ideals and strategies in art, architecture, and literature.

Unillustrated narratives and poems naturally find their place in the Getty Research Institute's collection along with those publications where the pictorial component is at least partially, if not exclusively, dominant, and they are thus included among the holdings presented here. These publications grew out of the same radical culture, even if the composition of words on the page was not, in itself, a site of innovation and subversion.[6] It would have been a mistake, for example, to exclude Mayakovsky's poetry collections from this survey of the Getty Research Institute's Russian holdings, since they also belong, if only by virtue of their covers, to the visual chronicle of the avant-garde.[7] In general, typography, with its varying effects determined by the choice of font, the pagination, and the margins and rules, is a communicative element in itself, distinct from the layout of the text and from the illustrations. Under certain conditions literary and typographical innovation coincide perfectly, as is the case in *Dlia golosa* (For voice), 1923, a collection of poems written by Mayakovsky and designed by Lissitzky. For the same reasons, a significant part of the Research Institute's children books has been included, this type of literature often having provided a framework for experimentation in typography and illustration.

I believe that the Getty Research Institute's Russian Modernist holdings are best characterized as a *study collection.* Like the curiosity cabinets of Enlightenment scholars, the collection both describes a certain state of knowledge and permits the development of new interpretations. Evoking the storage cases of natural scientists or archaeologists, the collection affords a useful reduction of a real world, the infinitely rich possibilities of which it cannot exhaust.

The task of describing the collection is made all the more delicate by the fact that the intensity of Russian literary and artistic production between the turn of the century and the Stalinist freeze is fully in keeping with the changes experienced by a country subject in turn to capitalist modernization, war, revolution, and a social and cultural fermentation abruptly fixed in place. If it is clear that the contradictory succession of initiatives in the modernization of Russian culture did not derive directly from the great political divides that cut across the first decades of the twentieth century, it is no less clear that these initiatives influenced and were influenced by successive political events, starting at least with the Revolution of 1905. In these few pages I cannot set forth a complete description of the many forms of affirmation and of crisis engaged in by the innovative groups represented in the Getty Research Institute's collection.[8] Instead, I will restrict myself to sketching out some specific conjunctures or *chronotopes*,[9] to use Mikhail Bakhtin's term, by which groups can be characterized and through which individuals can be situated. Each of the historical situations through which the ideals of the Russian intellectuals evolved is represented by a specific group of works featured in the collection.[10]

From the Revolution of 1905 to the outbreak of World War I, the first *chronotope* favored the development of new orientations among both writers and artists who worked independently and those who collaborated on projects. During this period the Russians assimilated European movements ranging from Symbolism to Neoclassicism and Art Nouveau. With the exhaustion of the production of the World of Art circle, younger artists established their identities in relation to Cubism or Futurism.[11] Valerii Briusov's *Urbi et orbi*, 1903—one of the earliest works in the collection—reflects the influence of Viennese typography in particular, and the volumes from the review *Apollon* after 1909 resemble the production of the World of Art artists. After a few somewhat limited initial attempts, Andrey Bely introduced in his prose poem *Chetvertaia simfoniia* (Fourth symphony) a decoupage of the text and a manipulation of the paragraphs that heralded a new era in the visual articulation of literary works. Although still limited by the constraints of typography, Kruchenykh broke with tradition in 1912 when he began to circulate handwritten books, well represented in the Getty Research Institute's collection by *Pomada* (Pomade), 1913, *Mirskontsa* (Worldbackward), 1912, *Starinnaia liubov'* (Old-fashioned love), 1912, and *Vzorval'* (Explodity), 1913. Contemporary collective works such as *Sadok sudei* (A trap for judges), 1910–1913, *Poshchechina obshchestvennomu vkusu* (A slap in the face of public taste), 1912, and the essays by Bubnovyi valet (Jack of diamonds), 1913, attest to the joint efforts of writers and artists to break the boundaries that divided Russian institutions and disciplines. During this period exceptional encounters between the explorers of new forms were marked by works such as the opera *Pobeda nad solntsem* (Victory over the sun), written by Kruchenykh, set to music by Mikhail Matiushin, and choreographed by Malevich in 1913 at the Luna Park Theater in Saint Petersburg. In addition, beginning in 1914, artists involved in the creation of *lubok* prints devoted to war propaganda produced many provocative images.

During the second *chronotope,* from 1914 to the beginning of the 1920s, different camps can be defined in exclusive relation to a radical culture, even though World War I, the Revolution of 1917, and the Civil War had altered the stakes of their initial explorations. After *Posledniaia futuristicheskaia vystavka kartin: 0.10* (The last Futurist exhibition: 0.10), held in 1915 in Petrograd, a division emerged between the followers of Malevich, who espoused his theory of Suprematism, and the partisans of Tatlin, who would develop Constructivism. Although this phase was less intense than both its predecessor and its successor, it is at this point that the fundamental breaks come to light and new political and artistic laboratories begin to emerge, starting in 1917. Malevich founded Affirmers of the New Art (UNOVIS) in Vitebsk, and the printed milestones that mark the thought of the founder of Suprematism constitute one of the jewels of the Research Institute's collection.

The third *chronotope*, which lasted through the 1920s, encompassed the cultural and institutional construction of a new social system issuing from the Revolution of 1917. It was a period during which the previous lines of research were consolidated, at least provisionally.[12] With the exhibition *5 × 5 = 25* and the third Society of Young Artists (OBMOKhU) exhibition, both held in 1921, the Constructivists fully emerged on the artistic scene. Slightly later, in the architectural arena, they opposed the rationalists, who had nonetheless already established their hegemony in the Higher State Artistic and Technical Workshops (VKhUTEMAS),[13] the new school created in 1920, represented by significant samples of works in the collection. The research of Nikolai Tarabukin, Aleksei Gan, and Boris Arvatov on the "art of production" combined with a taste for elementary figures that was shared by the entire avant-garde. Against this backdrop, the book and print played an essential role in the "cultural revolution" that seized the entire country. The didactic goal of this revolution was evident in books for children and in illustrated magazines. Collaborations between artists and writers took on a new dimension once the problem of "illustration" gave way to the "common work of the author and *Gestalter,*" as Lissitzky described it.[14] His little visual narrative, *Pro dva kvadrata* (Concerning two squares), 1922, for example, which he both wrote and illustrated, is presented as having been "constructed" rather than laid out on the page. Even the act of reading was described by Lissitzky as a piece of "construction" to be carried out "with scissors and glue."[15]

The fourth and final *chronotope*, the period from the end of the 1920s to the USSR's entry into World War II in 1941, was marked by the modernization of the Russian economy (introduced through the five-year plans) and was accompanied by the increasingly explicit politicization of literary, artistic, and architectural practices. For the most part, this new direction reflected the expectations formulated by the majority of the intellectuals who had rallied to the new regime. The celebration of the industrial epic was hardly difficult for the academic artists who had survived and prospered by virtue of the institutional commissions received in the twenties. Such a perspective, incidentally, would not in any way have startled the adherents of "literature of fact," which Sergei Tret'iakov and certain editors of the journal *Lef* invoked in their manifestos during the 1920s.[16] The work of Rodchenko and Klutsis answered the call for a literature that used the techniques of reporting and also explored the new practice of photomontage.[17] Far from stopping in 1932 with the "reorganization" of the literary and artistic unions through the decrees of the Central Committee of the Communist Party, artists experimented with many different approaches during the first stage of Constructivism until the war, particularly in illustrated publications such as *SSSR na stroike* (USSR in construction). It was thus logical to extend the period covered in the collection through the decade from 1932 to the war—a period during which the irresistible rise of "socialist" realism was accompanied by the late Constructivist strategies—and to include rare periodicals such as the weekly *Arkhitekturnaia gazeta* (Architectural gazette), which mirrors the takeover of the architectural community by Stalinist agents.[18]

The divisions set forth above are probably somewhat schematic. They cannot fully account for the activities of certain major figures of the avant-garde, such as Kruchenykh, Mayakovsky, or Malevich, even when their work betrays the effects of political circumstances that were internalized with varying degrees of ruse or sincerity. For example, shortly before his suicide in 1930, Mayakovsky joined the conservative Russian Association of Proletarian Writers (RAPP). This was an unexpected gesture from the perspective of his colleagues on the left. Malevich returned to a figurative painting style in the early 1930s. The changing relations with the West—which although productive were more difficult and less intense from 1925 on—influenced the thoughts of such intermediaries as Lissitzky and Il'ia Erenburg, as well as their less cosmopolitan contemporaries.

The identity of the Getty Research Institute's collection, placed in its historical context in the first part of this essay, is defined both by coherent groups of work and a profusion of isolated objects. It also places emphasis on certain genres whose growth was spurred by the October Revolution. I have already referred to the literary miscellanies and to the importance of collaborative works in the emergence of the avant-garde movements from Futurism to Constructivism. This group of documents constitutes one of the major resources of the collection. Some particularly remarkable pieces in this set are the handmade books of Kruchenykh and Khlebnikov and works such as *Avtografy* (Autographs), 1919, where every poem is written in longhand by the contributors, including Konstantin Bal'mont, Sergei Esenin, Boris Pasternak, and even Anatoly Lunacharsky, the future People's Commissar for Education. In these works, as well as in the two volumes of *Sadok sudei*, one sees the transcription of a poetic impulse that is sustained by the trembling of the hand, echoing Nikolai Feodorov's analyses of medieval manuscripts.[19] The use of rough and recycled papers, the lithographic impressions, and, on occasion, the addition of handwriting and rubber stamping, as well as drawing, all indicate the intentional primitivism of this corpus of works.

It is not only in the collaborative works but also in the individual publications that one sees the mutually enriching encounters between new literary and artistic themes, for example, in the collaboration between the poet Khlebnikov and the artist Pavel Filonov in Khlebnikov's *Izbornik stikhov* (Selected verse), 1915. The Getty Research Institute collection also contains important indices of the autonomous development of each practice: in the later editions of the great poetic texts, such as Aleksandr Blok's *Dvenadtsat'* (The twelve) and Il'ia Zdanevich's *lidantIU fAram* (Le-Dantiu as a lighthouse), which he published in Paris. The same holds true of the publications linked to exhibitions such as the collection authored by Bubnovyi valet, and to the theoretical writings of artists. One can thus trace Malevich's affirmation of Suprematism and Lissitzky's later break with Malevich's ideas in the sequence leading from Malevich's manifesto *Suprematizm: 34 risunka* (Suprematism: Thirty-four drawings), 1921, via Lissitzky's story *Pro dva kvadrata*, to the latter's portfolio of lithographs for *Sieg über die Sonne* (Victory over the sun), 1923.

As for the consolidation of Constructivist discourse, it is documented as much by the theoretical contributions of Gan (*Konstruktivizm*, 1922), Tarabukin (*Ot mol'berta k mashine* [From easel to machine], 1923), and Ginzburg (*Stil' i epokha* [Style and epoch], 1924), as it is by certain catalogs that in themselves constitute unique artworks. One example in the Research Institute's collection is the booklet that accompanied the exhibition *5 × 5 = 25*, held at the Club of the All-Russia Poets Union in Moscow in September 1921. In contrast to the accent on mechanical reproduction, which later became a major concern of the Constructivists, Varvara Stepanova used a typewriter to create twenty-five copies of the booklet in which were pasted original gouaches or drawings by each of the five participating artists (Stepanova, Rodchenko,

Aleksandr Vesnin, Liubov' Popova, and Alexandra Exter). In this booklet Stepanova calls for the passage from "composition" to "construction," echoing the contemporary discussions being held at the Institute of Artistic Culture (INKhUK). In this and other catalogs in the Research Institute's collection, the contributions of the artists and the Constructivist designers are most evident and even some exhibitions devoted to technological, professional, or political issues come to life.

Alongside these works more intimate material—such as several Lissitzky documents or the photographic album that Ekaterina Esenin, the sister of Sergei Esenin, published in 1928 after the poet's death—restores the human dimension to this otherwise literary chronicle. Smaller theoretical works without visual value, such as Markov's *Faktura* also help animate the discussion. In addition, developments in cinema and other new mass-communication genres are represented in the collection, for example in such books and periodicals as *Vestnik kinematografii* (Herald of cinematography), *Ekran* (Screen), *Kino i zhizn'* (Cinema and life), *Novaia rampa* (New footlights), and *Zrelishcha* (Spectacles), a journal that covered a wide range of disciplines. The theoretical and concrete transformations of architecture in the 1920s and 1930s are amply documented. The most important books recording the debate on the form of cities, such as Nikolai Miliutin's *Sotsgorod* (The socialist city), 1930, or on collective habitation, such as the publications of the *Stroikom* (Construction committee) studies, are in the Getty Research Institute's collection as well as the three portfolios of fantastic architecture by the visionary Iakov Chernikhov.[20] The very layout of the page of these architectural collections and journals constituted an important cultural contribution. For example, see Vesnin's design of the short-lived *Arkhitektura,* Gan's page layouts for *Sovremennaia arkhitektura*, and covers of the municipal journal *Stroitel'stvo Moskvy* (Construction of Moscow), which were often entrusted to the Stenberg brothers and to Klutsis.[21]

Other areas of postrevolutionary cultural politics are also well represented in the Getty Research Institute's collection. Art education, for example, had become one of the principal scenes of the confrontation between the adherents of an art consciously submitted to the agenda of industrial production and those of more conservative "applied" art. The *Distsipliny VKhUTEMAS* (The disciplines of VKhUTEMAS) portfolio and the booklet entitled *Arkhitektura: Raboty arkhitekturnogo fakul'teta VKhUTEMAS* (Architecture: Works by the architectural faculty of VKhUTEMAS) whose cover was designed by Lissitzky, attest to the founding moment of the new school as well as to the period of specialization of production.[22] In another area altogether, scholars can trace the Russian avant-garde's interest in aviation through a set of plates by Nataliia Goncharova, *Misticheskie obrazy voiny* (Mystical images of war), 1914, and the poetry collection *Lët* (Flight), published in 1923 with a cover by Rodchenko.[23]

Neither architecture, pedagogy, nor any other discipline, however, developed within an entirely Russian space. An extreme attention to Western currents is apparent at every turn in modernist Russian culture. Ivan Aksenov's book *Pikasso i okresnosti* (Picasso and environs), 1917, for example, reflects a knowledge of the Parisian scene.[24] The Russian idealization of America after 1917 can be read in productions as disparate as Marietta Shaginian's serial novel *Mess mend*, whose installments appeared with covers by Rodchenko (and in a cinematic version by Boris Barnet in 1926) and the Russian translation in 1929 of Richard Neutra's *Wie baut Amerika?* (How does America build?).[25] More generally, architects' interest in Western culture occasioned publications devoted specifically to the subject, represented in the collection by *Arkhitektura sovremennogo zapada* (Contemporary architecture of the West), edited by David Arkin, and *Iskusstvo bytovoi veshchi* (The art of everyday objects), 1932. Even the magazine *Arkhitektura za rubezhom* (Architecture abroad), published between 1934 and 1937, still concentrated on modernist currents in Europe and America, despite Russia's turn in 1932 toward cultural autarchy. *Planirovka goroda* (City planning), 1933, the belated translation of Le Corbusier's *Urbanisme*, 1924, and the only one of his books to reach the Russian public before the 1960s, is also found in the collection. Conversely, Russian publication for export is documented by the Soviet Union's catalog for the 1925 *Exposition des arts décoratifs et industriels* in Paris and in *Russland: Die Rekonstruktion der Architektur in der Sowjetunion*, 1930, published by Lissitzky as part of a monograph series for which he designed the covers.[26]

The documents that reveal the political and cultural transformations of the 1930s round out the Getty Research Institute's Russian Modernist collection. Such changes are sometimes best seen in the graphic design of a publication. Thus, for example, *Brigada khudozhnikov* (Artists' brigade), the organ of the Federation of Associations of Workers in the Spatial Arts, reflects the proletarian critique of "Art of the Left" insofar as the publication's typography evolved between 1931 and 1932 from a pseudo-Constructivist aesthetic to a far more conservatively organized page. Even more revealing are the Constructivists' page layouts after 1930, including special editions with large print runs such as the issue of *Ogonek* (Little fire) devoted to the subtropical regions on the banks of the Black Sea (designed by Lissitzky in 1934)[27] or the many issues of *SSSR na stroike*. In addition to Lissitzky, Rodchenko, Stepanova, and Telingater, many other "constructors" of books in the 1920s became associated with the latter review, which also published contributions by Tret'iakov and Isaak Babel'. The issue with foldouts on parachuting, designed by Stepanova and Rodchenko, and the issue devoted to the expedition of the icebreaker *Cheliuskin,* designed by Lissitzky, remain extraordinary examples of kinetic or interactive publications.[28] In order to publicize to the outside world Stalin's great construction projects, *SSSR na stroike* printed large-format photographs by Max Al'pert, Semen Fridliand, and Arkadii Shaikhet at the heliographic presses of Goznak, the ministry department that supervised the printing of bank notes.[29]

Between the Futurist almanacs distributed in elite circles before 1914 and later publications aimed at a wider public, one can trace not only the history of Russian Modernist culture but also the history of the press and the techniques of printing. The early subversive works that used woodcuts or lithography, sometimes on found paper, appear willful and provocative. This combination of willful primitivism and artistic experimentation was later supplanted by the prosaic reality of printed production in the Soviet era. If *SSSR na stroike* and a few art books escaped the effects of the economic depression that characterized the late 1920s, technical innovations were increasingly limited to the covers of publications—in the following decades the photoengraving and especially the typography of the inner pages would fade into a hopeless grisaille, a most unexpected result of the passage to industrial production that the Constructivists had expected would lead to a new liberation.

As a whole the Russian Modernist material in the Getty Research Institute collection illustrates the extraordinary cultural ferment in early twentieth-century Russia. Today these theoretical, poetic, and visual sources retain all their relevance even as the "Elektrobibliothek" that Lissitzky so boldly prophesied in 1923[30] takes form in conservation institutions storing microfilms and, in particular, digitized documents. And yet the smell of the ink, the imprint of the typographic press, the grain of the paper, the texture of the binding fabric, and especially the dimensions and weight of the volumes remain significant for scholarly research.

The very existence of such a collection, which permits a visual and *tactile* relation to this material, might seem to run counter to the concern of the Constructivists and certain avante-garde groups for the popular circulation of their work. In this context, however, we should recall the proposal that Stepanova made in the *5 × 5 = 25* catalog—she imagined that through the new reproducibility of objects museums would be transformed into open "archives."[31] Herein lies, ultimately, the identity and the destiny of the materials to be found in the list that follows.

Notes

1. El Lissitzky, "Unser Buch," in A. Ruppel, ed., *Gutenberg Jahrbuch 1927* (Mainz: Verlag der Gutenberg-Gesellschaft, 1926–1927), 178.

2. Among the very first generation of publications is Camilla Gray, *The Great Experiment: Russian Art, 1863–1922* (New York: Abrams, 1962).

3. Among the publications specifically devoted to the Western collections, see Susan P. Compton, *The World Backwards: Russian Futurist Books, 1912–16* (London: British Museum Publications, 1978); Edward Kasinec and Robert Davis, "Russian Book Arts on the Eve of World War One: The New York Public Library Collections," *The Journal of Decorative and Propaganda Arts*, no. 14 (Fall 1989): 94–111; and Irena Zantovská Murray, *Architectural Drawings of the Russian Avant-Garde, 1917–1935: Soviet Avant-Garde Publications* (Montreal: Canadian Centre for Architecture, 1991).

4. On the positive side, the new visibility of the publications of the Russian avant-garde has been supported by the Getty Research Institute's generous lending policy for recent exhibitions.

5. See the first monograph devoted to this artist: Hubertus Gassner and Roland Nachtigaeller, eds., *Gustav Klutsis: Retrospektive* (Stuttgart: G. Hatje, 1991).

6. For a pioneering discussion of this process see Gerald Janecek, *The Look of Russian Literature: Avant-Garde Visual Experiments, 1900–1930* (Princeton, N.J.: Princeton Univ. Press, 1984).

7. Mayakovsky also created a considerable number of illustrations and posters.

8. See, among the recent interpretations published in English, Evgenii Kovtun, "Experiments in Book Design by Russian Artists," *The Journal of Decorative and Propaganda Arts*, no. 5 (Summer 1987): 46–59.

9. The *chronotope* is for Bakhtin the place where and the time when an action is set in a literary text—concepts that are inseparable. See Mikhail Bakhtin, *The Dialogic Imagination: Four Essays*, ed. Michael Holquist, trans. Caryl Emerson and Michael Holquist (Austin: Univ. of Texas Press, 1981).

10. Richard Stites, *Revolutionary Dreams: Utopian Visions and Experimental Life in the Russian Revolution* (New York: Oxford Univ. Press, 1989).

11. Regarding the production of these latter individuals, see Evgenii Kovtun, *Russkaia futuristicheskaia kniga* (Moscow: Kniga, 1989).

12. Among recent interpretations of this phase, see Susan Compton, "The Art of the Soviet Book, 1922–1932," in *The Great Utopia: The Russian and Soviet Avant-Garde, 1915–1932* (New York: Solomon R. Guggenheim Museum, 1992).

13. Christina Lodder, *Russian Constructivism* (New Haven, Conn.: Yale Univ. Press, 1983).

14. El Lissitzky, "Do Not Separate Form from Content! The Polygraphic Design of

Newspapers, Magazines, and Books," transcript of a discussion at the House of the Soviet Press, Moscow, *Brigada khudozhnikov,* no. 4 (1931): 21.

15. The address books of Lissitzky held at the Research Institute bear witness to the wide range of contacts he had with intellectuals, as well as with architects and artists.

16. Benjamin H. D. Buchloh, "From Faktura to Factography," *October,* no. 30 (1984): 82–119.

17. Margarita Tupytsin, "From the Politics of Montage to the Montage of Politics: Soviet Practice 1919 through 1937," in Matthew Teitelbaum, ed., *Montage and Modern Life, 1919–1942* (Cambridge, Mass.: MIT Press, 1992).

18. See the detailed analysis of this process in Hugh D. Hudson, Jr., *Blueprints and Blood: The Stalinization of Soviet Architecture, 1917–1937* (Princeton: Princeton University Press, 1994).

19. Nikolai Fedorov, "O pismenakh," *Vesy* 1, no. 6 (1904): 1–5.

20. On the work of the latter, see Anatolii Strigalev and Arthur R. Sprague, *Iakov Chernikhov: The Logic of Fantasy* (New York: Graduate School of Architecture, Planning and Preservation, Columbia Univ., 1990).

21. On architectural periodicals during this period, see Vieri Quilici, "La rivista SA, un prodotto costruttivista," *Rassegna* 11, no. 38 (June 1989): 10–25; Jean-Louis Cohen, "Avant-garde et revues d'architecture en Russie, 1917–1941," *Revue de l'Art,* no. 89 (3rd quarter, 1990): 29–38. Mention should be made of the bibliography compiled by Anatole Senkevitch that provides a preliminary global approach to the production of architectural journals and an inventory of the articles on the principal Soviet architects. Anatole Senkevitch, *Soviet Architecture, 1917–1962: A Bibliographical Guide to Source Material* (Charlottesville: Univ. Press of Virginia, 1974).

22. Selim Omarovich Khan-Magomedov, *Vhutemas: Moscou, 1920–1930,* 2 vols. (Paris: Editions du Regard, 1990).

23. On the Russian fascination with aviation, see Felix Philipp Ingold, *Literatur und Aviatik: Europäische Flugdichtung, 1909–1927* (Basel: Birkhäuser, 1978).

24. The last work of Aksenov, who became the director of Vsevolod Meyerhold's theater school, was a monograph on Sergei Eisenstein, publication of which was forbidden in 1933 and which finally appeared sixty years later. Ivan Aleksandrovich Aksenov, *Sergei Eisenstein: Portret khudozhnika* (Moscow: Sciuz kinematografistov SSSR, 1991).

25. On the question of Russian *Amerikanizm,* see Jean-Louis Cohen, "L'Oncle Sam au pays des Soviets: Le temps des avant-gardes," in Jean-Louis Cohen and Hubert Damisch, eds., *Américanisme et modernité: L'idéal américain dans l'architecture* (Paris: Ecole des Hautes Etudes en Sciences Sociales, 1993).

26. This is the series *Neues Bauen in der Welt* published by Schroll. See *Rassegna* 11, no. 38 (June 1989), entitled *Neues Bauen in der Welt.*

27. In this superb publication featuring hazy color photographs, Lavrentii Beria, the future head of the political police, sets himself the task of "bringing lemons, oranges, and tangerines to the tables of Soviet workers." See the special issue of *Ogonek* entitled *Sovetskie Subtropiki* (1934): 13.

28. On parachuting, see *SSSR na stroike,* no. 12 (1935) and on the *Cheliuskin,* no. 10 (1934).

29. The Getty Research Institute collection includes, among the celebrated issues of the journal, issue no. 4, 1935, on Baku; nos. 4–5, 1936, on Georgia; no. 8, 1936, on the forests, with an imitation wood cover; no. 1, 1937, on the Red Navy, with a layout by Lissitzky; and no. 5, 1937, on gold, designed by Stepanova and Rodchenko.

30. El Lissitzky, "Topographie der Typographie," *Merz,* no. 4 (July 1923).

31. Varvara Stepanova, *5 × 5 = 25: Vystavka zhivopisi,* exh. cat. (Moscow: [Klub V.S.P.], 1921).

Ru

ssian

Modernism

Russian Modernism: The Collections of the Getty Research Institute

1. **Akademiia khudozhestv, Arkhitekturnyi fakul'tet** (Academy of Arts, Faculty of Architecture). *Sbornik kompozitsionnykh rabot studentov, 1* (Сборник композиционных работ студентов, 1 / Collection of student compositions, 1). Leningrad: Leningradskaia akademiia khudozhestv, 1929. 71 pp. 21 cm.
   Cover by Iakov Rubanchik.

2. **Akhmatova, Anna.** *Anno Domini MCMXXI.* St. Petersburg: Petropolis, 1921 (cover date 1922). 101 pp. 12 cm.
   Poems.

3. ***Akme: Pervyi sbornik Tiflisskogo tsekha poetov*** (Акмэ: Первый сборник Тифлисского цеха поэтов / Acme: First collection of the Tbilisi Poets' Workshop). Tbilisi: Tsekh poetov, 1919. 64 pp. 21 cm.
   Cover by Osip Sharleman'.
   Includes contributions by Anna Antonovskaia, Ripsime Asil'iants, Grigorii Bammel', N. Bel-Kon'-Liubomirskaia, Iurii Dantsiger, Magdalina De-Kaprelevich, Aleksandr Gerbsman, Sergei Gorodetskii, Nina Gratsianskaia, Ol'ga Kamaeva, Nikolai Kapranov, Aleksandr Kulebiakin, Maiia, Sof'ia Melikova, Konstantin Obraztsov, Tat'iana Poiarkova, Vladimir Prussak, Aleksandr Radike, Sergei Rafalovich, Vladimir Sapozhnikov, Nikolai Semeiko, and Vasilii Zota.

4. **Aksenov, Ivan.** *Korinfiane: Tragediia* (Коринфяне: Трагедия / The Corinthians: A tragedy). Moscow: Tsentrifuga, 1918. xiv, 66 pp. 18 cm.
   Frontispiece by Aleksandr Rodchenko.
   Tragedy in verse.
5. ———. *Neuvazhitel'nye osnovaniia* (Неуважительные основания / Insufficient grounds). Moscow: Tsentrifuga, 1916. 46 pp., [2] plates. 35 cm.
   Poems. Includes 2 etchings by Alexandra Exter.
   Copy 109 (or 104?) of 200. Rebound in molded rubber by Jean de Gonet, signed by him, and numbered 47/200.

6. ———. *Pikasso i okrestnosti* (Пикассо и окрестности / Picasso and environs). Moscow: Tsentrifuga, 1917. 62 pp. 27 cm.
   Cover by Alexandra Exter.
   Monograph on Picasso.

7. **Akul'shin, Rodion.** *O devochke Marishke, o noven'kom pal'tishke, o svin'e uzhasnoi, i o zvezdochke krasnoi* (О девочке Маришке, о новеньком пальтишке, о свинье ужасной, и о звездочке красной / About a little girl named Marishka, a new coat, a frightful pig, and a red star). [Moscow and Leningrad]: Gos. izd-vo, 1927. [12] pp. 21 cm.
   Children's book. Includes wood engravings by Georgii Echeistov, Andrei Goncharov, Z. Grigor'eva, and Mikhail Tarkhanov.

8. **Alekseeva, A.** *Shest'-desiat: Norvezhskaia skazka* (Шесть-десят: Норвежская сказка / Six-ty: A Norwegian folktale). Moscow: GIZ, 1930. 15 pp. 16 cm.
   Children's book. Includes illustrations by Nataliia Iznar.

9. ***Al'manakh Grif, 1903–1913*** (Альманах Гриф, 1903–1913 / The Griffin miscellany, 1903–1913). Edited by Sergei Krechetov. Moscow: Grif, [1914]. 184, x, iii pp. 30 cm.
   The fourth and last miscellany to be published by the Symbolist journal *Grif* (Griffin), the others having appeared in 1903, 1904, and 1905. The 29 contributors include nearly all of the writers published by *Grif* during the first 10 years of its existence, such as Innokentii Annenskii, Konstantin Bal'mont, Andrey Bely, Aleksandr Blok, Valerii Briusov, Viacheslav Ivanov, Aleksei Remizov, Igor' Severianin, Fedor Sologub, Aleksei Tolstoi, and Maksimilian Voloshin. The section devoted to each writer contains a small portrait, a reproduction of the author's signature, and, at the back, a brief bibliography of writings.

10. ***Al'manakh smert'*** (Альманах смерть / Death, a miscellany). St. Petersburg: Nov. zhurnal dlia vsekh, 1910. 283 pp., [2] plates. 23 cm.
   Cover by Vladimir Chembers.
   Poetry and prose on the theme of death. Includes contributions by Nikolai Abramovich, Nikolai Arkhipov, A. Boane, Georgii Chulkov, Vasilii Gippius, Viktor Gofman, Sergei Gorodetskii, Viacheslav Ivanov, Anatolii Kamenskii, Petr Kozhevnikov, Viktor Kozlov, Vladimir Lenskii, Viktor Muizhel', Nikolai Oliger, Petr Potemkin, Il'ia Repin, Aleksandr Roslavlev, Vasilii Rozanov, Dmitrii Tsenzor, and Viktor Zhirmunskii.
   Bears the ownership stamp of Vladimir Kranikhfel'd in purple ink.

11. **Al'tman, Natan.** *Lenin.* St. Petersburg: Izd. Otdela izobrazitel'nykh iskusstv Narkomprosa, 1921 (cover date 1920). 14 leaves. 23 cm.

Cover by Al'tman.

Sketches made by Alt'man while working on a portrait sculpture of Lenin.

Inscribed by Al'tman to Il'ia Shlepianov and dated 9 November 1945, "na pamiat' o vremenakh ne akademicheskogo iskusstva" (in remembrance of the times of nonacademic art).

12. [———]. **Boris Arvatov.** *Natan Al'tman.* Berlin: Petropolis, 1924. 61 pp., [41] plates. 33 cm.

From an edition of 500.

13. [———]. **Abram Efros.** *Portret Natana Al'tmana* (Портрет Натана Альтмана / Portrait of Natan Al'tman). Moscow: Shipovnik, 1922. 101 pp. 19 cm.

14. **Alvarez del Vayo, Julio.** *Krasnaia tropa* (Красная тропа / The red path). Moscow and Leningrad: GIZ, 1930. 166 pp. 20 cm.

Cover by Gustav Klutsis.

Translation of *La senda roja,* the journalist's reminiscences in novel form first published in Madrid by Espasa-Calpe in 1928.

15. **Annenkov, Iurii.** *1/4 deviatogo* (1/4 девятого / Quarter past eight). [Petrograd]: Segodnia, [1919]. [4] pp. 20 cm.

Contains a poem written and illustrated by Annenkov.

Not among the 125 hand-colored copies (Rozanov 1975, 127).

16. **Annenskii, Innokentii.** *Famira-Kifared: Vakkhicheskaia drama* (Фамира-Кифарэд: Вакхическая драма / Thamyras Citharoedus: A Bacchic drama). St. Petersburg: Z. I. Grzhebin, 1919. 91 pp. 20 cm.

Cover by Nikolai Radlov. Tailpieces by A. B., Veniamin Belkin, Dmitrii Mitrokhin, and Sergei Sudeikin.

From the second edition of 1919, which followed the 100-copy edition of 1913.

17. **[Antireligious playing cards].** [Russian SFSR.: n.p., ca. 1933]. [36] playing cards. 12 cm.

Pairs of playing cards numbered 1–18, forming a set of 36 that may be complete, though the Research Institute's copy retains no indication of the size of the set as issued. Each card has a picture, lithographed in color, and a brief caption. One card from each pair caricatures a religious custom or ritual while the other depicts the atheistic, Soviet equivalent. There is no indication of the artist or the source of the cards. The publisher could have been any of various groups active in promoting atheism in the 1930s,

such as the publisher of the newspaper and journal *Bezbozhnik* (The atheist).
Research Institute's copy lacks the atheistic card of the tenth pair and any container that may have originally been included.

18. ***Apollon*** (Аполлон / Apollo). St. Petersburg: Sergei K. Makovskii and M. K. Ushakov, 1909–1917. 25 cm.
Edited by Sergei Makovskii.
Typography supervised by Lev Bakst and Mstislav Dobuzhinskii.
Literary and artistic monthly (excluding the summer) of Russian Symbolism founded by Makovskii. Includes critical essays on Russian and Western art by Aleksandr Benua, Georgii Lukomskii, Makovskii, and Iakov Tugendkhol'd and poetry by Anna Akhmatova, Aleksandr Blok, Valerii Briusov, Mikhail Kuzmin, Osip Mandel'shtam, and Sergei Solov'ev. Wassily Kandinsky was the Munich correspondent from 1909 to 1910.
Research Institute's holdings: scattered issues.

19. **Apushkin, Iakov.** *Kamernyi teatr* (Камерный театр / The Kamerny Theater). Moscow and Leningrad: Kino-pechat', 1927. 63 pp. 17 cm.
Cover by 2-Stenberg-2 (Georgii and Vladimir Stenberg).

20. ***Arena: Teatral'nyi al'manakh*** (Арена: Театральный альманах / Arena: A theatrical miscellany). St. Petersburg: Vremia, 1924. 114 pp. 23 cm.
Cover by Valentina Khodasevich.

21. ***Arkhitektura: Ezhemesiachnik Moskovskogo arkhitekturnogo obshchestva*** (Архитектура: Ежемесячник Московского архитектурного общества / Architecture: Monthly of the Moscow Architectural Society). Moscow: MAO, 1923. 32 cm.
Edited by Moisei Ginzburg.
Includes illustrations of architectural projects by S. Chernyshev, Vladimir Shchuko, and Ivan Zholtovskii and essays by Slava Livshits, Aleksei Shchusev, and E. Shervinskii.
A total of 5 issues published.
Research Institute's holdings: scattered issues.

22. ***Arkhitektura Moskovskogo metro*** (Архитектура Московского метро / The architecture of the Moscow subway). Edited by Nikolai Kolli and Samuil Kravets. Moscow: Izd-vo Vsesoiuznoi akademii arkhitektury, 1936. 194 pp., [2] plates. 31 cm.
Layout, title page, and binding by Nikolai Il'in.
The plates are collotype portraits of Joseph Stalin and Lazar' Kaganovich.

23. ***Arkhitektura: Raboty arkhitekturnogo fakul'teta VKhUTEMASa, 1920–1927*** (Архитектура: Работы архитектурного факультета ВХУТЕМАСа, 1920–1927 / Architecture: Works by the architectural faculty of VKhUTEMAS, 1920–1927). Moscow: VKhUTEMAS, 1927. 45 pp. 24 cm.
Cover by El Lissitzky.

24. ***Arkhitektura sovremennogo zapada: Le Korbiuz'e, Bruno Taut, V. Gropius, I. P. Aud, Frank Reit, L. Gil'berseimer, i drugie*** (Архитектура современного Запада: Ле Корбюзье, Бруно Таут, В. Гропиус, И. П. Ауд, Франк Рейт, Л. Гильберсеймер, и другие / Contemporary architecture of the West: Le Corbusier, Bruno Taut, Walter Gropius, J. J. P. Oud, Frank Lloyd Wright, Ludwig Hilberseimer, and others). Edited by David Arkin. Moscow: Izogiz, 1932. 185 pp. 27 cm.
Cover, dust jacket, and title pages by El Lissitzky.

25. ***Arkhitektura SSSR*** (Архитектура СССР / USSR architecture). Moscow: Zhurnal'no-gazetnoe ob"edinenie, 1933–1941. 31 cm.
Edited by K. Alab'ian.
Monthly organ of the Union of Soviet Architects.
Includes reviews of foreign architectural journals and magazines, articles about current architectural developments in the West, and discussions about Moisei Ginzburg, Boris Iofan, Vladimir Shchuko, and their designs for the Palace of Soviets.
Research Institute's holdings: scattered issues.

26. ***Arkhitektura za rubezhom*** (Архитектура за рубежом / Architecture abroad). Moscow: Vsesoiuznaia akademiia arkhitektury pri TsIK SSSR, 1934–1937. 30 cm.
Edited by Ivan Matsa. Editorial committee included David Arkin, Hannes Meyer, and Adol'f Urban.
Contains discussions of city planning in Germany, Holland, Sweden, and Switzerland; articles on the Chicago World Exhibition of 1933; reviews of foreign architectural journals such as *Architectural Review*, *Der Baumeister*, and *La construction moderne*; and reports on architectural activity in Germany, including Fascist architecture. No. 1 (1934) bears the ownership stamp of Karel Teige.
Research Institute's holdings: scattered issues.

27. ***Arkhitekturnaia gazeta*** (Архитектурная газета / Architectural gazette). Moscow: Soiuz arkhitektorov SSSR, 1934–1939. 60 cm.
Organ of the Union of Architects of the USSR.
Provides a chronicle of daily events and developments in Soviet architecture. Includes articles by Soviet architects.

Merged with *Stroitel'nyi rabochii* (Construction worker) in March 1939 to form *Stroitel'naia gazeta* (Construction gazette).
Research Institute's holdings: scattered issues.

28. ***Arkhitekturnaia gazeta: Prilozhenie*** (Архитектурная газета: Приложение / Architectural gazette: Supplement). [Moscow: n.p.]. 47 cm.
Edited by M. O. Ol'shevets.
Design by V. Ninemiagi.
Contains various architectural schemes such as the design for the All-Union Agricultural Exhibition of 1937, a scenario for the reconstruction of Moscow in 1933, and plans for the building of the Academy of USSR, Moscow theaters and subway system, and architectural projects in other Soviet cities.
Research Institute's holdings: scattered issues.

29. **Arkin, David.** *Iskusstvo bytovoi veshchi: Ocherki noveishei khudozhestvennoi promyshlennosti* (Искусство бытовой вещи: Очерки новейшей художественной промышленности / The art of everyday objects: Essays on contemporary design). [Moscow]: Ogiz-Izogiz, 1932. 170 pp. 21 cm.
Cover by Solomon Telingater.

30. ***Armianskii sbornik*** (Армянский сборник / Armenian collection). Moscow: Zvezda, [1915]. 266, iv pp. 20 cm.
Cover by Nataliia Goncharova.
Essays on Armenian history and culture. They appeared in at least 2 previous editions.

31. **Aronson, Boris.** *Sovremennaia evreiskaia grafika* (Современная еврейская графика / Contemporary Jewish graphics). Berlin: Petropolis, 1924. 104 pp. 33 cm.
From an edition of 300.

32. **Arvatov, Boris.** *Iskusstvo i klassy* (Искусство и классы / Art and class). Moscow and Petrograd: Gos. izd-vo, 1923. 87 pp. 24 cm.
Cover signed "L. N."
Essay.
Title page inscribed by Iosif Brodskii in black ink and dated 1928.

33. ———. *Ob agit i proz iskusstve* (Об агит и проз искусстве / On agitation and production art). Moscow: Federatsiia, 1930. 223 pp. 17 cm.
Cover by Aleksandr Rodchenko.
Collection of articles written from 1921 to 1923.
Inscribed by Iosif Brodskii and dated 1928.

34. **Aseev, Nikolai.** *Bol'shoi chitatel'* (Большой читатель / Great reader). Moscow: Federatsiia, 1932. 134 pp. 17 cm.
Cover by Boris Titov.
Poems.

35. ———. *Izbrannye stikhi* (Избранные стихи / Selected verse). Moscow and Leningrad: Gos. izd-vo, 1930. 235 pp. 20 cm.
Cover by Aleksandr Rodchenko.

36. ———. *Izbran': Stikhi, 1912–1922* (Избрань: Стихи, 1912–1922 / Selections: Verse, 1912–1922). Moscow and St. Petersburg: Krug, 1923. 128 pp. 21 cm.
Cover by Aleksandr Rodchenko.

37. ———. *Izmoroz': Stikhi, 1925–1926* (Изморозь: Стихи, 1925–1926 / Hoar frost: Verse, 1925–1926). Moscow and Leningrad: Gos. izd-vo, 1927. 55 pp. 18 cm.

38. ———. *Maiakovskii nachinaetsia: Povest' v stikhakh v 17 glavakh s epilogom* (Маяковский начинается: Повесть в стихах в 17 главах с эпилогом / Mayakovsky begins: A verse tale in seventeen chapters and an epilogue). Moscow: Sov. pisatel', 1940. 137 pp., 16 plates. 22 cm.
Binding and title page by Ivan Nikolaevtsev.
Includes illustrations by Mariia Siniakova.

39. ———. "*Oi konin dan okein!*": *Chetvertaia kn. stikhov* («Ой конин дан окейн!»: Четвертая кн. стихов / "I love your eyes!": Fourth book of verse). Moscow: Liren', 1916. 16 pp. 21 cm.
Aseev claimed that "Oi konin dan okein" is "Gypsy" or perhaps "Tadzhik" (Markov 1968, 248 and 407 n. 34).
Rather than the usual drawing by Mariia Siniakova on the front cover, the Research Institute's copy has a collage in the form of a tree made from yellow satin, pink gauze, gold paper, and an artificial flower. According to a penciled annotation on the title page, this is a unique copy made by Siniakova for Nikolai Punin.

40. ———. *Rasstreliannaia zemlia: Fantasticheskie rasskazy* (Расстрелянная земля: Фантастические рассказы / The land that was shot: Fantastic stories). Biblioteka "Ogonek," no. 87. Moscow: Ogonek, 1925. 43 pp. 15 cm.

41. ———. *Semen Proskakov: Stikhotvornye primechaniia k materialam po istorii grazhdanskoi voiny* (Семен Проскаков: Стихотворные примечания к материалам по истории гражданской войны / Semen Proskakov: Observations in verse on material dealing with the history of the civil war). Moscow and Leningrad: Gos. izd-vo, 1928. 50 pp., [6] plates. 21 cm.

42. ———. *Sen'ka besprizornyi* (Сенька беспризорный / Sen'ka the homeless boy). [Leningrad]: Molodaia gvardiia, 1926. 29 pp. 17 cm.
Poem.

43. ———. *Sobranie stikhotvorenii* (Собрание стихотворений / Collected poems). 2nd ed., corr. Vols. 1 and 2 of 4. Moscow and Leningrad: Khudozhestvennaia lit-ra, 1931–1932. 15 cm.
Dust jacket and title page by Varvara Stepanova.

44. ———. *Stal'noi solovei* (Стальной соловей / Steel nightingale). MAF, Seriia poetov, no. 2. Moscow: VKhUTEMAS, 1922. 24 pp. 17 cm.
Poems.
Signed on the title page by Fedor Rusetskii in purple ink.

45. ———. *Stal'noi solovei* (Стальной соловей / Steel nightingale). MAF, Seriia poetov, no. 2. 2nd ed., enl. and corr. Moscow: VKhUTEMAS, 1922. 27 pp. 17 cm.
Poems.

46. ———. *Zapevaem!: Sbornik stikhov* (Запеваем!: Сборник стихов / Let's sing!: A collection of verse). Moscow and Leningrad: Gos. izd-vo, 1930. 99 pp. 20 cm.

47. ———. *Za riadom riad: Stikhi* (За рядом ряд: Стихи / Rank upon rank: Verse). Moscow: Moskovskii rabochii, 1925. 30 pp. 18 cm.

48. ———. *Zor* (Зор / Vision). Moscow: Liren', 1914. 16 pp. 15 cm.
Cover by Mariia Siniakova.
Poems.
Knizhnaia letopis' (1914, no. 21710) gives the edition size as 20, perhaps for 200. Text is handwritten in block characters and reproduced by lithography. Title page has a purple stamp depicting a moose, presumably an owner's mark.

49. **Aseev, Nikolai, and Vladimir Mayakovsky.** *Odna golova vsegda bedna, a potomu i bedna, chto zhivet odna* (Одна голова всегда бедна, а потому и бедна, что живет одна / A single man is always poor, and he's poor because he lives alone). Moscow: Kooperativnoe izd-vo, 1924. 28 pp. 22 cm.
Poem.
Bears the stamp of the Proletarian Writers Union in purple ink.

50. ———. *Pervyi Pervomai: Otkuda povel rabochii klass 1-oe maia v pervyi raz* (Первый Первомай: Откуда повел рабочий класс 1-ое мая в первый раз / The first May Day: Where the working class first got the idea of May Day). Leningrad: Priboi, 1926. 16 pp. 20 cm.
Poem.
Pp. 7–10 are missing.

51. **Aseev, Nikolai, and Grigorii Petnikov.** *Letorei: Kniga stikhov* (Леторей: Книга стихов / Summer soarer: A book of verse). Moscow: Liren', 1915. 32 pp. 23 cm.
Cover by Mariia Siniakova.

52. ***Asnova: Izvestiia Assotsiatsii novykh arkhitektorov. Mitteilungen der Assoziation Neuer Architekten. Revue de l'Association d'architectes contemporains*** (Аснова: Известия Ассоциации новых архитекторов / ASNOVA: Proceedings of the Association of New Architects). Moscow: VKhUTEMAS, 1926. [6] pp. 35 cm.
Edited by El Lissitzky and Nikolai Ladovskii.
Layout by Lissitzky.
Organ of the Association of New Architects (ASNOVA), formed in Moscow in 1923.
From an edition of 1,500.
A total of 1 issue published.

53. **Assotsiatsiia khudozhnikov revoliutsionnoi Rossii** (Association of Artists of Revolutionary Russia). *4 goda AKhRR, 1922–1926 g.: Sbornik 1* (4 года АХРР, 1922–1926 г.: Сборник 1 / Four years of AKhRR, 1922–1926: First collection). Moscow: Izd-vo AKhRR, 1926. 321, vi, 77 pp. 23 cm.
Sixteen essays by authors including Anatoly Lunacharsky. In addition the first sequence of pages contains extensive excerpts from newspaper and journal articles dealing with the Association of Artists of Revolutionary Russia (AKhRR), and the third sequence is devoted to AKhRR's eighth exhibition, *Zhizn' i byt narodov SSSR* (Everyday life of the peoples of the USSR). It consists largely of reproductions of exhibited works, many of them tipped-in gravures.

54. [———]. *Zhizn' i byt narodov SSSR: Vos'maia vystavka kartin i skul'ptury AKhRR—Spravochnik-katalog s illiustratsiiami* (Жизнь и быт народов СССР: Восьмая выставка картин и скульптуры АХРР—Справочник-каталог с иллюстрациями / Everyday life of the peoples of the USSR: Eighth AKhRR exhibition of pictures and sculpture—illustrated handbook and catalog). Leningrad: Assotsiatsiia khudozhnikov revoliutsionnoi Rossii, 1926. 121 pp. 23 cm.
Cover, headpieces, and tailpiece by Semen Pavlov.

55. ***Avtografy*** (Автографы / Autographs). Moscow: Imazhinisty, 1919. [16] pp. 30 cm.
The first of two miscellanies with this title, the second of which appeared in 1921. Each of the following poets contributed 1 poem and wrote it out in longhand: Konstantin Bal'mont, Sergei Esenin, Viacheslav Ivanov, Riurik Ivnev, Vasilii Kamenskii, Anatoly Lunacharsky, Anatolii Mariengof, Boris Pasternak, Ivan Rukavishnikov, and Vadim Shershenevich. Includes illustrations by Georgii Iakulov, Petr Konchalovskii, Aleksei Morgunov, N. B. Rozenfel'd, and M. Svetlov.
Reproduced by lithography on glass. Bears the ownership stamp of V. P. Il'in in blue ink.

56. ***Avto v oblakakh: Stikhi*** (Авто в облаках: Стихи / Auto in the clouds: Verse). Odessa: [n.p.], 1915. 64 pp. 22 cm.
Cover by S. Fazini.
Includes illustrations by Fazini and poems by Eduard Bagritskii, Isidor Bobovich, Anatolii Fioletov, Vadim Shershenevich, Petr Storitsyn, Sergei Tret'iakov, Georgii Tsagareli, and Nina Voskresenskaia.
From an edition of 300 (*Knizhnaia letopis'* 1915, no. 21871).

57. **Babel', Isaak.** *Istoriia moei golubiatni: Rasskazy* (История моей голубятни: Рассказы / The history of my dovecote: Stories). Moscow and Leningrad: Zemlia i fabrika, 1926. 78 pp. 19 cm.
Cover by Natan Al'tman.
Bears the ownership stamp of Hannes Meyer in red ink.

58. **Baian, Vadim, Konstantin Bol'shakov, and Mariia Kalmykova.** *Srublennyi potselui s gub vselennoi* (Срубленный поцелуй с губ вселенной / A kiss chopped off the lips of the universe). [Sevastopol]: Taran, [1922?]. 12 pp. 22 cm.
Poems.

59. **Balika, D.** *V laboratorii poeta: F. Sologub, A. Belyi, E. Zamiatin* (В лаборатории поэта: Ф. Сологуб, А. Белый, Е. Замятин / In the poet's laboratory: Fedor Sologub, Andrey Bely, Evgenii Zamiatin). Belebei: N. Ia. Frid'eva, 1917. 49 pp. 24 cm.

60. **Baruch, Dorothy.** *Doroga* (Дорога / The road). Translated by by Mikhail Gershenzon. Moscow and Leningrad: Gos. izd-vo, 1931. 14 pp. 22 cm.
Cover by Konstantin Vialov.
Children's book, a partial translation of *Big Fellow: The Story of a Road-Making Machine* (New York: Harper, 1929). Includes illustrations by Vialov.

61. **Bednyi, Demian.** *Tempy* (Темпы / Up to speed). Edited and with notes by A.V. Efremin. 2nd ed. Moscow and Leningrad: Khudozhestvennaia lit-ra, 1931. 71 pp. 20 cm.
Poem written for the opening of the sixteenth Congress of the Communist Party of the Soviet Union, 26 June 1930. Includes illustrations by Iulii Ganf and Konstantin Rotov.
First edition was published in 1930.

62. **Belenson, Aleksandr.** *Iskusstvennaia zhizn'* (Искусственная жизнь / Artificial life). St. Petersburg: Strelets, 1921. 88 pp. 21 cm.
Cover, headpieces, and tailpieces by Iurii Annenkov.
Includes an introduction by Nikolai Evreinov and selected articles by

Belenson that appeared in the periodical *Zhizn' iskusstva* (Art life) in 1920 and 1921.

Cover is missing.

63. ———. *Kino segodnia: Ocherki sovetskogo kino-iskusstva—Kuleshov, Vertov, Eizenshtein* (Кино сегодня: Очерки советского кино-искусства — Кулешов, Вертов, Эйзенштейн / The cinema today: Sketches of Soviet cinema art—Kuleshov, Vertov, Eisenstein). Moscow: Izd. avtora, 1925. 102 pp. 23 cm.

Cover by Bushkin.

64. ———. *Vrata tesnye: Vtoraia kniga stikhov* (Врата тесные: Вторая книга стихов / Strait is the gate: Second book of verse). St. Petersburg: Strelets, 1922. 45 pp. 18 cm.

Cover by Iurii Cherkesov.

Includes an illustration by Cherkesov and a portrait of Belenson by Nikolai Kul'bin.

From an edition of 300.

65. ***Belomorsko–Baltiiskii kanal imeni Stalina: Istoriia stroitel'stva*** (Беломорско–Балтийский канал имени Сталина: История строительства / The Stalin White Sea–Baltic canal: A history of its construction). [Moscow]: Istoriia fabrik i zavodov, 1934. 407 pp., 23 plates. 30 cm.

Cover and title pages by Nikolai Il'in.

The list of designers includes Aleksandr Rodchenko. The list of those responsible for maps includes Aleksandr Deineka.

66. **Bely, Andrey.** *Glossaloliia: Poema o zvuke* (Глоссалолия: Поэма о звуке / Glossalolia: A poem about sound). Berlin: Epokha, 1922. 131 pp. 18 cm.

Cover by S. A. Zalshupin.

Includes illustrations by Bely.

Inscribed by Bely to Vasilii Masiutin.

67. ———. *Masterstvo Gogolia: Issledovanie* (Мастерство Гоголя: Исследование / Gogol's craft: A study). Moscow and Leningrad: Khudozhestvennaia lit-ra, 1934. xv, 321 pp., 13 plates. 23 cm.

Binding and endpapers by Lev Miul'gaupt.

68. **Berdiaev, Nikolai.** *Krizis iskusstva* (Кризис искусства / The crisis in art). Moscow: G. A. Leman i S. I. Sakharov, 1918. 47 pp., [5] plates. 25 cm.

Originally given as a public lecture in Moscow on 1 November 1917. Also includes "Pikasso" (Picasso) and "Astral'nyi roman: Razmyshlenie po povodu romana A. Belogo *Peterburg*" (An astral novel: Reflections on Bely's *Petersburg*).

69. **Berendgof, Nikolai.** *Bunt veshchei: 4-ia kniga stikhov, 1922–1925* (Бунт вещей: 4-я книга стихов, 1922–1925 / The revolt of things: Fourth book of

verse, 1922–1925). Moscow: Kn-vo Moskovskogo tsekha poetov, 1926. 29 pp. 19 cm.

70. **Berman, L.** *Novaia Troia: Stikhotvoreniia* (Новая Троя: Стихотворения / New Troy: Poems). St. Petersburg: Erato, 1921. 79 pp. 15 cm.
Cover by Nikolai Kupreianov.
Inscribed by Berman and dated 22 May 1922.

71. **Beskin, Osip.** *Formalizm v zhivopisi* (Формализм в живописи / Formalism in painting). Moscow: Vsekokhudozhnik, 1933. 87 pp. 23 cm.

72. **"*Bezbozhnik u stanka*" *1923-V-1927*** («Безбожник у станка» 1923-V-1927 / Five years of *The Atheist at the Lathe*, 1923–1927). [Moscow]: Bezbozhnik u stanka, 1927. 154 sheets. 37 cm.
Portfolio of colored lithographs drawn from the first 5 years of *Bezbozhnik u stanka*. Most have titles at the top of the sheet and captions at the bottom, some of them in dialog or verse. Dmitrii Moor is the artist whose work appears most often, followed by Aleksandr Deineka and Nikolai Kogout, with a few prints each credited to Mikhail Cheremnykh, Mechislav Dobrokovskii, G. Golubev, Georgii Gugunava, and Vladimir Liushin.
Twenty-six of the prints are on folded double sheets. *Bezbozhnik u stanka* continued to appear until 1931.

73. **Bezymenskii, Aleksandr.** *Kak pakhnet zhizn'* (Как пахнет жизнь / The smell of life). Moscow: Krasnaia nov', Glavpolitprosvet, 1924. 87 pp. 20 cm.
Cover by Iurii Annenkov.
Poems. Includes a preface by Leon Trotsky.

74. ———. *Komsomoliia: Stranitsy epopei* (Комсомолия: Страницы эпопеи / The land of Komsomolia: Pages from an epic). 4th ed. Moscow and Leningrad: GIZ, 1928. 52 pp. 34 cm.
Design by Solomon Telingater.
Poem.

75. ———. *Komsomoliia: Stranitsy epopei* (Комсомолия: Страницы эпопеи / The land of Komsomolia: Pages from an epic). 5th ed. Moscow and Leningrad: Gos. izd-vo, 1929. 79 pp. 17 cm.
Cover signed "G. Sh."

76. ———. *Partbilet no. 224332: Stikhi o Lenine* (Партбилет но. 224332: Стихи о Ленине / Party membership card number 224332: Verses on Lenin). 3rd ed. Moscow and Leningrad: Gos. izd-vo, 1930. 93 pp., [9] plates. 17 cm.

77. ———. *Tragediinaia noch'* (Трагедийная ночь / Night of tragedy). [4th ed.] [Moscow]: Khudozhestvennaia lit-ra, 1935. 39 pp., [17] plates. 30 cm.
Design by Efim Pernikov.
Poem. Includes illustrations by Pernikov.

78. ***Biblioteka poetov, no. 2*** (Библиотека поэтов, но. 2 / Poets' library, number two). Edited by Vasilii Kamenskii. Moscow: Biblioteka poetov, 1923. 16 pp. 18 cm.

The second of 2 issues of *Biblioteka poetov,* the first of which appeared in 1922. Includes poems by Nikolai Berendgof, Kamenskii, Velimir Khlebnikov, Gurii Sidorov, and Sergei Tret'iakov.

79. ***Biulleten' avangardu*** (Бюллетень авангарду / Bulletin for the avant-garde). Kharkov: [n.p.], 1928? 28 cm.

Design by Vasyl' Iermilov and O. Levada.

Includes poetry, prose, and criticism.

Research Institute's holdings: scattered issues.

80. ***Biznes: Sbornik Literaturnogo tsentra konstruktivistov*** (Бизнес: Сборник Литературного центра конструктивистов / Business: Collection of the Literary Center of the Constructivists). Edited by Kornelii Zelinskii and Il'ia Sel'vinskii. Moscow: Gos. izd-vo, 1929. 260 pp. 23 cm.

Cover variously attributed to Aleksandr Rodchenko and Solomon Telingater (Compton 1992, 155 n. 113).

Poems and essays on literary theory. Includes contributions by Nikolai Aduev, Boris Agapov, Eduard Bagritskii, Evgenii Gabrilovich, G. Gauzner, Vera Inber, Aleksandr Kviatkovskii, Vladimir Lugovskoi, Nikolai Panov, Sel'vinskii, and Zelinskii.

Inscribed "A. Kviatkovskii."

81. **Blagov, Aleksandr.** *Rabochii gorod: Stikhi i pesni* (Рабочий город: Стихи и песни / Workers' city: Poems and songs). Moscow and Leningrad: Moskovskii rabochii, 1928. 92 pp. 17 cm.

Cover by Vladimir Roskin.

82. **Blok, Aleksandr.** *Dvenadtsat'* (Двенадцать / The twelve). 3rd ed. St. Petersburg: Alkonost, 1918. 61 pp. 34 cm.

Poem. Includes illustrations by Iurii Annenkov.

Research Institute's copy not among the 300 numbered copies, 25 of them hand-colored (Iatsunok 1980, 86).

83. ———. *Dvenadtsat'* (Двенадцать / The twelve). Sofiia: Rossiisko-bolgarskoe kn-vo, [1920]. 36 pp. 22 cm.

Cover signed "I. M." (?).

Includes an introduction by P. Suvchinskii.

84. ———. *Dvenadtsat'. Skify* (Двенадцать. Скифы / The twelve. The Scythians). Paris: Mishen', 1920. [51] pp. 24 cm.

Includes 2 illustrations by Nataliia Goncharova and 7 by Mikhail Larionov.

This "first Russian edition" to be published by Mishen' appeared in June

1920. Mishen' had published a French translation in April 1920 with 7 different illustrations by Larionov, reproduced from pencil drawings rather than ink drawings as here. The "second Russian edition" appeared at the same time as the first in June 1920; it had a total of 14 illustrations by both Larionov and Goncharova, selected from those of the French edition as well as the first Russian edition (Khardzhiev 1968, 316–17).

85. ———. [Dvenadtsat']. *The Twelve*. Translated by C. E. Bechhofer. London: Chatto & Windus, 1920. ix, 26 pp., [8] plates. 26 cm.
Cover design by Mikhail Larionov.
Translation of *Dvenadtsat'*. Includes illustrations by Larionov. The illustrations are those of the French translation published the same year in Paris by Mishen' (Khardzhiev 1968, 316 n. 1). The cover reproduces the first illustration from Mishen's "first Russian edition." (See no. 84.)

86. ———. [Dvenadtsat']. *Die Zwölf* (The twelve). Translated by Wolfgang Groeger. Berlin: Newa-Verlag, 1921. 34 pp. 26 cm.
Translation of *Dvenadtsat'*. Includes illustrations by Vasilii Masiutin.
Title leaf is missing.

87. ———. [Dvenadtsat']. *Dvanáct: Revoluční epos* (The twelve: A revolutionary epic). Translated by Bohumil Mathesius. Prague: Plamja, 1925. 47 pp. 28 cm.
Cover by Václav Mašek.
Translation of *Dvenadtsat'*. Includes illustrations by Mašek.

88. ———. *Ramzes: Stseny iz zhizni drevnego Egipta* (Рамзес: Сцены из жизни древнего Египта / Rameses: Scenes from the life of ancient Egypt). St. Petersburg: Alkonost, 1921. 26 pp. 18 cm.
Play.

89. ———. *Sedoe utro: Stikhotvoreniia* (Седое утро: Стихотворения / Gray morning: Poems). St. Petersburg: Alkonost, 1920. 103 pp. 16 cm.
Cover by Aleksandr Leo.

90. ———. *Za gran'iu proshlykh dnei: Stikhotvoreniia* (За гранью прошлых дней: Стихотворения / Beyond the edge of days gone by: Poems). St. Petersburg: Z. I. Grzhebin, 1920. 96 pp. 16 cm.

91. **Bobrov, Sergei.** *Liricheskaia tema: XVIII ekskursov v ee oblasti Sergeia Bobrova* (Лирическая тема: XVIII экскурсов в ее области Сергея Боброва / The lyrical theme: Eighteen digressions in its realm by Sergei Bobrov). Moscow: Tsentrifuga, 1914. 33 pp. 23 cm.
Criticism.

92. ———. *Vertogradari nad lozami* (Вертоградари над лозами / Gardeners at work on the vines). Moscow: Lirika, 1913. 162 pp., [10] double plates hinged at centerfold. 18 cm.
Cover and frontispiece by Nataliia Goncharova.
Poems. Includes 10 lithographs printed in blue and brown by Goncharova. From an edition of 500 (*Knizhnaia letopis'* 1913, no. 18037).

93. ———. *Vosstanie mizantropov* (Восстание мизантропов / Revolt of the misanthropes). Moscow: Tsentrifuga, 1922. 160 pp. 16 cm.
Cover by Liubov' Popova.
Novel.
An incompletely erased pencil inscription on the title page reads, "Ippolit Sokolov 1922."

94. **Bol'shakov, Konstantin.** *Serdtse v perchatke* (Сердце в перчатке / Gloved heart). Moscow: Mezonin poezii, 1913. [16] pp. 21 cm.
Cover by Nataliia Goncharova.
Poems.

95. ———. *Solntse na izlete: Vtoraia kniga stikhov, 1913–1916* (Солнце на излете: Вторая книга стихов, 1913–1916 / The sun in its decline: Second book of verse, 1913–1916). Moscow: Tsentrifuga, 1916. 63 pp. 24 cm.
Cover by El Lissitzky.
From an edition of 480 (*Knizhnaia letopis'* 1916, no. 10466).

96. ***Bol'shevistskii slet: 16 S"ezd VKP (b)*** (Большевистский слет: 16 Съезд ВКП (б) / Bolshevik rally: The sixteenth Congress of the Communist Party of the Soviet Union). Moscow and Leningrad: Gos. izd-vo, 1930. [32] pp. 22 cm.
Written and designed by a shock brigade (a highly motivated task force of workers in the early 1930s) of the Children's Literature Section of Gosizdat RSFSR.

97. **Bond, Alexander.** *Geroi tekhniki* (Герои техники / Heroes of technology). Populiarnaia tekhnicheskaia biblioteka. Moscow: Gos. izd-vo, [1924]. 303 pp. 18 cm.
Cover by Aleksandr Rodchenko.
Translation of *With the Men Who Do Things,* made from an earlier German translation by S. S. Tsetlin.

98. **Borisov, Leonid.** *2 Leonardi 2.* [Leningrad]: Izd-vo pisatelei v Leningrade, 1928. 135 pp. 19 cm.
Cover by Nikolai Akimov.
Includes the title story and the story "Zavival'shchik Vol'demar" (Waldemar the hairdresser).

99. **Borodin, A., and D. Dolev.** *Tekhnika raboty nad malymi formami: V pomoshch' klubnomu dramaturgu* (Техника работы над малыми формами: В помощь клубному драматургу / The technique of work on minor forms: An aid for the club dramatist). Moscow: Teakinopechat', 1930. 93 pp. 21 cm.

Among the minor forms discussed are vaudeville and the review and variety and club performances such as the living newspaper, the dramatized lecture, and the literary montage.

100. **Bozhidar.** *Buben* (Бубен / Tambourine). Moscow: Liren', 1914. 12 pp. 18 cm.
Poems.

101. **Braun, Nikolai, Aleksandr Prokof'ev, and Vissarion Saianov.** *Maiakovskomu* (Маяковскому / To Mayakovsky). [Leningrad]: Izd-vo pisatelei v Leningrade, [1931]. 51 pp. 18 cm.
Cover, half-title, and title page by Mark Kirnarskii.
Verse reminiscences of Mayakovsky and his recent death.

102. ***Brigada khudozhnikov: Ezhemesiachnyi zhurnal Federatsii ob"edinenii rabotnikov prostranstvennykh iskusstv*** (Бригада художников: Ежемесячный журнал Федерации объединений работников пространственных искусств / Artists' brigade: Monthly journal of the Federation of Associations of Workers in the Spatial Arts). Moscow: Izogiz, 1931–1932. 22 cm.
Editorial board included such artists as Aleksandr Deineka, Ivan Matsa, Dmitrii Moor, Pavel Sokolov-Skalia, and Petr Vil'iams.
Covers by El Lissitzky, Georgii and Vladimir Stenberg, and Solomon Telingater.
Organ of the Federation of Associations of Workers in the Spatial Arts (FOSKh; later known as the Federation of Soviet Artists' Associations [FOSKh]), founded in 1930.
Features discussions of the themes and problems of socialist construction in the context of Socialist Realism, and Marxist-Leninist theory and criticism of exhibitions, performing arts, and fine and applied arts in the Soviet Union and abroad. Contains works by Walter Gropius, Gustav Klutsis, and Aleksandr Tyshler and essays by David Arkin and Aleksei Fedorov-Davydov.
Research Institute's holdings: scattered issues.

103. **Brik, Osip.** *Ne poputchitsa* (Не попутчица / No fellow-traveler she). Moscow and Petrograd: Gos. izd-vo, Lef, 1923. 36 pp. 23 cm.
Cover by Anton Lavinskii.
Novella.

104. **Briusov, Valerii.** *Dali: Stikhi 1922 goda* (Дали: Стихи 1922 года / Distances: Verse of 1922). Moscow: Gos. izd-vo, 1922. 87 pp. 19 cm.

105. ———. *Mea: Sobranie stikhov, 1922–1924* (Меа: Собрание стихов, 1922–1924 / Mea: Collected verse, 1922–1924). Moscow: Gos. izd-vo, [1924]. 107 pp. 20 cm.

106. ———. *Mig: Stikhi, 1920–1921 g.* (Миг: Стихи, 1920–1921 г. / A moment: Verse, 1920–1921). Berlin, St. Petersburg, and Moscow: Z. I. Grzhebin, 1922. 80 pp. 14 cm.
107. ———. *Urbi et orbi: Stikhi, 1900–1903 g.* (—Стихи, 1900–1903 г. / — Verse, 1900–1903). [Moscow]: Skorpion, [1903]. 190, iv pp. 24 cm.
108. ———. *Zerkalo tenei: Stikhi, 1909–1912 g.* (Зеркало теней: Стихи, 1909–1912 г. / A mirror of shadows: Verse, 1909–1912). Moscow: Skorpion, 1912. 212, xii pp. 24 cm.
    Cover by Dmitrii Mitrokhin.

109. **Broderson, Moses.** *Sihes hulin: Eyne fun di geshikhten* (Ordinary tales: One of the stories). Moscow: Ferlag Haber, 1917. [18] pp. 24 × 30 cm.
    Cover by El Lissitzky.
    Children's story in Yiddish. Includes illustrations by Lissitzky.

110. **Bubnovyi valet** (Jack of Diamonds). *Sbornik statei po iskusstvu* (Сборник статей по искусству / Collection of essays on art). No. 1. [Moscow]: Bubnovyi valet, 1913. 78 pp. 22 cm.
    Includes paintings by Alexandra Exter, Robert Fal'k, Petr Konchalovskii, Aleksandr Kuprin, Henri Le Fauconnier, Fernand Léger, Aristarkh Lentulov, Ivan Mashkov, and Vasilii Rozhdestvenskii; articles by Ivan Aksenov, Guillaume Apollinaire, and Le Fauconnier; and reviews of exhibitions by the groups Union of Russian Artists and World of Art.

111. **Burliuk, David.** *Desiatyi Oktiabr'* (Десятый октябрь / The tenth October). New York: Mariia Nikiforovna Burliuk, 1928. 24 pp. 25 cm.
    Criticism and a poem on the occasion of the tenth anniversary of the October Revolution of 1917.
112. ———. *Galdiashchie "benua" i novoe russkoe natsional'noe iskusstvo: Razgovor g. Burliuka, g. Benua i g. Repina ob iskusstve* (Галдящие "бенуа" и новое русское национальное искусство: Разговор г. Бурлюка, г. Бенуа и г. Репина об искусстве / Noisy "Benoises" and the new Russian national art: A conversation between Mr. Burliuk, Mr. Benois, and Mr. Repin on art). St. Petersburg: Soiuz molodezhi, 1913. 20 pp. 24 cm.
    Includes Nikolai Burliuk's "O parodii i o podrazhanii" (On parody and imitation), a discussion of the collection of poems and drawings in *Neo-futurizm*. (See no. 584.)
113. [———]. Erik Gollerbakh. *Poeziia Davida Burliuka* (Поэзия Давида Бурлюка / The poetry of David Burliuk). New York: M. N. Burliuk, 1931. 32 pp., [7] plates. 23 cm.

114. ***Byt protiv menia*** (Быт против меня / Everyday life is against me). Leningrad: Izd-vo "Krasnaia gazeta," 1928. 32 pp. 28 cm.

An attack in words and pictures on the resurgence of bourgeois vulgarity in Soviet culture, by Vladimir Bogdanovich, Evgenii Ryss, Il'ia Segal', and Vsevolod Voevodin.

115. **Chaikin, Vladimir.** *Bal Satany* (Бал Сатаны / Satan's ball). Warsaw: Izd. avtora, 1928. 31 pp. 17 cm.
Poems.

116. **Charchoune, Serge.** *Dadaizm: Kompiliatsiia* (Дадаизм: Компиляция / Dada: A compilation). [Berlin]: Evropa Gomeopat, [1922]. [16] pp. 16 cm.
Discussion of Dada consisting chiefly of brief quotations from Dadaist writers.

117. ***Chasy, 1: Chas pervyi*** (Часы, 1: Час первый / Clock, one: The first hour). St. Petersburg: [n.p.], 1922. 88 pp. 14 cm.
Cover by Vladimir Milashevskii.
Miscellany of poetry and fiction. Includes works by I. Evert, Iurii Iurkun, Velimir Khlebnikov, Mikhail Kuzmin, B. Paparigopulo, Anna Radlova, and Viktor Shklovskii.

118. **Chekhov, Mikhail.** *Put' aktera* (Путь актера / An actor's path). Teatral'nye memuary, no. 4. Leningrad: Academia, 1928. 176 pp. 15 cm.
Research Institute has 2 different copies, with covers by Valentina Khodasevich and El Lissitzky respectively.

119. **Cheliuskin Expedition, 1933–1934.** *Pokhod "Cheliuskina"* (Поход «Челюскина» / The voyage of the *Cheliuskin*). Vols. [1–2]. *Kak my spasali cheliuskintsev* (Как мы спасали челюскинцев / How we saved the crew of the *Cheliuskin*). Vol. [3]. Geroicheskaia epopeia. Moscow: Izd. red. "Pravdy," 1934. 26 cm.
Design by P. Freiberg, Solomon Telingater, and Nikolai Sedel'nikov.
The first 2 volumes contain an account of the Cheliuskin Expedition to the Arctic Ocean off eastern Siberia. The third is an account of the rescue of its surviving members by Soviet aviators after the ship became trapped in the ice and sank.
From an edition of 100,000.

120. [———]. *Geroicheskaia epopeia* (Героическая эпопея / Epic of heroism). Moscow: Izd. red. "Pravdy"; Partizdat TsK VKP (b), 1935. [x], 153 pp., [24] plates (1 printed on clear plastic). 37 cm.
Design by Paula Freiberg, Nikolai Sedel'nikov, and Solomon Telingater.
A more ambitious publication on the same subject as *Pokhod "Cheliuskina,"* which was published one year earlier. (See no. 119.)
From an edition of 5,000. In a gray, cloth-covered slipcase.

121. ***Chempionat poetov*** (Чемпионат поэтов / Championship of poets). St. Petersburg: Severnye pleiady, [1913]. 15 pp. 24 cm.

Cover by Ivan Mozalevskii.

Poems, at least some of them parodies directed at the Futurists, by the group Championship of Poets (Markov 1968, 213). The participants are Ivan Evdokimov, Cheslava Mal'tanskaia, Gleb Marev, Anatolii Puchkov, Boris Skorobogatko, and F. S. Solov'ev.

From an edition of 300 (*Knizhnaia letopis'* 1913, no. 28231). Title page inscribed by Aleksandr Tiniakov in black ink and dated 7 November 1913, St. Petersburg.

122. **Cheremnykh, Mikhail.** *Antireligioznaia azbuka* (Антирелигиозная азбука / Antireligious alphabet). Moscow: Ogiz-Izogiz, [1932]. 28 color plates. 41 cm.

Twenty-eight color lithographs by Cheremnykh with captions by his wife, Nina Cheremnykh. Each antireligious image is explained in a caption of 4 words that all start with the same letter, a different letter for each image.

Lithographs laid down on heavy stock. In a pasteboard box (44 cm).

123. ———. *K zazhitochnoi zhizni! 19 risunkov khudozhnika M. Cheremnykh k rechi t. Stalina na I Vsesoiuznom s"ezde kolkhoznikov-udarnikov* (К зажиточной жизни! 19 рисунков художника М. Черемных к речи т. Сталина на I Всесоюзном съезде колхозников-ударников / Toward a prosperous life! Nineteen drawings by the artist M. Cheremnykh illustrating Comrade Stalin's speech at the first All-Union Congress of Shock-Worker Members of Collective Farms). Moscow: Ogiz-Izogiz, 1934. [1] leaf, 19 plates. 33 cm.

The illustrations are color relief halftones, and most have legends taken from Stalin's speech. The verses on plate 12 are by Nina Cheremnykh.

Inscribed on the title leaf by Mikhail Cheremnykh to the satirical magazine *Krokodil* (Crocodile) and dated 5 February 1934.

124. **Chernikhov, Iakov.** *Arkhitekturnye fantazii: 101 kompozitsiia v kraskakh, 101 arkhitekturnaia miniatiura, ispolneny pri uchastii D. Kopanitsyna i E. Pavlovoi* (Архитектурные фантазии: 101 композиция в красках, 101 архитектурная миниатюра, исполнены при участии Д. Копаницына и Е. Павловой / Architectural fantasies: 101 compositions in color, 101 architectural miniatures, realized with the participation of D. Kopanitsyn and E. Pavlova). Leningrad: Izd. Leningradskogo obl. otd-niia Vses. ob"edineniia "Mezhdunarodnaia kniga," 1933. 102 pp., 101 color plates. 31 cm.

Research Institute's copy signed on the title page "Molchanov" and dated 24 January 1936.

125. ———. *Iskusstvo nachertaniia* (Искусство начертания / The art of draftsmanship). Leningrad: Akademiia khudozhestv, 1927. 77 pp. 17 cm.

126. ———. *Konstruktsiia arkhitekturnykh i mashinnykh form* (Конструкция архитектурных и машинных форм / Construction of architectural and machine forms). [Leningrad]: Leningradskoe ob-vo arkhitektorov, 1931. 232 pp., 40 plates. 31 cm.
127. ———. *Ornament: Kompozitsionno-klassicheskie postroeniia* (Орнамент: Композиционно-классические построения / Ornament: Classically composed structures). Leningrad: Izd. avtora, 1930. 221 pp., 8 plates. 30 cm.
128. ———. *Osnovy sovremennoi arkhitektury: Eksperimental'no-issledovatel'skie raboty* (Основы современной архитектуры: Экспериментально-исследовательские работы / Foundations of modern architecture: Experimental research studies). Leningrad: Leningradskoe ob-vo arkhitektorov, 1930. 123 pp., 5 plates. 28 cm.
129. ———. *Osnovy sovremennoi arkhitektury: Eksperimental'no-issledovatel'skie raboty* (Основы современной архитектуры: Экспериментально-исследовательские работы / Foundations of modern architecture: Experimental research studies). 2nd ed., enl. Leningrad: Leningradskoe ob-vo arkhitektorov, 1931. 96 pp., 46 plates. 31 cm.

130. **Chernyi, Sasha.** *Detskii ostrov* (Детский остров / Children's island). Gdansk: Slovo, 1921. 158 pp., 32 cm.
Cover by Boris Grigor'ev.
Children's book in verse. Includes illustrations by Grigor'ev.

131. ***Chetvero: "Krasnye d'iavoliata"—sbornik, stat'i, fel'etony, stikhi*** (Четверо: «Красные дьяволята»—сборник, статьи, фельетоны, стихи / The foursome: *Red imps*—A miscellany of criticism, feuilletons, verse). Edited by St. Asilov. Moscow: Kinopechat', 1926. [8] pp., including cover. 23 × 26 cm.
Design by Konstantin Vialov. Back cover by Vasilii Sur'ianinov.
Brochure on the 1923 film produced and directed by Ivan Perestiani. "The foursome" refers to the film's 4 main actors.
Front cover is stamped "probnye ekzempliary" (trial copies).

132. **Chukovskii, Kornei.** *Futuristy: Igor' Severianin, Kruchenykh, Vl. Khlebnikov, Vas. Kamenskii, Vl. Maiakovskii* (Футуристы: Игорь Северянин, Крученых, Вл. Хлебников, Вас. Каменский, Вл. Маяковский / The Futurists: Igor' Severianin, Kruchenykh, Velimir Khlebnikov, Vasilii Kamenskii, Vladimir Mayakovsky). St. Petersburg: Poliarnaia zvezda, 1922. 84 pp. 20 cm.
Criticism.

133. **Churilin, Tikhon.** *Vesna posle smerti: Stikhi* (Весна после смерти: Стихи / Springtime after death: Verse). Moscow: Al'tsiona, 1915. 90 pp. 33 cm.

Includes 7 tipped-in lithographs by Nataliia Goncharova.
Copy 9 of 240.

134. ***Daesh'*** (Даешь / Let's produce!). Moscow: Rabochaia Moskva, 1929–1930. 30 cm.
Cover designs by Aleksandr Deineka, Dmitrii Moor, Aleksandr Rodchenko, and others. Artistic direction by Moor.
Social, political, literary, and artistic biweekly for the working class.
A total of 14 issues published.

135. **Debabov, Dmitrii.** *Po taige i tundre: Fotoocherk* (По тайге и тундре: Фотоочерк / Through taiga and tundra: A photo essay). Moscow: Soiuzfoto, Studiia "Fotokhudozhnik," 1937. 40 leaves. 24 × 30 cm.
Cover by Aleksandr Rodchenko and Varvara Stepanova.
Includes text by El-Registan.

136. **[Deineka, Aleksandr].** Boris Nikiforov. *A. Deineka.* [Moscow]: Izogiz, 1937. 121 pp., [5] plates. 30 cm.

137. **Deni, Viktor.** *Deni.* Moscow: Ogiz-Izogiz, 1934. [4] pp., [20] plates. In portfolio. 15 cm.
Posters for the group October.

138. **Derzhavin, Konstantin.** *Kniga o Kamernom teatre, 1914–1934* (Книга о Камерном театре, 1914–1934 / Book about the Kamerny Theater, 1914–1934). Leningrad: Khudozhestvennaia lit-ra, 1934. 239 pp., [78] plates. 25 cm.
Cover, ornamental capitals, and dust jacket by M. Grigor'ev.

139. ***Deviatyi smotr: Deviatyi vsesoiuznyi s"ezd Leninskogo kommunisticheskogo soiuza molodezhi*** (Девятый смотр: Девятый всесоюзный съезд Ленинского коммунистического союза молодежи / Ninth review: The ninth All-Union Congress of the Komsomol). [Moscow]: Ogiz, Molodaia gvardiia, 1931. 30 pp. 22 cm.
Written and designed by a shock brigade (a highly motivated task force of workers in the early 1930s) of the Children's Section of the publisher Molodaia gvardiia.

140. ***Distsipliny VKhUTEMAS*** (Дисциплины ВХУТЕМАС / The disciplines of VKhUTEMAS). [Moscow: n.p., 1920]. [6] sheets. In portfolio. 23 cm.
Caricatures in Constructivist style of instructors at the Higher State Artistic and Technical Workshops (VKhUTEMAS) in Moscow. Each incorporates a large numeral and a 2- or 4-line verse epigram on the subject of the

caricature. According to notes made by Galina Chichagova and preserved in a private archive in Moscow, the epigrams were composed by Chichagova and Aleksei Babichev, and the lithographs were done by A. Akhtyrko (Lodder 1983, 288 n. 142, 305).

Irregularly trimmed white-on-black lithographs mounted on cream-colored sheets of paper. Research Institute's copy is incomplete, including only the lithographs with the numerals 1, 2, 4, 5, 7, and 8. Their subjects are: (1) Aleksandr Vesnin and Liubov' Popova; (2) Aleksandr Osmerkin; (4) Ivan Kliun; (5) Aleksandr Rodchenko; (7) "Nadia" (for Nadezhda Udal'tsova); and (8) Vladimir Baranov-Rossiné. These are the instructors in charge of 6 of the 8 basic disciplines as constituted in 1920, the missing third discipline being directed by Alexandra Exter and the sixth by Aleksandr Drevin (Khan-Magomedov 1990, 69).

Front and back covers of portfolio each have a Constructivist lithograph printed in red and black. In Research Institute's copy they are mounted on a sheet of printer's waste on which it is possible to discern the words "Russkie drevnosti po snimkam I. F. Barshchevskogo. Vypusk 18. Izdanie Imperatorskogo Stroganovskogo [tsentral'nogo khudozhestvenno-promyshlennogo uchilishcha]" (Russian antiquities in photographs by I. F. Barshchevskii. Issue 18. A publication of the Imperial Stroganov [Central School of Applied Art]). The Stroganov Art School was an institutional predecessor of VKhUTEMAS.

141. ***Dokhlaia luna: Stikhi, proza, stat'i, risunki, oforty*** (Дохлая луна: Стихи, проза, статьи, рисунки, офорты / Dead moon: Verse, prose, essays, drawings, prints). 2nd ed., enl. Moscow: Pervyi zhurnal russk. futuristov, 1914. 123 pp., 19 plates. 24 cm.

Includes lithographs by David and Vladimir Burliuk, an article on literary theory by Benedikt Livshits, and poems by Konstantin Bol'shakov, David and Nikolai Burliuk, Vasilii Kamenskii, Velimir Khlebnikov, Aleksei Kruchenykh, Livshits, Vladimir Mayakovsky, and Vadim Shershenevich.

The lithographs are mostly printed in blue ink on white coated paper, and Vladimir Burliuk's frontispiece is in blue, green, and red.

142. ***Dvorets Sovetov*** (Дворец Советов / Palace of Soviets). Moscow: Mosoblispolkom, 1931. 17 cm.

Edited by M. V. Kriukov.

Bulletin contains descriptions and drawings from 15 entries in the international competition for the design of the Palace of Soviets. Includes entries from members of architectural associations such as the Association of New Architects (ASNOVA), the Society of Urban Architects (ARU), the All-Union Association of Proletarian Architects (VOPRA), and the Division of Architects for Socialist Construction (SASS) and architectural projects by Boris and Dmitrii Iofan (whose design for the Palace of Soviets was accepted and

approved in 1932 but never realized), Nikolai Ladovskii, and Aleksei Shchusev.
Research Institute's holdings: scattered issues.

143. ***Dvorets sovetov*** (Дворец советов / Palace of Soviets). Populiarnaia biblioteka po arkhitekture. Compiled by the Technical Propaganda Department of the Palace of Soviets Construction Project. Moscow: Izd-vo Vsesoiuznoi akademii arkhitektury, 1939. 47 pp. 22 cm.
Popular brochure on the construction of the Palace of Soviets up to 1939, in accordance with the final design by Vladimir Gel'freikh, Boris Iofan, and Vladimir Shchuko. Work stopped the following year because of World War II and never resumed.

144. **Edschmid, Kasimir.** *Baski, byki, araby: Kniga ob Ispanii i Marokko* (Баски, быки, арабы: Книга об Испании и Марокко / Basques, bulls, Arabs: A book about Spain and Morocco). Translated by Elena Eikhengol'ts. Moscow and Leningrad: Gos. izd-vo, 1929. 234 pp. 20 cm.
Design by Fain Tagirov.
Translation of *Basken, Stiere, Araber*.

145. **Efros, Abram.** *Profili* (Профили / Profiles). Moscow: Izd-vo "Federatsiia," 1930. 306 pp., [14] plates. 21 cm.
Essays on 14 Russian artists, with a portrait of each.

146. **Efros, Nikolai.** *Teatr "Letuchaia mysh'" N. F. Balieva: Obzor desiatiletnei khudozhestvennoi raboty pervogo russkogo teatra-kabare* (Театр «Летучая мышь» Н. Ф. Балиева: Обзор десятилетней художественной работы первого русского театра-кабарэ / N. F. Baliev's theater "The Bat": A survey of ten years' artistic work of the first Russian cabaret theater). [Moscow: n.p.], 1918. 48 pp. 30 cm.
Cover, headpieces, and tailpieces by Sergei Chekhonin.
Includes photographs by P. Orlov and Mikhail Sakharov.
Research Institute's copy is bound in dark red floral satin brocaded in gold and green with the spine in dark red velvet.

147. **[Eisenstein, Sergei]. Viktor Shklovskii, Lev Kuleshov, and Eduard Tisse.** *Eizenshtein: "Bronenosets Potemkin"* (Эйзенштейн: «Броненосец Потемкин» / Eisenstein: *The Battleship Potemkin*). Moscow: Kinopechat', 1926. 15 pp. 15 cm.
Cover signed "P. S. G.," probably for Petr Stepanovich Galadzhev.
Short essays by Kuleshov, Shklovskii, and Tisse, the film's cinematographer.

148. ***Ekran kino-gazety*** (Экран кино-газеты / The screen of movie-gazette). Moscow: Sovkino, 1925. 27 cm.

Edited by V. Erofeev and Kirill Shutko.

Illustrated supplement to *Kino-gazeta* (Movie-gazette). Includes photomontages by Petr Galadzhev featuring his numerous movie posters.

A total of 10 issues published. Continued as *Sovetskii ekran.* (See no. 745.)

149. ***Ekran: Vestnik teatra, iskusstva, kino, sporta*** (Экран: Вестник театра, искусства, кино, спорта / Screen: Herald of theater, art, film, and sport). Moscow: M. Dolinov i N. Khessin, 1921–1922. 36 cm.

Edited by I. I. and Z. I. Dobuzhskie, Mario Dolinov, and Nikolai Khessin.

Weekly journal dedicated to art, literature, and music. Includes contributions by Iakov Apushkin and Iakov Tugendkhol'd.

A total of 32 issues published.

Research Institute's holdings: scattered issues.

150. ***Ekspressionisty*** (Экспрессионисты / Expressionists). Moscow: Sad Akadema, 1921. 16 pp. 18 cm.

Poems by Evgenii Gabrilovich, Boris Lapin, Ippolit Sokolov, and Sergei Spasskii.

151. **El'sberg, Iakov. *Obshchestvennyi smysl russkogo literaturnogo futurizma: Neo-narodnichestvo russkoi literatury XX veka*** (Общественный смысл русского литературного футуризма: Нео-народничество русской литературы XX века / The social meaning of Russian literary Futurism: Neopopulism in twentieth-century Russian literature). Moscow: A. G. Mironov, 1922. 80 pp. 21 cm.

Cover signed "A. Shch."

Includes a foreword by Anatoly Lunacharsky.

Cover and title page bear the stamp "Pravda."

152. ***Epopeia*** (Эпопея / Epic). Berlin: Gelikon, 1922–1923. 273 pp. 21 cm.

Edited by Andrey Bely.

Literary monthly. Includes poetry by Bely and S. Klychkov, reminiscences about Aleksandr Blok by Bely, and fiction by Aleksandr Kusikov, Boris Pil'niak, and Aleksei Remizov. Research Institute's copy of no. 1 (1922), the cover of which was designed by El Lissitzky, is signed by the artist.

A total of 4 issues published.

Research Institute's holdings: scattered issues.

153. **Erenburg, Il'ia.** *A vse-taki ona vertitsia* (А все-таки она вертится / Eppur si muove [Nevertheless, it does move]). Moscow and Berlin: Gelikon, 1922. 139 pp., [16] plates. 22 cm.

Cover by Fernand Léger.

Essay defending Constructivism in art.

154. ———. *Budni: Stikhi* (Будни: Стихи / Work days: Verse). Paris: [n.p.], 1913. [54] pp. 19 cm.

155. ———. *Detskoe* (Детское / Things of childhood). Paris: [n.p.], 1914. 20 pp. 13 cm.
   Cover by E. Shiriaev.
   Rhyming prose.

156. ———. *Ispaniia* (Испания / Spain). 2 vols. [Moscow and Leningrad]: Ogiz-Izogiz, 1937. 31 cm.
   Vol. 1 designed by Evgenii Goliakhovskii. Vol. 2 designed by El and Es (Sophie) Lissitzky.
   Reportage in words and photographs from the Spanish civil war.

157. ———. *Lik voiny* (Лик войны / The face of war). 2nd ed. Berlin: Gelikon, 1923. 186 pp. 19 cm.
   Cover by Natan Al'tman.
   Reminiscences of France during World War I.

158. ———. *Materializatsiia fantastiki* (Материализация фантастики / The materialization of fantasy). Kinopechat', no. 126. Moscow and Leningrad: Kinopechat', 1927. 30 pp. 17 cm.
   Cover by Aleksandr Rodchenko.
   Essay on film.

159. ———. *Moi Parizh* (Мой Париж / My Paris). Moscow: Izogiz, 1933. 235 pp. 17 cm.
   Design by El Lissitzky.
   Impressions of Paris in words and pictures. Includes a photomontage by Lissitzky and photographs and text by Erenburg.

160. ———. *Molitva o Rossii* (Молитва о России / Prayer for Russia). Moscow: Severnye dni, 1918. 45 pp. 18 cm.
   Poems.

161. ———. *Shest' povestei o legkikh kontsakh* (Шесть повестей о легких концах / Six tales with easy endings). Moscow and Berlin: Gelikon, 1922. 163 pp. 21 cm.
   Cover by El Lissitzky.
   Includes illustrations by Lissitzky.

162. ———. *Trest D. E.: Istoriia gibeli Evropy* (Трест Д. Е.: История гибели Европы / The D. E. Trust: History of the destruction of Europe). Berlin: Gelikon, 1923. 197 pp. 23 cm.
   Cover by Vladimir Konstantinovskii.
   Novel.

163. ———. *Trinadtsat' trubok* (Тринадцать трубок / Thirteen pipes). Moscow and Berlin: Gelikon, 1923. 257 pp. 19 cm.
   Cover by Liubov' Kozintsova.
   Stories.

164. ———. *Trubka* (Трубка / Pipe). Leningrad: Krasnaia nov', 1924. 35 pp. 15 cm.

Cover by Ruvim Mazel'.
Story. Includes illustrations by Mazel'.

165. ———. *V Protochnom pereulke: Roman* (В Проточном переулке: Роман / In Protochny Lane: A novel). Paris: Gelikon, 1927. 224 pp. 20 cm.
Cover by Otakar Mrkvička and Karel Teige.

166. ———. *Zarubezhnye razdum'ia* (Зарубежные раздумья / Thoughts while abroad). Moscow: Kostry, 1922. 29 pp. 16 cm.
Poems.

167. ***Erste Russische Kunstausstellung*** (First Russian art exhibition). Berlin: Internationale Arbeiterhilfer, [1922]. 31 pp., [45] plates. 23 cm.
Cover by El Lissitzky.
Catalog of exhibition at the Galerie Van Diemen in Berlin.

168. **Esenin, Sergei.** *Ispoved' khuligana* (Исповедь хулигана / The confession of a hooligan). [Moscow: Imazhinisty], 1921. 12 pp. 21 cm.
Poems.

169. ———. *Isus mladenets* (Исус младенец/ Baby Jesus). [Petrograd]: Segodnia, [1918]. [8] pp., including cover. 20 cm.
Cover by Elena Turova.
Poems. Includes illustrations by Turova.

170. ———. *Kliuchi Marii* (Ключи Марии / Mary's keys). [Moscow]: Moskovskaia trudovaia artel' khudozhnikov slova, 1920. 42 pp. 15 cm.
Criticism.
On p. 4 the date of printing is given as 1919.

171. ———. *O Rossii i revoliutsii: Stikhotvoreniia i poemy* (О России и революции: Стихотворения и поэмы / On Russia and revolution: Poems short and long). Moscow: Sovremennaia Rossiia, 1925. 94 pp. 18 cm.

172. ———. *Persidskie motivy* (Персидские мотивы / Persian motifs). Moscow: Sovremennaia Rossiia, [1925]. 48 pp. 18 cm.
Poems.

173. ———. *Radunitsa* (Радуница / Ceremony for the dead). [Moscow]: Imazhinisty, 1921. 45 pp. 22 cm.
The third collection of Esenin's poetry to appear under this title. The first appeared in 1916 (Petrograd: M. V. Aver'ianov), the second in 1918 (Moscow: Moskovskaia trudovaia artel' khudozhnikov slova).

174. ———. *Strana sovetskaia* (Страна советская / Soviet land). Tbilisi: Sov. Kavkaz, 1925. 62 pp. 21 cm.
Cover by Kirill Zdanevich.
Poems.

175. ———. *Treriadnitsa* (Трерядница / Three-keyboard accordion). [Moscow]: Imazhinisty, 1921. [29] pp. 18 cm.
Poems.
Previously published by Zlak in Moscow, 1920.

176. [———]. Ivan Gruzinov. *S. Esenin razgovarivaet o literature i iskusstve* (С. Есенин разговаривает о литературе и искусстве / S. Esenin talks about literature and art). Moscow: Vseros. soiuz poetov, 1927. 22 pp. 23 cm.

177. [———]. *Sergei Esenin.* Moscow: Izdano Ekaterinoi Eseninoi, 1928. [44] leaves. 28 cm.

Album of photographs of the poet, published by his sister 3 years after his death.

178. **Esenin, Sergei, Anatolii Mariengof, and Vadim Shershenevich.** *Plavil'nia slov* (Плавильня слов / Foundry of words). Moscow: Imazhinisty pri Vseros. soiuze poetov, 1920. [43] pp. 18 cm.

Poems.

179. **Evreinov, Nikolai.** *"Chto takoe teatr": Knizhka dlia detei* («Что такое театр»: Книжка для детей / "What is theater": A little book for children). St. Petersburg: Svetozar, 1921. 76 pp., [1] plate. 30 cm.

Headpieces and tailpieces by Sergei Chekhonin.

Includes illustrations by Chekhonin and Vladimir Milashevskii.

180. ———. *K postanovke "Khil'perika"* (К постановке «Хильперика» / On the production of *Chilpéric*). [St. Petersburg]: Direktsiia Palas-Teatra, 1913. 55 pp., [4] plates. 24 cm.

Study of Hervé's operetta read by Evreinov to the company of the Palace Theater on 1 August 1913. Includes costume sketches by Nikolai Kalmakov.

181. ———. *Predstavlenie liubvi: Monodrama v 3-kh deistviiakh* (Представление любви: Монодрама в 3-х действиях / A representation of love: A monodrama in three acts). St. Petersburg: N. I. Butkovskaia, [1916?]. Pp. 52–127. 29 cm.

Cover by Iurii Annenkov.

Offprint from *Studiia impressionistov* (Impressionists' studio) of 1910. Includes the original illustrations by Nikolai Kul'bin, Liudmilla Shmit-Ryzhova, and Evgenii Vashchenko and a new portrait of Evreinov by Annenkov.

182. ———. *Proiskhozhdenie dramy: Pervobytnaia tragediia i rol' kozla v istorii ee vozniknoveniia* (Происхождение драмы: Первобытная трагедия и роль козла в истории ее возникновения / The origin of drama: Primitive tragedy and the role of the goat in the history of its rise). Teatr: Monografii po istorii i teorii teatra, no. 1. St. Petersburg: Petropolis, 1921. 58 pp. 18 cm.

183. ———. *Teatralizatsiia zhizni: Poet, teatralizruiushchii zhizn'* (Театрализация жизни: Поэт, театрализирующий жизнь / Adapting life for the theater: A poet who does so). Moscow: Vremia, 1922. 15 pp. 22 cm.

Cover by Aleksandr Iakimchenko.

Study of Vasilii Kamenskii.

184. ———. *Teatral'nye inventsii* (Театральные инвенции / Theatrical inventions). Moscow: Vremia, 1922. 14 pp. 23 cm.

185. ———. *Teatr dlia sebia* (Театр для себя / Theater for oneself). 3 vols. Petrograd: N. I. Butkovskaia, 1915–1917. 22 cm.
Essays. Vols. 1 and 3 are illustrated by Nikolai Kul'bin. Vol. 2 is illustrated by Iurii Annenkov.

186.———. *Teatr u zhivotnykh: O smysle teatral'nosti s biologicheskoi tochki zreniia* (Театр у животных: О смысле театральности с биологической точки зрения / Theater among the animals: On the biological meaning of theatricality). Leningrad and Moscow: Kniga, 1924. 72 pp. 21 cm.
Cover by Nikolai Ushin.

187. **Exposition internationale des arts décoratifs et industriels modernes.** *L'art decoratif et industriel de l'URSS*. Moscow: Comité de la Section de l'URSS, 1925. 94 pp., [13] plates. 27 cm.
Cover by Aleksandr Rodchenko.

188. ***Ezhegodnik Moskovskogo arkhitekturnogo obshchestva*** (Ежегодник Московского архитектурного общества / Annual of the Moscow Architectural Society). Moscow: Moskovskoe arkhitekturnoe ob-vo, 1909–1930. 33 cm.
Annual of the Moscow Architectural Society (MAO). Divided into 4 sections: architecture, painting, sculpture, and decorative arts. No. 5 (1928), a special issue marking the sixtieth anniversary of MAO, founded in 1867, was published in both Russian and German to provide Western readers with an overview of Soviet architecture. It contains an introductory essay by Ivan Mashkov that discusses the history and accomplishments of the association. No. 6 (1930), edited by Grigorii Barkhin, covers the achievements of Soviet architecture from the middle of 1928 through 1929 and includes sections on architectural projects for libraries, schools, sanitariums, administrative buildings, and apartment complexes.
A total of 6 issues published. Publication suspended from 1917 to 1927.
Research Institute's holdings: scattered issues.

189. ***Ezhegodnik Obshchestva arkhitektorov-khudozhnikov*** (Ежегодник Общества архитекторов-художников / Annual of the Society of Artist-Architects). St. Petersburg: OAKh, 1906–1935. 29 cm.
Covers by Evgenii Lansere.
Includes illustrations, drawings, and photographs of architectural projects and restoration work conducted in Russia since 1906. No. 8 (1913) celebrates the 100th anniversary of the death of architect Thomas Jean de Thomon, who participated in various Russian architectural projects and was appointed the court architect in 1802.
A total of 14 issues published. Publication suspended from 1917 to 1926.

Continuation of *Ezhegodnik Imperatorskogo obshchestva arkhitektorov-khudozhnikov* (Annual of the imperial society of artist-architects [1906–1916]).

190. ***Ezhenedel'naia gazeta 41°*** (Еженедельная газета 41° / Weekly gazette 41°). Tbilisi: 41°, 1919. 4 pp. 59 cm.

Organ of 41°, formed in Tbilisi on the initiative of Aleksei Kruchenykh. Although the group existed from late 1917 until 1920, it was formally announced only in 1919 with the publication of their newspaper.

Contains the group's manifesto, signed by Nikolai Cherniavskii, Iliazd, Kruchenykh, and Igor' Terent'ev (Markov 1968, 338).

A total of 1 issue published.

191. **Fedorov-Davydov, Aleksei.** *Russkoe iskusstvo promyshlennogo kapitalizma* (Русское искусство промышленного капитализма / Russian art of industrial capitalism). Istoriia i teoriia iskusstv, no. 11. Moscow: Gos. akademiia khudozhestvennykh nauk, 1929. 246 pp. 24 cm.

Cover signed "E."

Cover printed in red and black.

192. **Feinberg, Il'ia.** *1914-i: Dokumental'nyi pamflet* (1914-й: Документальный памфлет / The year 1914: A documentary pamphlet). Moscow: MTP, 1934. 92 pp., [7] plates. 25 × 18 cm.

Design by Solomon Telingater.

Plates have guard tissues with quotations from Lenin and Stalin in red letterpress. Slips tipped in at intervals have quotations from Lenin printed in white on red. The foreword tipped in at p. [3] consists of 4 narrower pages, each 25 × 12 cm.

193. ***Feniks*** (Феникс / The phoenix). Tbilisi: [n.p.], 1918–1919 [?]. 22 cm.

Edited by Iurii Degen.

Covers by Igor' Terent'ev.

Artistic and literary monthly. Includes linoleum cuts by Vladimir Gudiashvili and Terent'ev; articles by Boris Korneev, Aleksei Kruchenykh, and Terent'ev; and poems by Georgii Deshkin, Georgii Evangulov, Iuliia Makovskaia, Aleksandr Poroshin, and Sergei Rafalovich.

Research Institute's holdings: scattered issues.

194. ***Film und Filmkunst in der UdSSR, 1917–1928*** (Film and the art of film in the USSR, 1917–1928). [Moscow]: Gesellschaft für kulturelle Verbinding der Sowjetunion mit dem Auslande, [1928?]. 55 pp. 21 cm.

Cover by Gustav Klutsis and Sergei Sen'kin.

Catalog for the Soviet section of a proposed international exhibition of cinematography to be held at the Hague. Contains text in English, French, and German.

195. **Filonov, Pavel.** *Propeven' o prorosli mirovoi* (Пропевень о прорасли мировой / Sermon-chant on universal sprouting). Petrograd: Izd. Mirovyi raztsvet, [1915]. 24 pp., 3 plates. 23 cm.

Transrational verse drama illustrated with 4 relief halftones of Filonov's drawings, one of them mounted on the front cover.

From an edition of 300 (*Knizhnaia letopis'* 1915, no. 8482). Bears the ownership stamp of D. Gordeev on the front cover.

196. **Finkel', Aleksandr.** *Sukhoi blesk: Stikhi, 1919–1924* (Сухой блеск: Стихи, 1919–1924 / Dry luster: Verse, 1919–1924). Kharkov: Geraklit, 1925. 38 pp. 15 cm.

Cover signed "SR," perhaps for Stepan Rzhetskii.

Cover is in the Constructivist style.

197. **Finkel', Aleksandr, Ester Papernaia, and Aleksandr Rozenberg.** *Parnas dybom: Pro kozlov, sobak i veverleev* (Парнас дыбом: Про козлов, собак и веверлеев / Parnassus upended: Concerning goats, dogs, and Waverleys). 2nd ed., enl. [Kharkov]: Kosmos, 1927. 82 pp. 15 cm.

Cover by Stepan Rzhetskii.

Literary parodies.

198. **Forsh, Ol'ga.** *Ravvi: P'esa v trekh deistviiakh* (Равви: Пьеса в трех действиях / Rabbi: A play in three acts). Berlin: Skify, 1922. 62 pp. 20 cm.

Cover by El Lissitzky.

199. ***Futuristy: Pervyi zhurnal russkikh futuristov*** (Футуристы: Первый журнал русских футуристов / Futurists: First journal of Russian Futurists). Moscow: David Burliuk, 1914. 160 pp. 27 cm.

Edited by Vasilii Kamenskii.

Contains introductory statement that journal was to appear 6 times a year. Includes color lithographs by David and Vladimir Burliuk; paintings by Alexandra Exter; criticism; prose by Nikolai Burliuk, Benedikt Livshits, and Vadim Shershenevich; poetry by Konstantin Bol'shakov, David and Vladimir Burliuk, Kamenskii, and Vladimir Mayakovsky, including several of Kamenskii's Ferroconcrete poems such as "Sketin rin" (Skating rink) and "Tango s korovamy" (Tango with cows).

A total of 1 issue published, which appeared as a double issue (no. 1/2).

200. **Gabo, Naum.** Archive of Jan Tschichold. Letter. N.d.

One handwritten letter from Gabo to Tschichold, sent from Paris after 1932. Gabo discusses the possibility of making Constructivist art in Paris, his difficulties in adapting to French culture, and the lack of people like Tschichold, who adhered to the ideas of Constructivism.

201. **Gan, Aleksei.** *Konstruktivizm* (Конструктивизм / Constructivism). [Tver]: Tverskoe izd-vo, 1922. 70 pp. 24 cm.

Cover attributed to Aleksandr Rodchenko (Khan-Magomedov 1986, 131). Artistic theory.

There is a lengthy dedicatory inscription by Gan on the title page, dated 9 August 1926. The addressee is not named, but Gan concludes, "Tvoe imia sviazano s pervymi shagami konstruktivizma—sviazhis' s nim snova" (Your name is linked with the first steps of Constructivism—join it again).

202. ***Gazeta futuristov*** (Газета футуристов / Gazette of the Futurists). Moscow: Assotsiatsiia sotsialisticheskogo iskusstva, 1918. 1 sheet. 71 cm.

Edited by David Burliuk, Vasilii Kamenskii, and Vladimir Mayakovsky.

This newspaper, issued on 15 March 1918, was the last place in which the three poets appeared as a group. Although it was printed and published by the poets themselves using funds provided by Lev Grinkur (Jangfeldt 1976, 17), its publisher was announced as the Association of Socialist Art (ASIS). Includes Mayakovsky's poems "Revoliutsiia" (Revolution) and "Nash marsh" (Our march); poems by Burliuk and Kamenskii; a short piece on Café Pittoresque, one of the Futurists' favorite gathering places; 2 poems by a younger Futurist poet, Sergei Spasskii; a poem by the Ego-Futurist Vasilisk Gnedov; a short poem by Dokto; and three manifestos: "Dekret o demokratizatsii iskusstva" (A decree on the democratization of art) and "Manifest Letuchei federatsii futuristov" (A manifesto of the Flying Federation of Futurists), signed by all three poets, and "Otkrytoe pis'mo rabochim" (An open letter to the workers), signed by Mayakovsky alone. The text was printed on both sides of a sheet the size of a daily newspaper.

A total of 1 issue published.

203. **Ginsburger, Roger.** *Frankreich: Die Entwicklung der neuen Ideen nach Konstruktion und Form* (France: The development of new ideas of construction and form). Neues Bauen in der Welt, vol. 3. Vienna: Anton Schroll, 1930. 132 pp. 28 cm.

Cover and dust jacket by El Lissitzky.

204. **Ginzburg, M.** *Na vostok* (На восток / Go east). Leningrad: Izd. avtora, 1926. 31 pp. 17 cm.

Poems.

From an edition of 500.

205. **Ginzburg, Moisei.** *Arkhitektura sanatoriia NKTP v Kislovodske* (Архитектура санатория НКТП в Кисловодске / Architecture of the

NKTP sanitorium in Kislovodsk). Moscow: Izd-vo Akademii arkhitektury SSSR, 1940. 85 pp., [3] plates. 30 cm.

The first plate is missing.

206. ———. *Ritm v arkhitekture* (Ритм в архитектуре / Rhythm in architecture). Moscow: Sredi kollektsionerov, 1923. 116 pp. 28 cm.

Cover signed "I. R.," perhaps for Ivan Rerberg.

207. ———. *Stil' i epokha: Problemy sovremennoi arkhitektury* (Стиль и эпоха: Проблемы современной архитектуры / Style and epoch: Problems of contemporary architecture). Moscow: Gos. izd-vo, 1924. 238 pp. 23 cm.

208. **Globa, Andrei.** *Famar': Tragediia* (Фамарь: Трагедия / Tamar: A tragedy). Moscow and Petrograd: Gos. izd-vo, 1923. 100 pp. 24 cm.

Cover by Vladimir Favorskii.

Includes illustrations by Favorskii.

209. **Gnedov, Vasilisk.** *Gostinets sentimentam* (Гостинец сентиментам / A treat for the sentiments). [St. Petersburg]: Peterburgskii glashatai I. V. Ignat'eva, 1913. 4 pp. 27 cm.

Poems.

210. **Gogol', Nikolai.** *Nos: Povest'* (Нос: Повесть / The nose: A tale). Moscow and Berlin: Gelikon, 1922. 68 pp. 22 cm.

Cover by Vasilii Masiutin.

Includes illustrations by Masiutin.

211. **Goll, Claire, and Ivan Goll.** *Poèmes d'amour*. Collection surréaliste. Paris: Jean Budry, 1925. 60 pp. 19 cm.

Contains 4 illustrations by Marc Chagall.

Copy 325 of 625.

212. **Goncharova, Nataliia.** *Misticheskie obrazy voiny: 14 litografii* (Мистические образы войны: 14 литографий / Mystical images of war: Fourteen lithographs). Moscow: V. N. Kashin, 1914. [3] p., [14] plates. In portfolio. 32 cm (lithographs); 37 cm (portfolio).

Cover includes a lithographed vignette by Goncharova.

Cover title is *Voina* (War). Lower right-hand corner of cover has roman numeral "I," suggesting that a continuation was planned.

213. **Gorlov, Nikolai.** *Futurizm i revoliutsiia: Poeziia futuristov* (Футуризм и революция: Поэзия футуристов / Futurism and revolution: The poetry of the Futurists). Moscow: Gos. izd-vo, [1924]. 85 pp. 19 cm.

214. ***Gosplan literatury: Sbornik Literaturnogo tsentra konstruktivistov*** (LTsK) (Госплан литературы: Сборник Литературного центра конструктивистов (ЛЦК) / The state plan for literature: A collection of the Literary Center of the Constructivists). Edited by Il'ia Sel'vinskii and Kornelii Zelinskii. Moscow and Leningrad: Krug, 1925. 144 pp. 23 cm.

Cover by Nikolai Kupreianov.

Includes contributions by Boris Agapov, Ivan Aksenov, Vera Inber, Sel'vinskii, Dir Tumannyi (pseudonym for Nikolai Panov), and Zelinskii. Inserted is a copy of *Izvestiia LTsK* (The LTsK news), a single 46 × 66 cm sheet folded to 23 × 16 cm.

215. ***Gostinitsa dlia puteshestvuiushchikh v prekrasnom*** (Гостиница для путешествующих в прекрасном / Hotel for travelers in the beautiful). Moscow: Vol'nitsa, 1922–1924. 20–31 cm.

Edited by N. Savkin.

Primary journal of the Imagists, a group active from 1919 to 1927. Contains numerous illustrations by Vasilii Chekrygin and Georgii Iakulov; the stage design by Konstantin Medunetskii and Georgii and Vladimir Stenberg for *Zheltaia kofta* (Yellow blouse), a play performed in 1922 by the Kamerny Theater in Moscow; an article by Fernand Léger in no. 3 (1923) on his costume design for the ballet *Sotvorenie mira* (Creation of the world); and poetry and prose by Nikolai Erdman, Sergei Esenin, Pavel Kuznetsov, Osip Mandel'shtam, Anatolii Mariengof, and Vadim Shershenevich. Page 1 of no. 3 (1924) contains an illegible inscription by Riurik Ivnev.

Irregularly published. A total of 4 issues published. Publisher varies.

216. ***Gosudarstvennoe izdatel'stvo za piat' let*** (Государственное издательство за пять лет / Five years of the State Publishing House). Edited by L. I. Ruzer. Moscow: Gos. izd-vo, 1924. 172, ii pp., [32], 30 plates. 22 cm.

Cover by Boris Titov.

Seventeen essays by various authors on the beginnings of the State Publishing House. In addition to portraits, views, and illustrated graphs (the last by A. Kurovskii), the first series of plates includes samples from 2 relatively modest, early publications of 1919–1920. The second series of plates consists of title pages and illustrations from later, more accomplished publications, some in color.

217. **Gosudarstvennyi muzei novogo zapadnogo iskusstva** (State Museum of New Western Art). *Illiustrirovannyi katalog* (Иллюстрированный каталог / Illustrated catalog). Moscow: [n.p.], 1928. 130 pp., 32 plates. 17 cm.

218. **Gosudarstvennyi muzei novogo zapadnogo iskusstva** (I Shchukinskoe otdelenie) (State Museum of New Western Art [first Shchukin section]). *Vystavka novykh priobretenii (graviury i litografii): Podrobnyi illiustrirovannyi katalog* (Выставка новых приобретений (гравюры и литографии): Подробный иллюстрированный каталог / Exhibition of new acquisitions [engravings and lithographs]: A detailed illustrated catalog). Moscow: [n.p.] 1927. 49 pp. 18 cm.

219. **Gosudarstvennyi muzei novogo zapadnogo iskusstva** (II Morozovskoe otdelenie) (State Museum of New Western Art [second Morozov section]). *Vystavka novykh priobretenii (zhivopis', risunok): Podrobnyi illiustrirovannyi katalog* (Выставка новых приобретений (живопись, рисунок): Подробный иллюстрированный каталог / Exhibition of new acquisitions [painting and drawing]: A detailed illustrated catalog). Moscow: [n.p.], 1927. 70 pp. 18 cm.

220. **Gosudarstvennyi teatr imeni Meierkhol'da** (Meyerhold State Theater). *Staatstheater W. Meyerhold: Auslandstournee, 1930* (The V. Meyerhold State Theater: Foreign tour, 1930). Berlin: Petropolis, 1930. 46 pp. 27 cm.

Cover by Gustav Klutsis.

221. ***Govorit Il'ich*** (Говорит Ильич / Lenin speaking). Moscow: Ogiz, Molodaia gvardiia, 1932. 32, [32] pp. 22 cm.

Design by Solomon Telingater.

Devoted to Lenin's speech before the third All-Union Congress of the Komsomol in 1920 and to the organization's subsequent progress through its ninth congress in 1931.

222. **Gozzi, Carlo.** *Printsessa Turandot: Teatral'no-tragicheskaia kitaiskaia skazka v 5 aktakh* (Принцесса Турандот: Театрально-трагическая китайская сказка в 5 актах / Princess Turandot: A theatrico-tragic Chinese tale in five acts). Translated by Mikhail Osorgin. Moscow and Petrograd: Gos. izd-vo, [1923]. 222 pp., [26] plates. 32 cm.

Design and cover by Ignatii Nivinskii.

Printsessa Turandot was directed by Evgenii Vakhtangov for the Third Studio of the Moscow Art Theater, now the Vakhtangov Theater. Includes vignettes, and sketches for costumes and scenery by Nivinskii.

223. **Gralitsa, Iurii.** *Detskii Internatsional* (Детский Интернационал / Children's International). Moscow and Leningrad: Gos. izd-vo, 1926. 32 pp. 23 cm.

Cover by Georgii Echeistov.

Children's book. Includes illustrations by Echeistov.

Entire volume is reproduced by lithography.

224. **Grigor'ev, Boris.** *Intimité* (Intimacy). St. Petersburg: V. M. Iasnyi, 1918. 87 pp. 35 cm.

Drawings of women by Grigor'ev and essays by Vsevolod Dmitriev and Vsevolod Voinov on his work.

Copy 135 of 1,000.

225. ———. *Raseia* (Расея / Rooshia). St. Petersburg: V. M. Iasnyi, 1918. 42 pp., 33 plates. 34 cm.

Images of Russian peasants. Includes tipped-in plates, most of which are on sheets made from 2 pieces of wallpaper pasted back to back.

Copy 448 of 750. Research Institute also has copies of the Russian-language edition published in Berlin by S. Efron and the German-language edition published in Potsdam by Müller Verlag, both in 1922.

226. ———. *Visages de Russie* (Faces of Russia). Paris: P. Ollendorff, 1923. 100 pp. 37 cm.

Includes relief halftones of paintings and drawings by Grigor'ev, depicting Russian peasants, landscapes, and actors in costume for parts in Russian plays and texts by André Antoine, André Levinson, Louis Réau, and Clare Sheridan.

Copy 223 of 500. Research Institute also has a copy of the English-language edition published in London in 1924 under the title *Faces of Russia*.

227. **Grishchenko, Aleksei.** *"Krizis iskusstva" i sovremennaia zhivopis': Po povodu lektsii N. Berdiaeva* («Кризис искусства» и современная живопись: По поводу лекции Н. Бердяева / The "crisis in art" and contemporary painting: Apropos of a lecture by N. Berdiaev). Voprosy zhivopisi, no. 4. Moscow: Izd. avtora, 1917. 29 pp. 25 cm.

228. ———. *O sviaziakh russkoi zhivopisi s Vizantiei i Zapadom XIII–XX vv.: Mysli zhivopistsa* (О связях русской живописи с Византией и Западом XIII–XX вв.: Мысли живописца / On the links of Russian painting with Byzantium and the West, thirteenth through twentieth centuries: Thoughts of a painter). Moscow: Izd. A. Grishchenko, 1913. 89 pp. 27 cm.

229. ———. *Russkaia ikona kak iskusstvo zhivopisi* (Русская икона как искусство живописи / The Russian icon and the art of painting). Voprosy zhivopisi, no. 3. Moscow: Izd. avtora, 1917. 165 pp. 26 cm.

230. **Griuntal', Vladimir, and G. Iablonovskii.** *Chto eto takoe?* (Что это такое? / What is that?). [Moscow]: Ogiz, Molodaia gvardiia, 1932. [32] pp. 17 × 24 cm.

Children's book. The first section consists of photographs of common objects, taken from angles that make the objects hard to recognize. Each photograph is associated with an arithmetic problem. In the second section the correct answers to the problems provide the key to locating photographs of the same objects, taken from more revealing angles.

231. **Gruzinov, Ivan.** *Imazhinizma osnovnoe* (Имажинизма основное / The basis of Imagism). Moscow: Imazhinisty, 1921. 21 pp. 26 cm.

232. ———. *Seraficheskie podveski* (Серафические подвески / Seraphic pendants). Petrograd: Imazhinisty, 1922. [7] pp. 18 cm.

Poems.

From an edition of 100.

233. **Gumilev, Nikolai.** *Farforovyi pavil'on: Kitaiskie stikhi* (Фарфоровый павильон: Китайские стихи / The porcelain pavilion: Chinese poetry). 2nd ed., enl. Petrograd: Mysl', 1922. 28 pp. 17 cm.

234. ———. *Koster: Stikhi* (Костер: Стихи / The campfire: Verse). Berlin, St. Petersburg, and Moscow: Z. I. Grzhebin, 1922. 59 pp. 14 cm.

235. [———]. *Gil'gamesh: Vavilonskii epos* (Гилгамеш: Вавилонский эпос / Gilgamesh: The Babylonian epic). Translated by Nikolai Gumilev. St. Petersburg: Z. I. Grzhebin, 1919. 78 pp. 20 cm.

236. **Guro, Elena.** *Nebesnye verbliuzhata* (Небесные верблюжата / Baby camels of the sky.) [St. Petersburg]: Zhuravl', 1914. 126 pp. 22 cm.

A posthumous collection of poems and short prose sketches. Includes a photograph of Guro and 15 illustrations (some of which are tipped in) and 15 headpieces and tailpieces by her.

From an edition of 750 (*Knizhnaia letopis'* 1914, no. 6463). Thick, light-green paper is used throughout. Research Institute also has a copy of the publisher's announcement for *Nebesnye verbliuzhata.*

237. ———. *Osennii son: P'esa v chetyrekh kartinakh* (Осенний сон: Пьеса в четырех картинах / Autumn dream: A play in four pictures). St. Petersburg: [Zhuravl'], 1912. 57 pp., [5] plates. 20 cm.

The play is followed by 5 short prose pieces and 2 poems. Includes 3 tipped-in color relief halftones of paintings by Guro's husband, Mikhail Matiushin, an excerpt from his suite for violin and piano (also entitled *Osennii son*), and 2 relief halftones of pencil drawings by Guro of her son V. V. Notenberg, who died as a child. The drawings show him as he might have appeared had he lived to about the age of 18 (Markov 1968, 17).

238. ———. *Sharmanka: P'esy, stikhi, proza* (Шарманка: Пьесы, стихи, проза / The hurdy-gurdy: Plays, verse, prose). St. Petersburg: [Zhuravl'], 1909. 218, [15] pp. 20 cm.

Cover by Guro.

Includes illustrations by Guro, 3 illustrations by N. I. Liubavina, and Mikhail Matiushin's music for the harlequin's canzonet from Guro's play *Nishchii arlekin* (The poor harlequin).

Research Institute's copy has 2 impressions of a giraffe stamped in black ink on pp. [1] and [3], presumably an owner's mark.

239. **Gusman, Boris.** *100 poetov: Literaturnye portrety, s prilozheniem bibliograficheskogo ukazatelia russkoi poezii za poslednee desiatiletie* (100 поэтов: Литературные портреты, с приложением библиографического указателя русской поэзии за последнее десятилетие / One hundred poets: Literary portraits, together with a bibliographical index to Russian poetry of the last decade). [Tver]: Oktiabr', 1923. 291, xxix pp. 21 cm.
Cover by Mikhail Sokolov.

240. **Gutman, L.** *Strana zhivykh kukol: Pro tsarei, pro soldat, pro voinu, pro chuzhie strany* (Страна живых кукол: Про царей, про солдат, про войну, про чужие страны / The land of living puppets: About tsars, soldiers, war, foreign lands). Moscow and Leningrad: Molodaia gvardiia, 1931. 63 pp. 22 cm.
Cover by P. Suvorov.
Many of the illustrations are taken from Kurt Tucholsky's *Deutschland, Deutschland über Alles* (Germany, Germany above all), designed by John Heartfield. The remainder are from various Soviet sources.

241. **Hofstein, David.** *Troyer* (Mourning). Kiev: Kultur-lige, 1922. xxiii pp., 4 plates. 33 cm.
Poems in Yiddish. Includes illustrations by Marc Chagall.

242. **Iakubovskii, Georgii.** *Kul'turnaia revoliutsiia i literatura* (Культурная революция и литература / Cultural revolution and literature). Moscow: Moskovskoe t-vo pisatelei, 1928. 206 pp. 18 cm.
Cover by P. Liubarskii.

243. ***Iaponskoe kino: Vystavka*** (Японское кино: Выставка / Japanese cinema: An exhibition). Moscow: Vses. ob-vo kul'turnoi sviazi s zagranitsei, 1929. 23 pp. 15 × 21 cm.
Design and cover by El Lissitzky.

244. ***Iav': Stikhi*** (Явь: Стихи / Reality: Verse). [Moscow]: Iav', 1919. 69 pp. 27 cm.
Cover by Aristarkh Lentulov.
Includes contributions by Andrey Bely, Sergei Esenin, Riurik Ivnev, Vasilii Kamenskii, Anatolii Mariengof, Aleksandr Olenin, Petr Oreshin, Boris Pasternak, Sergei Reksin, Vadim Shershenevich, Sergei Spasskii, Ivan Startsev, and Galina Vladychina (spelled *Vladygina* on the cover and in the table of contents).

245. **Iermilov, Vasyl'.** *Ukraïnske maliarstvo* (Українське малярство / Ukrainian painting). Tretia seriia monohrafii pro Ukrainske maliarstvo pid zah. redaktsieiu A. Berezins'koho. Kharkov: Rukh, 1931. 57 pp. 25 cm.

Design by Iermilov.
Includes text by Valeriian Polishchuk.

246. **Ignat'ev, Ivan.** *Ego-futurizm* (Эго-футуризм / Ego-Futurism). [St. Petersburg]: SPb. Glashatai, 1913. 16 pp. 27 cm.
Historical and theoretical discussion of the literary movement Ego-Futurism.

247. **Ignatov, Sergei.** *"Fedra" v Moskovskom Kamernom teatre* («Федра» в Московском Камерном театре / *Phèdre* at the Moscow Kamerny Theater). Moscow: Izd. avtora, 1925. 23 pp. 17 cm.
Includes gravures of costume sketches by Georgii and Vladimir Stenberg.

248. **Iliazd.** *Ianko, krul' albanskai* (Янко, круль албанскай / Ianko, king of Albania). Aslaablich'ia, 1. Tbilisi: Sindikat, 1918. [28] pp. 15 cm.
Play.
From an edition of 105. The copy number is nearly illegible, but it may be 62.

249. ———. *lidantIU fAram* (лидантЮ фАрам / Le-Dantiu as a lighthouse). Aslaab"lIch'ia, dEistva 5. Paris: 41°, 1923. 61 pp. 19 cm.
Cover by Naum Granovskii.
Play. Dedicated to the painter Mikhail Le-Dantiu, who had recently died at the age of 26. Includes Georges Ribemont-Dessaignes's separately bound, 8-page preface in French.
Copy 282 of 530. Chapon reports that the edition actually consisted of only 150 copies, the remainder being pulped (1978, 110). Inscribed in verse by Iliazd in black ink on p. 1 to Jean Lebedeff and dated 18 January 1924. Inserted in Research Institute's copy is a classified advertisement torn from *Paris-Soir* for 14 February 1924 announcing the publication of *lidantIU fAram,* written in "un dialecte russe dadaïsé . . . tuméfié d'avenir" (a dadaizing Russian dialect... pregnant with the future).

250. ———. *Nataliia Goncharova, Mikhail Larionov.* Moscow: Ts. A. Miunster, 1913. 39 pp., [46], [8] plates, xxi pp. 30 cm.
The second sequence of plates consists of tipped-in lithographs by Goncharova and Larionov, 4 by each artist.
From an edition of 525.

251. ———. *Ostraf Paskhi* (Остраф Пасхи / Easter Island). [Tbilisi: 41°, 1919]. 31 pp. 21 cm.
A play, the third in the pentalogy *Aslaablich'ia* (Aspects of a donkey).

252. ***Illiustrirovannoe prilozhenie k Stroitel'noi gazete*** (Иллюстрированное приложение к Строительной газете / An illustrated supplement to the *Construction* newspaper). Moscow: [n.p., n.d]. 30–44 cm.

Newspaper. Each issue is dedicated to a specific architectural project or competition and has its own title. Documents the major projects of high Stalinist architecture, including designs for the party buildings, apartment and industrial complexes, concert halls, theaters, and public dining places.
Research Institute's holdings: scattered issues.

253. ***Imazhinisty*** (Имажинисты / Imagists). Moscow: Izd. avtorov, 1925. 38 pp. 22 cm.
Cover montage by Georgii Stenberg.
Second collection of poetry with this title published by the Imagists, the earlier appearing in 1921. Includes photographs by Moisei Nappel'baum and contributions by Riurik Ivnev, Anatolii Mariengof, Matvei Roizman, and Vadim Shershenevich. The cover montage incorporates photographs of the 4 poets by Nappel'baum.

254. ***Industriia sotsializma*** (Индустрия социализма / The industry of socialism). Moscow: Stroim, Izogiz, 1935. 6 fascicles, 2 maps. In portfolio. 37 cm.
Design by El Lissitzky.
Two maps with key.

255. **Institut khudozhestvennoi kul'tury** (Institute of Artistic Culture). Receipts.
Eighteen receipts for purchases of art supplies, signed by students and staff from 1923 and 1924.

256. **Internationale Presse-Ausstellung, Köln 1928** (International Press Exhibition, Cologne 1928). *Katalog des Sowjet-Pavillons auf der Internationalen Presse-Ausstellung, Köln 1928* (Catalog of the Soviet pavilion at the International Press Exhibition, Cologne 1928). Cologne: Komitee des Sowjet-Pavillons, 1928. 111 pp. 21 cm.
Design by El Lissitzky.
Exhibition catalog. The illustrations consist of a single foldout plate of photomontages circa 230 cm in length. It is gravure printed in sepia, with titles of sections of the exhibition and numbers corresponding to paragraphs of the catalog printed in red.

257. ———. *Union der Sozialistischen Sowjet-Republiken. Pressa Köln 1928* (Union of Soviet Socialist Republics: Pressa Cologne 1928). Cologne: Komitee des Sowjet-Pavillons, 1928. 16 pp. 29 cm.
Design by El Lissitzky.
Brochure.

258. **Ioffe, Ieremiia.** *Kul'tura i stil': Sistema i printsipy sotsiologii iskusstv; literatura, zhivopis', muzyka natural'nogo, tovarno-denezhnogo, industrial'nogo khoziaistva* (Культура и стиль: Система и принципы социологии

искусств; литература, живопись, музыка натурального, товарно-денежного, индустриального хозяйства / Culture and style: Systematics and principles of the sociology of the arts; literature, painting, and music in natural, barter-money, and industrial economies). Leningrad: Priboi, 1927. 366 pp. 23 cm.

259. ———. *Novyi stil'* (Новый стиль / The new style). Moscow and Leningrad: Gos. izd-vo izobrazitel'nykh iskusstv, 1932. 156 pp. 18 cm.
Criticism.

260. ***Iskhod: Al'manakh*** (Исход: Альманах / Exodus: A miscellany). Moscow and Petrograd: Khudozhestv. klub, 1918. 28 pp., [6] plates. 23 cm.
Cover by Vitalii Usenko.
Includes lithographs by E. Ravdel', A. Slavin, N. Tsitskovskii, and Usenko (4 of them colored by hand); stories by Iulii Khozhalkin, Grigorii Kolobov, and S. Stogov; and poems by Osip Mandel'shtam, Anatolii Mariengof, Ivan Startsev, and Boris Virganskii.

261. ***Iskusstvo*** (Искусство / Art). Moscow and Leningrad: Ogiz-Izogiz, 1933–1990. 25 cm.
Edited by Osip Beskin.
Design by Grigorii Bershadskii.
Organ of the Union of Soviet Artists (SSKh), an association dedicated to uniting Marxist critics and art historians.
Research Institute's holdings: scattered issues.

262. ***Iskusstvo: Ezhemesiachnyi zhurnal Glaviskusstva Narkomprosa RSFSR*** (Искусство: Ежемесячный журнал Главискусства Наркомпроса РСФСР / Art: A monthly journal of Narkompros RSFSR). Moscow: Tea-Kino-Pechat', 1929.
Edited by Anatoly Lunacharsky.
Cover by Boris Titov.
A total of 8 issues published, from March to October 1929. Continuation of *Khudozhnik i zritel'* (Artist and viewer [1924]).
Research Institute's holdings: scattered issues.

263. ***Iskusstvo i narod*** (Искусство и народ / Art and the people). Edited by Konstantin Erberg. St. Petersburg: Kolos, 1922. 229 pp. 27 cm.
Cover, headpieces, and tailpieces by Kuz'ma Petrov-Vodkin.
Essays by 9 authors.
Research Institute's copy signed on front cover and on first leaf by B. Golvuev.

264. ***Iskusstvo kommuny*** (Искусство коммуны / The art of the commune). Petrograd: Otdel izobrazitel'nykh iskusstv Komissariata narodnogo prosveshcheniia, 1918–1919. 44 cm.

Weekly publication.

A total of 19 issues published.

265. ***Iskusstvo rabochikh: Kruzhki IZO rabochikh klubov Leningrada i masterskie IZO Oblpolitprosveta pri DPR im. Gertsena*** (Искусство рабочих: Кружки ИЗО рабочих клубов Ленинграда и мастерские ИЗО Облполитпросвета при ДПР им. Герцена / Workers' art: Art circles in Leningrad workers' clubs and art studios of the Oblpolitprosvet at Hertsen DPR). Leningrad: Russkii muzei, 1928. 72 pp. 18 cm.

Cover by Moisei Brodskii.

Published in conjunction with an exhibition at the Russian Museum in Leningrad.

266. ***Iskusstvo v massy: Zhurnal Assotsiatsii khudozhnikov revoliutsii*** (Искусство в массы: Журнал Ассоциации художников революции / Art to the masses: Journal of the Association of Artists of the Revolution). Moscow: Assotsiatsiia khudozhnikov revoliutsii, 1929–1930. 30 cm.

Edited by A. A. Antonov, L. O. Chetyrkin, E. A. Katsman, and Lev Viaz'menskii.

Organ of the Association of Artists of the Revolution (AKhR), formerly known as the Association of Artists of Revolutionary Russia (AKhRR). AKhRR was one of the most influential groups of artists in Russian during the mid-1920s. Cover of no. 2 (1930) designed by M. Raiskaia.

A total of 8 issues published in 1929 and 12 in 1930. Continued by *Za proletarskoe iskusstvo*. (See no. 852.)

Research Institute's holdings: scattered issues.

267. ***Iskusstvo v proizvodstve*** (Искусство в производстве / Art in production). Moscow: Khudozhestvenno-proizvodstvennyi sovet Otdela IZO Narkomprosa, 1921. 42 pp. 23 cm.

Cover by David Shterenberg.

Organ of the Department of Visual Arts of the People's Commissariat for Education (IZO Narkompros). Prepared by a special IZO Narkompros committee (founded in August 1918 and first led by Ol'ga Rozanova) that was dedicated to the problem of art and production.

Contains articles by David Arkin, Osip Brik, A. Filippov, Shterenberg, A. K. Toporkov, and Vasilii Voronov.

A total of 1 issue published.

268. ***I. Stalin: Zhivopis', plakat, grafika, skul'ptura*** (И. Сталин: Живопись, плакат, графика, скульптура / J. Stalin: Painting, posters, graphics, sculpture). Moscow: Ogiz-Izogiz, 1934. [34] leaves. 35 cm.

Design by Gustav Klutsis. Cover by Sergei Mograchev.

Includes a silhouette of Stalin by Nataliia Pinus. Cover features an embossed head of Stalin.

269. ***Iugo Lef: Zhurnal levogo fronta iskusstv Iuga SSSR.*** (Юго Леф: Журнал левого фронта искусств юга СССР / South Lef: Journal of the Left Front of the Arts of the southern USSR). Odessa: Iugo-Lef, 1924. 27 cm.

Edited by L. Nedolia-Goncharenko.

Established in Odessa in 1924 and affiliated with the group Left Front of the Arts (LEF), *Iugo Lef* includes poetry; prose; theoretical essays on theater, literature, and art; and work by such writers as Z. Barantsevich, S. Bondarin, N. Danilov, Semen Kirsanov, E. Pokudin, M. Sanin, and N. Sokolov. Kirsanov was secretary of the group.

Irregularly published from September through December. A total of 4 issues published. Kirsanov indicated in his memoirs published in *Novyi Lef*, no. 8 (1927) that *Iugo Lef* had a fifth issue. (See no. 593.)

270. **Iurkun, Iurii.** *Durnaia kompaniia* (Дурная компания / Bad company). St. Petersburg: Felana, 1917. 185 pp. 17 cm.

Novel. Includes illustrations by Iurii Annenkov.

Inscribed by Iurkun to Avgusta Natanovna Razhnovskaia and dated 1 February 1920.

271. **Ivanitskii, Ivan.** *Izobrazitel'naia statistika i venskii metod* (Изобразительная статистика и венский метод / Representational statistics and the Vienna method). Moscow and Leningrad: Ogiz-Izogiz, 1932. 43 pp. 19 × 26 cm.

A presentation of Otto Neurath's method of conveying relations between statistical quantities by varying numbers of pictographs. Ivanitskii also recommends the use of pictorial backgrounds and caricatures in graphs to clarify their social and political significance.

272. **Ivanov, Viacheslav.** *Mladenchestvo* (Младенчество / Infancy). St. Petersburg: Alkonost, 1918. 57 pp. 15 cm.

Poems.

273. ———. *Prometei: Tragediia* (Прометей: Трагедия / Prometheus: A tragedy). St. Petersburg: Alkonost, 1919. xxiv, 76 pp. 21 cm.

274. **Ivanov, Vsevolod, and Viktor Shklovskii.** "Taina golubia" («Тайна голубя» / The pigeon's secret). Part 5 of *Iprit: Roman* (Иприт: Роман / Mustard gas:

A novel). Moscow: Gos. izd-vo, 1925. 19 cm.
Cover by Solomon Telingater.
The complete novel has 9 parts.

275. ***Iz batarei serdtsa*** (Из батареи сердца / From the battery of the heart). [Sevastopol]: Taran, 1922. 15 pp. 22 cm.
Includes poems by Vadim Baian, Konstantin Bol'shakov, Mariia Kalmykova, and Georgii Zolotukhin.

276. ***Izobrazitel'noe iskusstvo*** (Изобразительное искусство / Visual art). St. Petersburg: Otdel izobrazitel'nykh iskusstv komissariata narodnogo prosveshcheniia, 1919. 87 pp. 35 cm.
Cover by David Shterenberg.
Organ of the Department of Visual Arts of the People's Commissariat for Education (IZO Narkompros).
Includes works by Natan Al'tman, Kazimir Malevich, Nikolai Punin, Ol'ga Rozanova, Shterenberg, and Vladimir Tatlin; an article by Osip Brik, "Khudozhnik i kommuna" (The artist and the commune); an article by Wassily Kandinsky, "O stsenicheskoi kompozitsii" (On theatrical composition), written in 1913 and published earlier in *Der Blaue Reiter*; articles by Malevich, "Nashi zadachi" (Our tasks) and "O poezii" (On poetry); an article by Punin, "Iskusstvo i proletariat" (Art and proletariat); and an article by Vladimir Solov'ev, "O teatral'no-dekorativnoi zhivopisi i o khudozhnike-dekoratore" (On theatrical and decorative painting and on the scene-painter).
A total of 1 issue published.

277. ***Izofront: Klassovaia bor'ba na fronte prostranstvennykh iskusstv*** (Изофронт: Классовая борьба на фронте пространственных искусств / Art front: Class war on the visual arts front). Edited by Pavel Novitskii. Moscow and Leningrad: Ogiz-Izogiz, 1931. 159 pp. 17 cm.
Collection of essays by authors associated with the artists' group October.

278. ***Izo rabochei molodezhi Leningrada*** (Изо рабочей молодежи Ленинграда / Art by young Leningrad workers). [Moscow]: Gos. Tret'iakovskaia gallereia, 1929. 68 pp. 16 cm.
Published on the occasion of an exhibition at the Tretyakov Gallery in Moscow.

279. ***Kachestvennaia stal' SSSR*** (Качественная сталь СССР / High-quality steel of the USSR). Edited by A. A. Tsvetaev. Moscow and Leningrad: Glavnaia redaktsiia lit-ry po chernoi metallurgii, 1935. 262 pp., [31] plates. 26 cm.
Design by Solomon Telingater.

Includes 3-color illustrations by Mechislav Dobrokovskii and photographs by Vladimir Griuntal'. The frontispiece consists of a thin sheet of stainless steel inserted between 2 sheets of heavy paper stock, in each of which there has been cut an outline of Stalin's head in profile. The head of Stalin, a name is derived from the Russian word for steel, thus appears as a silhouette of steel on both recto and verso, on the recto over a printed graph of rising steel production.

Research Institute's copy has a special binding. The covers are 2 additional thin sheets of stainless steel, attached with 3 rivets each to the stubs of a truncated case binding that holds the text block. The title is etched on the metal of the front cover in Constructivist style. In a gray, cloth-covered slipcase.

280. **Kamenskii, Vasilii.** *Ego-moia biografiia velikogo futurista* (Его-моя биография великого футуриста / His-my biography of the great Futurist). Moscow: Kitovras, 1918. 228 pp., [3] plates. 24 cm.

Memoirs and literary theory.

281. ———. *Emil'ian Pugachev: Poema Vasiliia Kamenskogo* (Емельян Пугачев: Поэма Василия Каменского / Emilian Pugachev: A poem by Vasilii Kamenskii). [Moscow]: Federatsiia, 1932. 157 pp. 30 cm.

Includes illustrations by Boris Titov.

282. ———. *Iunost' Maiakovskogo* (Юность Маяковского / Mayakovsky's youth). Tbilisi: Zakkniga, 1931. 83 pp., [1] plate. 18 cm.

Cover signed "Bor. R."

283. ———. *Put' entuziasta* (Путь энтузиаста / The path of an enthusiast). Moscow: Federatsiia, 1931. 268 pp., [1] plate. 18 cm.

Cover by Boris Titov.

Memoirs. Includes a portrait of Kamenskii by Vladimir Mayakovsky.

284. ———. *Saryn' na kichku: Stikhi izbrannye* (Сарынь на кичку: Стихи избранные / Scum to the bow!: Selected verse. Moscow: Federatsiia, 1932. 111 pp. 17 cm.

Cover by Fisher, perhaps Georgii Ivanovich Fisher.

The title is the traditional command of Volga pirates to the crew of a captured vessel.

285. ———. *Zvuchal' vesneianki: Stikhi* (Звучаль веснеянки: Стихи / Soundsong of the pipe of spring: Verse). Moscow: Kitovras, 1918. 160 pp. 26 cm.

286. **Kamenskii, Vasilii, and Andrei Kravtsov.** *Nagoi sredi odetykh: Stikhi Kravtsova* (Нагой среди одетых: Стихи Кравцова / Naked among the clad: Verse by Kravtsov). [Moscow: Izd. Rossiiskikh futuristov, 1914]. [14] leaves. 21 cm.

Includes illustrations variously attributed to Kamenskii (Markov 1968, 200) and Kravtsov (Compton 1978, 83).

From an edition of 300 (*Knizhnaia letopis'* 1914, no. 5074). Printed on paste side of sheets of wallpaper. The upper right corner of each printed page is trimmed at a 45-degree angle, producing 5-sided pages with 3 short and 2 long sides. The first page in the copy reproduced in Compton (1977) is cut at the upper left, allowing the decorated side of the wallpaper to form the front cover, but this is not the case in the Research Institute's copy (which may be missing a first leaf). Although the Research Institute's copy has 14 leaves, *Knizhnaia letopis'* (1914, no. 5074) calls for 18, and Tarasenkov reports the same (1966, 167). The copy reproduced in Compton 1977 has 14 leaves, like the Research Institute's, but its order is considerably different. The Research Institute's copy also lacks 2 of the leaves of that copy—a leaf with a portrait of Kratsov and a leaf with the heading "Stikhi Kratsova" (Verse by Kratsov)—and includes 2 others not there present—those with Kamenskii's Ferro-concrete poems "Konstantinopol'" (Constantinople) and "Tsirk Nikitina" (Nikitin's circus). These leaves are discussed by Janecek (1984, 136) as part of Kamenskii's "Tango s korovami" (Tango with cows), another work on 5-sided pieces of wallpaper, also published in 1914. "Konstantinopol'," the first leaf in Research Institute's copy, differs from that reproduced by Janecek from *Nagoi sredi odetykh* in that it has Kamenskii's name printed in the top margin at left (1984, 125). Three wallpaper patterns were used in Research Institute's copy of *Nagoi sredi odetykh*. There are 5 leaves of the pattern with animals in vegetation that predominates in the Compton (1977) copy and 3 leaves of the pattern with blue flowers alternating with brackets in half-drop rows that occurs in it once. In addition there are 6 leaves of a third pattern with large stylized flowers over dotted black triangles that does not occur in the Compton copy. All 3 patterns are in the same tones of red, green, blue, and black.

287. **Kamernyi teatr** (Moscow Kamerny Theater). *Kamernyi teatr i ego khudozhniki, 1914 XX 1934* (Камерный театр и его художники, 1914 XX 1934 / The Moscow Kamerny Theater and its artists, 1914—twenty years—1934). Moscow: Vseross. teatral'noe ob-vo, 1934. xlvii, 211 pp. 31 cm.

Includes an introduction by Abram Efros.

288. ———. *Kto, chto, kogda v Moskovskom Kamernom teatre* (Кто, что, когда в Московском Камерном театре / Who, what, when in the Moscow Kamerny Theater). [Moscow: Kamernyi teatr, 1924.] [39] pp. 25 cm.

Includes an illustration on the title page by Georgii Stenberg and text by Aleksandr Gorin.

289. **Kandinsky, Wassily.** *Kandinsky, 1901–1913*. Berlin: Verlag der Sturm, [1913]. 67 leaves, xxxxi pp. 24 × 27 cm.

Cover has title and abstract vignette by Kandinsky embossed in gold.

Title page inscribed by H. H. Waechter in black ink.

290. ———. *Klänge* (Sounds). Munich: R. Piper, [1913]. [113] pp. 28 cm.

Contains 38 brief prose poems by Kandinsky and 56 woodcuts, 12 of them full-page in color and 13 full-page in black and white. Front and back covers each have an abstract vignette by Kandinsky embossed in gold.

Copy 93 of 300, signed and numbered by Kandinsky. Bound in red paper over pasteboard, quarter purple cloth (faded).

291. ———. *Tekst khudozhnika* (Текст художника / An artist's text). Moscow: Izd. Otdel izobrazitel'nykh iskusstv Narkomprosa, 1918. 56 pp. 30 cm.

Essay.

Inscribed by Kandinsky to Konstantin Iuon and dated December 1919.

292. ———. *Über das Geistige in der Kunst, insbesondere in der Malerei* (On the spiritual in art, particularly in painting). 2nd ed. Munich: R. Piper, 1912. 125 pp., 8 plates, 3 tables. 24 cm.

Cover woodcut by Kandinsky.

Includes 10 headpieces by Kandinsky.

Research Institute's copy is rebound in vellum, with the lettering and woodcut of the original front cover drawn on the new cover. The original wrappers have been placed loosely around the new binding. The 8 plates are inserted in a pocket at the back cover. Research Institute also has a copy of the third edition (same imprint) and of Michael Sadler's English-language translation *The Art of Spiritual Harmony* (London: Constable, 1914).

293. ———. *Xylographies*. Paris: Edition des tendances nouvelles, [1909]. [2] leaves, 5 plates. In portfolio. 32 cm.

Five black-and-white line gravures on Russian folk themes from woodcuts of 1907 (Roethel 1970, nos. 54, 55, 59, 60, 65). Two additional vignettes on front and back covers of portfolio may have been printed from the woodcut blocks (Roethel 1970, nos. 70, 71).

294. **Kandinsky, Wassily.** Archive. Bauhaus teaching materials.

Written material comprising approximately 200 pp. of typed and handwritten lecture notes from Kandinsky's years at the Bauhaus (1925–1933). The collection also includes reading lists, class rosters, graphic teaching aids such as detailed drawings that illustrate theories of form and color, and more than 50 colored cutouts of various geometric shapes with which Kandinsky attempted to establish that primary colors correspond to elemental geometric patterns.

295. ———. Archive. Manuscript and typescript pages.

Outlines of 2 of Kandinsky's projected essays, "Razvitie zhivopisnoi idei v sovremennom iskusstve" (The development of painterly idea in contemporary art) and "Sushchnost' formy i formal'nyi metod v zhivopisi" (The essence of form and the formal element in painting), and a fragment of the proposed updated Russian edition of *O dukhovnom v iskusstve* (On the spiritual in art), which consists of 3 components—manuscript, typescript, and proof pages. The fragment includes the title page, preface, introduction; untitled section A with chapters 2, 3, and 4 titled "Dvizhenie" (Movement), "Povorot"

(Turning point), and "Piramida" (The pyramid), respectively; section B "Zhivopis'" (Painting) with chapters five and six, "Deistvie kraski" (Effects of color) and "Iazyk form i krasok," corrected to read "Iazyk risunka i tsveta" (The language of form and color, corrected to read, The language of drawing and color), respectively; and other manuscript and typescript pages.

296. **Karpov, Pimen.** *Russkii kovcheg* (Русский ковчег / A Russian ark). Moscow: Novaia zhizn', 1922. 62 pp. 25 cm.
Cover by Nikolai Vysheslavtsev.
Poems.

297. ***Kartinki—voina russkikh s nemtsami*** (Картинки—война русских с немцами / Lubok prints—Russians' war with Germans). Petrograd: [F. G. Shilov, Sklad izdaniia u V. I. Uspenskago, 1914]. 1 portfolio, [1] folded sheet, [100] leaves of plates, 35 cm.
Hand-colored, lithographed, anti-German *lubki.* Plates lithographed by Petrograd firms, including Sh. Bussel', V. M. Shmigel'skii, and A. Pavlova.

298. **Kataev, Valentin.** *Kvadratura kruga: Vodevil' v 3-kh deistviiakh* (Квадратура круга: Водевиль в 3-х действиях / Squaring the circle: A vaudeville in three acts). Moscow and Leningrad: MODPIK, 1928. 46 pp. 22 cm.

299. ***Katalog peredvizhnoi vystavki: Zhivopis', risunok, grafika, plakat, tekstil'*** (Каталог передвижной выставки: Живопись, рисунок, графика, плакат, текстиль / Catalog of a traveling exhibition: Paintings, drawings, graphics, posters, textiles). Moscow: Khudozhnik, 1931. 31 pp., [23] plates. 17 cm.
Catalog of the third traveling exhibition organized by the Arts Section of the People's Commissariat for Education of the RSFSR (Narkompros RSFSR).

300. ***Katalog pervoi vystavki leningradskikh khudozhnikov*** (Каталог первой выставки ленинградских художников / Catalog of the first exhibition of Leningrad artists). Leningrad: Gos. Russkii muzei zhivopisi, skul'ptury i grafiki, 1935. 79 pp. 18 cm.

301. ***Katalog priobretenii Gosudarstvennoi komissii po priobreteniiam proizvedenii rabotnikov izobrazitel'nykh iskusstv*** (Каталог приобретений Государственной комиссии по приобретениям произведений работников изобразительных искусств / Catalog of acquisitions by the State Commission for Acquiring Works of Visual Art). Moscow: Glaviskusstvo, 1928. 44 pp. 23 cm.
Catalog of an exhibition of works acquired primarily in 1927 and 1928. Includes text by Aleksei Fedorov-Davydov.

302. ***Katalog vystavki revoliutsionnogo iskusstva Zapada*** (Каталог выставки революционного искусства Запада / Catalog of an exhibition of revolutionary Western art). Moscow: Gos. Akademiia khudozhestvennykh nauk, Vses. ob-vo kul'turnoi sviazi s zagranitsei, 1926. 81 pp. 17 cm.

The exhibition was organized by the State Academy of Artistic Sciences and included both visual arts and literature.

303. **Katanian, Vasilii.** *Ubiistvo na romanicheskoi pochve: Stikhi* (Убийство на романической почве: Стихи / Crime of passion: Verse). Tbilisi: Feniks, 1919. 15 pp. 17 cm.

Cover by Katanian.

Includes linoleum prints from blocks, cut by Katanian, of drawings by Vladimir Gudiashvili and Sigizmund Valishevskii. Cover is a linocut of a drawing by Kirill Zdanevich.

304. **Kerzhentsev, Platon.** *Gazeta: Organizatsiia i tekhnika gazetnogo dela* (Газета: Организация и техника газетного дела / The newspaper: Organization and technical aspects of newspaper production). 3rd ed., enl. Moscow: Krasnaia nov', 1924. 174 pp. 23 cm.

Cover by Gustav Klutsis.

305. **Kharms, Daniil.** *Vo-pervykh i vo-vtorykh* (Во-первых и во-вторых / In the first place and in the second). Moscow and Leningrad: Gos. izd-vo, 1929. 23 pp. 27 cm.

Cover by Vladimir Tatlin.

Children's book. Includes illustrations by Tatlin.

306. **Khlebnikov, Velimir.** *Doski sud'by* (Доски судьбы / Tablets of destiny). 3 vols. [Moscow: n.p.], 1922. [48] pp. 25 cm.

Covers of vols. 1 and 2 by Anatolii Borisov (Sillov 1926, 32).

An exposition of Khlebnikov's numerological theories and their application to human history. Other "tablets of destiny" remain unpublished in the Russian State Archive for Literature and Art (RGALI) in Moscow (Vroon 1993).

From an edition of 500. Covers of vols. 1 and 2 are missing.

307. ———. *Izbornik stikhov, 1907–1914, s poslesloviem rechiaria* (Изборник стихов, 1907–1914, с послесловием речаря / Selected verse, 1907–1914, with an afterword by the speecher). [Petrograd]: EUY, 1915. 48 pp., [16] leaves. 21 cm.

Cover by Vladimir Mayakovsky.

The first section consists of letterpress poems and Khlebnikov's afterword. The second section consists of a lithographed excerpt from his "Dereviannye idoly" (Wooden idols), hand-lettered and illustrated by Pavel Filonov. The illustration by Kazimir Malevich on p. [38] appeared previously in *Troe.* (See no. 318.) The cover illustration is a portrait of Khlebnikov that is credited to Nadezhda Burliuk, but it appeared previously in *Trebnik troikh* (see no. 775), leaf [4], where it is credited to Vladimir Mayakovsky and is apparently by him (Kovtun 1989, 164).

308. ———. "*Nastoiashchee*": *Poema.* («Настоящее»: Поэма / "The real": A poem). Al'vek. *Stikhi* (Стихи / Verse). Moscow: V. V. Khlebnikova, 1926. 39 pp. 22 cm.

Includes a bibliography of Khlebnikov's works from 1908 to 1925, compiled by V. A. Sillov.

309. ———. *Neizdannyi Khlebnikov* (Неизданный Хлебников / Unpublished Khlebnikov). Edited by Aleksei Kruchenykh. Vols. 1–19. Moscow: Izd. Gruppy druzei Khlebnikova, 1928–1933. 18 × 22 cm.

Covers of vols. 3, 5, 7, 9, 15, and 19 by Ivan Kliun. Cover of vol. 10 by Igor' Terent'ev. Covers of vols. 11–14 and 16 by Kirill Zdanevich. Covers of vols. 17 and 18 by Nataliia Goncharova.

Vol. 3 includes vignettes by Kliun. The cover of vol. 18 is after an illustration from the first edition of *Igra v adu.* (See no. 398.) A total of 30 volumes were prepared for publication by lithography on glass under the editorship of Kruchenykh, but only 24 were published (Vrcon 1993).

Edition sizes range from 95 or 100 for the earlier volumes to 150 for the later ones. Vols. 1–13 are numbered by hand. Research Institute's copy of vol. 1 contains penciled emendations. The letters of the word *rychag* (lever) on the cover of vol. 15 (copy 1) are colored red and accompanied by a roman "I."

310. ———. *Noch' v okope* (Ночь в окопе / Night in a trench). [Moscow]: Imazhinisty, 1921. [11] pp. 22 cm.

Poem.

311. ———. *Riav!: Perchatki 1908–1914 g.g.* (Рявъ!: Перчатки 1908–1914 г.г. / Roar!: Gauntlets of 1908–1914). [St. Petersburg]: EUY, [1914]. 29 pp. 26 cm.

Poems, essays, and short plays. Includes 2 gravures by Malevich that appeared previously in *Troe* (see no. 318) and 2 linocuts (?) by David Burliuk that appreared previously in *Sadok sudei* (see no. 693), vol. 2, pp. [47] and [91]. Here, however, the first Burliuk illustration is oriented horizontally on the page rather than vertically, and the second has been inverted.

312. ———. *Tvoreniia, 1906–1908* (Творения, 1906–1908 / Creations, 1906–1908). Moscow: Izd. "Pervogo zhurnala russkikh futuristov," 1914. 106 pp., [8] plates. 21 cm.

Includes illustrations by David and Vladimir Burliuk and articles on Khlebnikov by David Burliuk and Vasilii Kamenskii.

From an edition of 480 (*Knizhnaia letopis'* 1914, no. 6814).

313. ———. *Vsem. Nochnoi bal* (Всем. Ночной бал / To everyone. Night ball). Al'vek. *Nakhlebniki Khlebnikova: Maiakovskii-Aseev* (Нахлебники

Хлебникова: Маяковский-Асеев / Khlebnikov's spongers: Mayakovksky-Aseev). Moscow: Izd. avtora, 1927. 29 pp. 18 cm.

Includes 5 poems by Al'vek and Petr Miturich's "*Otkrytoe pis'mo Maiakovskomu*" (Open letter to Mayakovsky) in addition to the 2 poems by Khlebnikov and the article by Al'vek. Cover illustration by Miturich is a drawing of Khlebnikov on his deathbed.

314. ———. *Vzor na 1923-i god* (Взор на 1923-й год / A look at the year 1923). [1922]. 1 sheet. 36.8 × 45.5 cm, trimmed.

A lithograph on glass produced by Khlebnikov, probably in the last year of his life, with the help of his brother-in-law, the graphic artist Petr Miturich. It expresses Khlebnikov's notion that the course of human history can be reduced to powers of 2 and 3 and takes the form of a diagram branching from left to right along a time axis, ending with several possibilities for 1923. Khlebnikov's preparatory sketch for *Vzor na 1923-i god* is preserved in the Russian State Archive for Literature and Art (RGALI) (Vroon 1993).

315. ———. *Zangezi* (Зангези) Moscow: [n.p.], 1922. 35 pp. 24 cm.

Cover by Petr Miturich.

Dramatic poem.

316. ———. *Zapisnaia knizhka Velimira Khlebnikova* (Записная книжка Велимира Хлебникова / Velimir Khlebnikov's notebook). Moscow: Vseros. soiuz poetov, 1925. 30 pp. 20 cm.

Cover by Valentina Kulagina.

Compiled and annotated by Aleksei Kruchenykh.

Inscribed by Kruchenykh to Konstantin Iuon, his painting teacher, on the sixtieth anniversary of Khlebnikov's birth (1945).

317. ———. *Zverinets* (Зверинец / Menagerie). Edited by Aleksei Kruchenykh. Moscow: Izd. "Gruppy druzei Khlebnikova," 1930. 17 leaves. 21 cm.

Cover by Kirill Zdanevich.

Poem. Includes a foreword by Iurii Olesha. Published on the twentieth anniversary of the initial appearance of *Zverinets* in vol. 1 of *Sadok sudei*. (See no. 693.)

From an edition of 130.

318. **Khlebnikov, Velimir, Aleksei Kruchenykh, and Elena Guro.** *Troe* (Трое / Threesome). St. Petersburg: Zhuravl', [1913]. 96 pp. 20 cm.

Front and back covers by Kazimir Malevich.

Poems and prose. Dedicated to Guro, who had died earlier in 1913. Includes 4 illustrations by Malevich.

From an edition of 500 (*Knizhnaia letopis'* 1913, no. 24569).

319. **Khovin, Viktor.** *Segodniashnemu dniu* (Сегодняшнему дню / To the present day). St. Petersburg: Ocharovannyi strannik, 1918. 7 pp. 20 cm.

Essay on Russian Futurism.

320. ***Khudozhestvennoe oformlenie massovykh prazdnestv v Leningrade, 1918–1931*** (Художественное оформление массовых празднеств в Ленинграде, 1918–1931 / The artistic design of mass celebrations in Leningrad, 1918–1931). Moscow and Leningrad: Ogiz-Izogiz, 1932. 31 pp., 48 plates. In portfolio. 15 cm.

The first 30 plates (most of them in color) reproduce projects for temporary structures and street decorations drawn by a variety of artists and architects working under the sponsorship of various institutions. The occasions most frequently celebrated are anniversaries of the October Revolution and May Day. The last 18 plates are black and white and reproduce photographs of some of the projects as realized. Includes text by Aleksandr Gushchin. Projects by the following artists, among others, are featured: Leonid Akishin, Natan Al'tman, Vladimir Baranov-Rossiné, Kseniia Boguslavskaia, Mstislav Dobuzhinskii, Vladimir Kozlinskii, Boris Kustodiev, Vladimir Lebedev, Sarra Lebedeva, Kazimir Malevich, Mikhail Matiushin, Kuz'ma Petrov-Vodkin, Anatolii Proshkin, Varvara Raevskaia, and David Shterenberg. Projects by the following architects are included: David Buryshkin, P. S. Duplitskii, Lev Rudnev, and Noi Trotskii. Projects sponsored by the following institutions are included: (Leningrad) City Council Art Brigade, Brigade of October (the artists' group), Decorative Arts Institute, (Leningrad) Young Workers' Art Movement (IZORAM), (Leningrad) Proletarian Culture, and Suprematists, from Vitebsk.

Portfolio is pasteboard printed with title, publisher, and price. The plates are loose and mounted on a light stock. Research Institute's copy lacks plate 38 and has 2 copies of plate 40.

321. ***Khudozhestvennyi trud*** (Художественный труд / Artistic labor). Moscow and Petrograd: Khud. trud, 1923. 26 cm.

Edited by Anatoly Lunacharsky.

Covers by Boris Titov.

Biweekly journal. Includes poetry and prose by Iurii Annenkov, Nikolai Aseev, V. Erofeev, L. Ginzburg, Erik Gollerbakh, and Sergei Gorodetskii. No. 1 (1923) contains 2 actual samples of an Oriental textile design.

A total of 4 issues published.

Research Institute's holdings: scattered issues.

322. ***Kino*** (Кино / Cinema). Kharkov: Vseukrainskoe foto-kino upravlenie, 1925–1933. 29 cm.

Edited by Benedikt Livshits.

Biweekly journal of All-Ukrainian Organization of Cinema Workers (VUORRK) and the Society of Friends of Soviet Photography and Cinematography (ODSFK).

Research Institute's holdings: scattered issues.

323. ***Kino: Dvukhnedel'nik o-va kinodeiatelei*** (Кино: Двухнедельник о-ва кинодеятелей/ Cinema: Biweekly of the Society of Cinema Workers). Moscow: O-vo kinodeiatelei, 1922–1923. 30 cm.
A total of 5 issues published, the first 4 during 1922.
Research Institute's holdings: scattered issues.

324. ***Kino: Ezhenedel'naia gazeta*** (Кино: Еженедельная газета / Cinema: A weekly gazette). Moscow: Kino-izd. RSFSR, 1925–? 45 cm.
Became the organ of the Society of Friends of Soviet Cinema and Photography (ODSK) in 1927.
Irregularly published.
Research Institute's holdings: scattered issues.

325. ***Kino i zhizn'*** (Кино и жизнь / Cinema and life). Moscow: Teakinopechat', 1929–1930. 29 cm.
A total of 4 issues published in 1929 and 36 in 1930. Continuation of *Sovetskii ekran.* (See no. 745.) Continued as *Proletarskoe kino: Organ Assotsiatsii rabotnikov revoliutsionnoi kinematografii.* (See no. 650.) Publisher varies.
Research Institute's holdings: scattered issues.

326. ***Kino-nedelia*** (Кино-неделя / Cinema week). Leningrad: Sevzapkino, 1924–1925. 35 cm.
Edited by K. Arshavskii and A. I. Syrkin.
Organ of the International Workers Relief, the Scholarly and Artistic Council of North-West Cinema, the Executive Bureau of the Leningrad Gubernia Council of Cinema Workers, and the United Publishing House of North-West Cinema.
A total of 47 issues published in 1924 and 13 in 1925. Publisher and place of publication varies.
Research Institute's holdings: scattered issues.

327. ***Kinovar': Sbornik stikhov*** (Киноварь: Сборник стихов / Cinnabar: Collection of poetry). Ryazan: Riazanskoe otd-nie Vseros. soiuza poetov; Gos. izd-vo, Riazanskoe gubernskoe otd-nie, 1921. 42 pp. 21 cm.
Includes contributions by Iakov Apushkin, Riurik Ivnev, Veniamin Kisin, Nataliia Kugusheva, Taras Machtet, Dmitrii Maizel's, and Boris Pasternak.

328. **Kipling, Rudyard.** *Otkuda u kita takaia glotka* (Откуда у кита такая глотка / How the whale got his throat). Translated by Kornei Chukovskii and Samuil Marshak. Moscow: Gos. izd-vo, 1926. 10 pp. 28 cm.
One of the tales from the *Just So Stories.* Includes illustrations by Eduard Krimmer.

329. **Kirsanov, Semen.** *Chetyre tetradi* (Четыре тетради / Four notebooks). Moscow: Sov. pisatel', 1940. 127 pp. 21 cm.
Poems.

330. ———. *Moia imeninnaia: Poema* (Моя именинная: Поэма / My name-day poem). Moscow and Leningrad: Zemlia i fabrika, 1928. 50 pp. 20 cm.
Cover by E. Rozhdestvenskaia.

331. ———. *Piatiletka: Poema* (Пятилетка: Поэма / The five-year plan: A poem). Moscow and Leningrad: Khudozhestvennaia lit-ra, 1931. 173 pp., [8] plates. 20 cm.
Includes photographs and a folded "Karta stroitel'stva sotsializma" (Map of the building of socialism) in black and red.

332. ———. *Poslednii sovremennik* (Последний современник / My last contemporary). Moscow: Federatsiia, 1930. 95 pp. 18 cm.
Cover by Aleksandr Rodchenko.
Poems.

333. ———. *Slovo predostavliaetsia Kirsanovu* (Слово предоставляется Кирсанову / Kirsanov has the floor). Moscow: Gos. izd-vo, 1930. [84] pp. 20 cm.
Design by Solomon Telingater.
Poems.

334. ———. *Tetrad', 1932* (Тетрадь, 1932 / Notebook, 1932). Moscow: Sov. lit-ra, 1933. 98 pp. 25 cm.
Poems.

335. ———. *Udarnyi kvartal: Stikhi* (Ударный квартал: Стихи / The shock-workers' quarter: Verse). [Moscow]: Ogiz, Molodaia gvardiia, 1931. 92 pp. 17 cm.

336. **Klutsis, Gustav.** Archive of Jan Tschichold. Photomontages.
Six printed examples of Klutsis's photomontages, including designs for his posters.

337. ———. Archive of Jan Tschichold. Postcards.
One handwritten postcard by Klutsis describing the Soviet pavilion at the *Internationale Presse-Ausstellung* (International press exhibition) held in Cologne in 1928 and 1 typewritten postcard addressed to Jan Tschichold and dated 28 June 1930. The handwritten card, numbered 10, has the caption, "Pavillon der Union der Sozialistischen Sowjet Republiker. Anchauungsmodel. Der Siebenstundentag. Pressa, Köln, 1928" (The pavilion of the Union of Soviet Socialist Republics. Model for a display case. The seven-hour day. Pressa, Cologne, 1928). Klutsis's handwritten note reads: "Prostranstvennaia konstruktsiia dlia vystavki 'Pressa' v Kel'ne. Razmer: 4.5 metra vysota, 4 metra v diametre" (Spatial construction for the Pressa exhibition in Cologne. Dimensions: 4.5 meters high, 4 meters in diameter).

338. ***Kniga o knigakh*** (Книга о книгах / A book about books). Moscow: GIZ, 1924. 25 cm.

Edited by S. D. Mstislavskii.

Covers by Aleksandr Rodchenko.

Biweekly bibliographical journal. Includes reviews of foreign publications, children's books, and publications on history, economics, literature, and art. No. 7/8 (July 1924) includes a bibliography of Aleksandr Blok's works and a speech by Leon Trotsky given at an All-Union Congress of Librarians.

A total of 8 issues published.

Research Institute's holdings: scattered issues.

339. ***Knizhnye znaki russkikh khudozhnikov*** (Книжные знаки русских художников / Bookplates by Russian artists). St. Petersburg: Petropolis, 1922. 238 pp. 28 cm.

Cover by Dmitrii Mitrokhin.

Copy 136 of 500.

340. **[Konchalovskii, Petr].** *Katalog vystavki proizvedenii P. P. Konchalovskogo* (Каталог выставки произведений П.П. Кончаловского / Catalog of an exhibition of works by P. P. Konchalovskii). Leningrad: Izd. Gos. russkogo muzeia, 1929. 28 pp. 18 cm.

341. [———]. *Vystavka proizvedenii P. P. Konchalovskogo, 1933–1934* (Выставка произведений П.П. Кончаловского, 1933–1934 / Exhibition of works by P. P. Konchalovskii, 1933–1934). Moscow: Vsekokhudozhnik, 1935. 8 pp., [16] plates. 18 cm.

Exhibition catalog.

Bears the ownership stamp of Anatolii Sergeevich Vasil'ev, Leningrad.

342. **Kondrat'ev, Aleksandr.** *Chernaia Venera: Stikhi, kniga vtoraia* (Черная Венера: Стихи, книга вторая / Black Venus: Verse, second book). St. Petersburg: Golike i Vil'borg, 1909. 78 pp. 19 cm.

Cover signed "Ia. B.," for Iakov Bel'zen.

343. ***Konnitsa bur': Stikhi*** (Конница бурь: Стихи / Cavalry of storms: Verse). Moscow: Div, 1920. [35] pp. 23 cm.

Cover by Vasilii Kamardenkov.

This first Imagist collection contains poems by Sergei Esenin, Mikhail Gerasimov, Riurik Ivnev, Nikolai Kliuev, Anatolii Mariengof, and Petr Oreshin.

344. ***Konnitsa bur': Vtoroi sbornik imazhinistov*** (Конница бурь: Второй сборник имажинистов / Cavalry of storms: The second Imagist collection). [Moscow]: Div, 1920. 31 pp. 16 cm.

Includes poems by Sergei Esenin, Aleksei Ganin, and Anatolii Mariengof.

345. ***Koster: Stikhi*** (Костер: Стихи / Campfire: Verse). [Vladikavkaz]: Terkavtsentropechat', 1920. 40 pp. 21 cm.
Includes contributions by G. A., Liudmila Beridze, Georgii Evangulov, Konstantin Iust, and Riurik Ivnev. The cover illustration is a linoleum print, cut by Skril'nikov, of an illustration by Ivan Ivanov.

346. **Kovalevskii, Viacheslav.** *Tsyganskaia vengerka* (Цыганская венгерка / Hungarian gypsy dance). Moscow: Ozar', 1922. 15 pp. 19 cm.
Cover and frontispiece by Georgii Echeistov.
Poem. Two wood engravings in the text are credited to M. N. Vladimirova, though the first bears what appears to be the monogram "GE," implying that Vladimirova's role may have been limited to carrying out the engravings of Echeistov's drawings.

347. ***Krasnaia Armiia*** (Красная Армия / The Red Army). Moscow: Ogiz-Izogiz, 1938. [232] pp. 36 cm.
Design by Aleksandr Rodchenko and Varvara Stepanova.
Published to honor the twentieth anniversary of the Red Army.

348. ***Krasnaia niva*** (Красная нива / Red grain field). Moscow: Izvestiia VTsIK, 1923–1931. 31 cm.
Edited by Anatoly Lunacharsky.
Covers by the Georgii and Vladimir Stenberg and Valentina Kulagina.
Literary and artistic weekly.
Irregularly published.
Research Institute's holdings: scattered issues.

349. **Kreitan, Georgii.** *Chelovek na kryshe: Vtoraia kniga stikhov* (Человек на крыше: Вторая книга стихов / Someone's on the roof: Second book of verse). Tbilisi: Zakkniga, 1928. 91 pp. 20 cm.

350. **Kriuchkov, Dmitrii.** *Padun nemolchnyi* (Падун немолчный / Incessant faller). [St. Petersburg]: Peterburgskii glashatai, 1913. 24 pp. 23 cm.
Poems.

351. **Kruchenykh, Aleksei.** *Apokalipsis v russkoi literature* (Апокалипсис в русской литературе / Apocalypse in Russian literature). MAF, Seriia teorii, no. 3. Moscow: Moskovskaia assotsiatsiia futuristov, [1922] (cover date 1923). 46 pp. 19 cm.
Kruchenykh's 122nd book. Contains an illustration by Natal'ia Nagorskaia and 4 texts previously published separately.
Inscribed by Kruchenykh in blue pencil and dated 14 September 1928.

352. ———. *Chetyre foneticheskikh romana* (Четыре фонетических романа / Four phonetic novels). Moscow: Izd. avtora, 1927. 38 pp. 25 cm.

Cover by Gustav Klutsis.

Poems. Kruchenykh's "Production no. 142." Includes lithographs by Mariia Siniakova, 4 poems, and "Deklaratsiia no. 6 o segodniashnikh iskusstvakh" (Declaration number six on the arts of today). The first of the poems, "Razboinik Van'ka-Kain i Son'ka-manikiurshchitsa," appeared previously (with "Deklaratsiia") in the separate edition of 1925. (See no. 378.) The dark blue linocuts on the front and back covers are entitled *Chetyrekhkoordinatnyi neboskreb* (Four-coordinate skyscraper).

From an edition of 500. The poem "Dun'ka-Rubikha," which appeared in 1926 as part of *Na bor'bu s khuliganstvom v literature* (see no. 368) and as a separate edition (see no. 355), is listed on the title page as an addendum. Research Institute's copy is one of a number that do not have it, however (Golubeva 1977, 11:381).

353. ———. *Chornaia taina Esenina* (Чорная тайна Есенина / Esenin's dark secret). Moscow: Izd. avtora, 1926. 24 pp., [1] plate. 19 cm.

Cover portrait of Sergei Esenin by Valentina Kulagina.

Criticism. Kruchenykh's "Production no. 136." Frontispiece is a second portrait of Esenin by Kulagina.

354. ———. *Chort i rechetvortsy* (Черт и речетворцы / The devil and the poets). [St. Petersburg: EUY, 1913]. 16 pp. 23 cm.

Cover by Ol'ga Rozanova.

Criticism.

355. ———. *Dun'ka-Rubikha* (Дунька-Рубиха / Dun'ka the chopper). Moscow: Izd. avtora, 1926. 12 pp. 17 cm.

Cover by Gustav Klutsis.

A "crime novel" in verse. Kruchenykh's "Production no. 140/b." It appeared previously as the last item in *Na bor'bu s khuliganstvom v literature.* (See no. 368.) The cover repeats Klutsis's illustrations for the cover of *Na bor'bu s khuliganstvom v literature,* but here the image of Dun'ka and her ax is on the front cover and that of the skull with knife and pistol is on the back, rather than vice versa.

356. ———. *Esenin i Moskva kabatskaia. Liubov' khuligana. Dve avtobiografii Esenina* (Есенин и Москва кабацкая. Любовь хулигана. Две автобиографии Есенина / Esenin and the Moscow of low taverns. A hooligan's love. Two autobiographies by Esenin). 3rd ed., enl. Moscow: Izd. avtora, 1926. 31 pp., [1] plate. 18 cm.

Kruchenykh's "Production no. 135B."

357. ———. *Faktura slova: Deklaratsiia* (Фактура слова: Декларация / Verbal texture: A declaration). MAF, Seriia teorii, no. 1. Moscow: Moskovskaia assotsiatsiia futuristov, 1922 (cover date 1923). [24] pp. 17 cm.

Headpieces and tailpieces by Ivan Kliun.

Criticism. Kruchenykh's 120th book.

One copy is inscribed by Kruchenykh in blue pencil and dated 14 September 1928. A second copy, which bears the publication date 1923, is inscribed by Kruchenykh to N. N. Orlov.

358. ———. *Fonetika teatra* (Фонетика театра / Phonetics of the theater). Introduction by Boris Kushner. Moscow: 41°, 1923. 42 pp. 18 cm.

Front cover by Natal'ia Nagorskaia. Back cover by Mikhail Plaksin.

Essays on transrational language in the theater and film, with numerous examples from Kruchenykh's own work and from Iliazd, Vladimir Mayakovsky, Aleksandr Olenin, and Igor' Terent'ev. Kruchenykh's 123rd book. Includes illustrations by Nagorskaia.

359. ———. *Fonetika teatra* (Фонетика театра / Phonetics of the theater). 2nd ed. Moscow: Izd-vo Vseros. soiuza poetov, 1925. 42 pp. 18 cm.

Includes illustrations by Natal'ia Nagorskaia and an introduction by Boris Kushner.

360. ———. *Gibel' Esenina: Kak Esenin pereshel k samoubiistvu* (Гибель Есенина: Как Есенин перешел к самоубийству / The death of Esenin: How Esenin came to suicide). 3rd ed., enl. Moscow: Izd. avtora, 1926. 18 pp., [1] leaf of plates. 18 cm.

Kruchenykh's "Production no. 134b."

361. ———. *Golodniak* (Голодняк / Hunger). Moscow, 1922. [24] pp. 17 cm.

Poems.

Inscribed by Kruchenykh.

362. ———. *Govoriashchee kino: 1-aia kniga stikhov o kino* (Говорящее кино: 1-ая книга стихов о кино / The talking cinema: First book of verse about the cinema). Moscow: Izd. avtora, 1928. 63 pp. 17 cm.

Kruchenykh's "Production no. 150."

363. ———. *Iazyk Lenina: Odinnadtsat' priemov leninskoi rechi* (Язык Ленина: Одиннадцать приемов ленинской речи / Lenin's language: Eleven devices of Lenin's speech). Moscow: Izd. Vseros. soiuza poetov, 1925. 60 pp. 19 cm.

Cover by Valentina Kulagina.

Includes illustrations by Gustav Klutsis.

364. ———. *Ironiada: Lirika, mai–iun' 1930 g.* (Ирониада: Лирика, май–июнь 1930 г. / The ironiad: Lyrics, May–June 1930). Moscow: Izd. avtora, 1930. 19 leaves. 18 × 22 cm.

Cover by Ivan Kliun.

Poems. Includes a portrait by Igor' Terent'ev. Edition size given variously as 150 (leaf 1) and 250 (leaf 19).

Text is written in longhand and reproduced by lithography on glass. Inscribed by Kruchenykh "D. Kal'mu v pamiat' 'nedostupnykh' videnii" (To D. Kal'm, in memory of "inaccessible" visions) and dated June–August 1930.

365. ———. *Kalendar'* (Календарь / Calendar). Moscow: Izd. Vseros. soiuza poetov, 1926. 16 pp. 18 cm.

Poems. Kruchenykh's "Production no. 133." Includes an introduction by Boris Pasternak. Cover portrait is a relief halftone of a photograph of 1925.

366. ———. *"Lef" agitki Maiakovskogo, Aseeva, Tret'iakova* («Леф» агитки Маяковского, Асеева, Третьякова / Propaganda pieces by the *Lef* poets Mayakovsky, Aseev, Tret'iakov). Moscow: Izd. Vseros. soiuza poetov, 1925. 61 pp. 19 cm.

Cover by Valentina Kulagina.

367. ———. *Liki Esenina ot kheruvima do khuligana: Esenin v zhizni i portretakh* (Лики Есенина от херувима до хулигана: Есенин в жизни и портретах / Esenin's faces from cherub to hooligan: Esenin in life and in portraits). Moscow: Izd. avtora, 1926. 24 pp. 19 cm.

Kruchenykh's "Production no. 137." Includes portraits by Valentina Kulagina.

368. ———. *Na bor'bu s khuliganstvom v literature* (На борьбу с хулиганством в литературе / To war with literary hooliganism). Moscow: Izd. avtora, 1926. 32 pp. 17 cm.

Cover by Gustav Klutsis.

Kruchenykh's "Production no. 140," dealing in part with the poet Sergei Esenin. Contains 4 essays in literary criticism and the poem "Dun'ka-Rubikha." (See no. 355.)

369. ———. *Ozhirenie roz: O stikhakh Terent'eva i drugikh* (Ожирене роз: О стихах Терентьева и других / Obesity in roses: On the poetry of Terent'ev and others). [Tbilisi: n.p., 1918.] 30 pp. 20 cm.

Cover by Kirill Zdanevich (Le Gris-Bergmann 1987, 39).

Unlike the cover illustrated in Le Gris-Bergmann, the Research Institute's copy is purely typographical and is not decorated.

370. ———. *15 let russkogo futurizma, 1912–1927 gg.: Materialy i kommentarii* (15 лет русского футуризма, 1912–1927: Материалы и комментарии / Fifteen years of Russian Futurism, 1912–1927: Source materials and commentaries). Moscow: Izd. Vseros. soiuza poetov, 1928. 67 pp. 17 cm.

Kruchenykh's "Production no. 151." Includes a photomontage of Kruchenykh by Gustav Klutsis, a self-portrait by Velimir Khlebnikov, a self-caricature by Igor' Terent'ev, portraits of Emiliia Ink and V. Kashnitskii by Terent'ev, and caricatures of Nikolai Aseev and Sergei Tret'iakov by Mariia Siniakova.

371. ———. *500 novykh ostrot i kalamburov Pushkina* (500 новых острот и каламбуров Пушкина / Five hundred new witticisms and puns of Pushkin). Moscow: Izd. avtora, 1924. 71 pp. 18 cm.

Inscribed as follows: "Ser. Nel'dikhenu ot Pushkina-Kruchenykh 7/VII 24" (To Sergei Nel'dikhen from Pushkin-Kruchenykh, 7 July 1924).

372. ———. *Pobeda nad solntsem* (Победа над солнцем / Victory over the sun). [St. Petersburg: EUY, 1913]. 23 pp. 25 cm.

Front cover illustration by Kazimir Malevich (Karshan 1975, no. 15). Back cover illustration by David Burliuk.

Libretto of the Futurist opera produced in December 1913 at the Luna Park Theater in St. Petersburg. The words are by Kruchenykh, the music is by Mikhail Matiushin, and the prologue is by Velimir Khlebnikov. Malevich's illustration is a sketch for a set design used in the opera. Burliuk's illustration had been used previously in the second volume of *Sadok sudei* (vol. 2, p. [51]), where it was oriented vertically rather than horizontally as here. (See no. 693.)

373. ———. *Poluzhivoi* (Полуживой / Half alive). Moscow: Izd. G. L. Kuz'min i S. D. Dolinskii, 1913. 17 leaves. 19 cm.

Poem. Includes 6 full-page drawings by Mikhail Larionov and additional drawings in the margins of the handwritten text and on the front and back covers.

From an edition of 480 (*Knizhnaia letopis'* 1913, no. 5549). Entire volume is reproduced by lithography.

374. ———. *Pomada* (Помада / Pomade). Moscow: G. L. Kuz'min i S. D. Dolinskii, [1913]. [15] leaves. 16 cm.

Poems. Includes illustrations by Mikhail Larionov mounted on gold paper and text written by hand in small capitals and longhand. According to a note on leaf [13], the last 3 poems were written jointly with E. Lunev, a pseudonym that Kruchenykh used to sign works written with others (Golubeva 1977, 11:379 n. 1).

From an edition of 480 (*Knizhnaia letopis'* 1913, no. 5548). Cover is of red paper on which the title, illustration, and author statements have been mounted, each on a separate slip of buff paper. Entire volume is reproduced by lithography. Golubeva (1977, 11:380) gives the foliation as [16] leaves. The copy reproduced in Compton (1977) has 17 leaves, and Tarasenkov gives 18 "pages" (1966, 196). Compared to the Compton microfiche with its 9 leaves of text and 8 plates, the Research Institute's copy lacks the first and last of the plates, the place of the first being taken by what is the seventh in the Compton copy. In addition, the second plate in Research Institute's copy, a Cubist standing figure, is not mounted upside down as it is in the Compton copy, and the sixth plate is bound after the eighth leaf of text rather than after the seventh. The text leaves in the 2 copies are identical. Research Institute's copy is not among the 25 copies hand colored by Larionov (Compton 1978, 81).

375. ———. *Priemy leninskoi rechi: K izucheniiu iazyka Lenina* (Приемы ленинской речи: К изучению языка Ленина / Devices of Lenin's speech: A study of Lenin's language). Moscow: Izd. Vseros. soiuza poetov, 1927. 60 pp. 17 cm.

Kruchenykh's "Production no. 143." Includes illustrations by Gustav Klutsis.

376. ———. *Priemy leninskoi rechi: K izucheniiu iazyka Lenina* (Приемы ленинской речи: К изучению языка Ленина / Devices of Lenin's speech: A study of Lenin's language). 3rd ed. Moscow: Izd. Vseros. soiuza poetov, 1928. 60 pp. 17 cm.

Cover by Gustav Klutsis.

Includes illustrations by Klutsis.

377. ———. *Pustynniki; Pustynnitsa: Dve poemy* (Пустынники; Пустынница: Две поэмы / Anchorites; Anchoress: Two poems). [Moscow: G. L. Kuz'min i S. D. Dolinskii, 1913.] [48] pp. 21 cm.

Kruchenykh stated that Mikhail Larionov did the cover and first illustration, although he is not credited in the published work (Khardzhiev 1968, 311 n. 1). The remaining illustrations are by Nataliia Goncharova.

Entire volume is reproduced by lithography, including the text, which is handwritten in block letters.

From an edition of 480 (*Knizhnaia letopis'* 1913, no. 3995).

378.———. *Razboinik Van'ka-Kain i Son'ka-Manikiurshchitsa: Ugolovnyi roman* (Разбойник Ванька-Каин и Сонька-Маникюрщица: Уголовный роман / Van'ka Cain the robber and Son'ka the manicurist: A crime novel). Moscow: Izd. Vseros. soiuza poetov, 1925 (cover date 1926). 27 pp. 27 cm.

Cover by Mariia Siniakova.

Kruchenykh's 132nd book. Includes drawings by Siniakova and introductory remarks by Boris Nesmelov. A shorter version originally appeared in the journal Lef (1924). (See no. 436.) This edition also includes "Deklaratsiia no. 6 o segodniashnikh iskusstvakh" (Declaration number 6 on the arts of today).

379. ———. *Rubiniada: Lirika, avgust–sentiabr' 1930 g.* (Рубиниада: Лирика, август–сентябрь 1930 г. / The rubyad: Lyrics, August–September 1930). Moscow: Izd. avtora, 1930. 18 leaves. 19 × 23 cm.

Cover by Ivan Kliun.

Kruchenykh's "Production no. 178."

From an edition of 130. Reproduced by lithography on glass.

380. ———. *Sdvigologiia russkogo stikha: Traktat obizhal'nyi* (traktat obizhal'nyi i pouchal'nyi) (Сдвигология русского стиха: Трактат обижальный (трактат обижальный и поучальный) / The theory of displacement in Russian verse: A provocative tract [a provocative and didactic tract]). MAF, Seriia teorii, no. 2. Moscow: Moskovskaia assotsiatsiia futuristov, 1922 (cover date 1923). 46 pp. 19 cm.

Kruchenykh's 121st book. Includes 2 illustrations by Ivan Kliun.

Inscribed by Kruchenykh and dated 14 September 1928.

381. ———. *Sobstvennye rasskazy detei* (Собственные рассказы детей / Children's own stories). Moscow: 41°, 1923. 16 pp. 19 cm.

Children's stories, poems, and songs gathered by Kruchenykh in 1921 and 1922. Child's drawing on cover engraved by Natal'ia Nagorskaia.

Inscribed by Kruchenykh to Boris Zemenkov and dated 1 January 1923.

382. ———. *Sobstvennye rasskazy i risunki detei* (Собственные рассказы и рисунки детей / Children's own stories and drawings). Moscow: [Zhuravl'], 1914. 48 pp. 23 cm.

The drawings are lithographed in black on orange, machine-made paper and appear on one side only of the leaves that make up pp. [1]–[32]. The text occupies pp. 33–48 and is letterpress on light green machine-made paper. The publisher's name has been lined out on the back cover of the Research Institute's copy.

383. ———. *Starinnaia liubov'* (Старинная любовь / Old-fashioned love). [Moscow: Kuz'min i Dolinskii, 1912.] 13 leaves. 14 cm.

Poems. Includes illustrations by Mikhail Larionov.

From an edition of 300 (*Knizhnaia letopis'* 1912, no. 27431).

384. ———. *Tainye poroki akademikov* (Тайные пороки академиков / Secret vices of academicians). Moscow: [n.p.], 1916. 32 pp., [1] plate. 23 cm.

Cover, headpiece, and tailpiece by Ivan Kliun.

Criticism. Includes illustrations and a plate by Kliun, *Ozonator (elektricheskii perenosnyi ventiliator)* (Ozonizer [electric transferential ventilator]), 3 essays by Kruchenykh, and 1 each by Kliun and Kazimir Malevich.

The actual date of publication was 1915 (Golubeva 1977, 11:381). From an edition of 450 (*Knizhnaia letopis'* 1915, no. 19059).

385. ———. "*Tsement*" *Gladkova i khuliganstvo* («Цемент» Гладкова и хулиганство / Gladkov's *Cement* and hooliganism). Moscow: Izd. avtora, 1926. 11 pp. 17 cm.

Kruchenykh's "Production no. 140v," an offprint of 1 section from his *Na bor'bu s khuliganstvom v literature.* (See no. 368.)

386. ———. *Tsvetistye tortsy* (Цветистые торцы / Paving blocks in bloom). [Baku]: 41°, 1920. [56] pp. 16 cm.

Poems and drawings.

Publication date is given as 1921 in a publisher's announcement in Kruchenykh's *Zudesnik* (see no. 394) and also in a bibliography of Kruchenykh's works appended to *Zaumnyi iazyk u Seifullinoi, Vs. Ivanova, Leonova, Babelia, I. Sel'vinskogo, A. Veselogo, i dr.* (See no. 392.) The text consists of hand-lettered poems reproduced on a hectograph in greenish or black typescript and in greenish carbon typescript. The cover is black letterpress. Of the 4 hectographed drawings, 1 is signed in the hectograph by Vladimir Burliuk and 2 by Kirill Zdanevich. The fourth is unsigned but is in the style of those by Zdanevich. The drawing by Burliuk, a portrait of S. Miasoedov, appeared previously on leaf [75] of the first volume of *Sadok sudei.* (See no. 693.) A variety of found papers were used. The most common are several sorts of machine-made, now yellowish. There are 6 leaves of a coarse machine-made paper ruled with faint blue lines, apparently from a writing tablet. Two other leaves seem to be of ledger paper, as they have blue and black lines that cross at right angles. There are 2 leaves of smoother, whiter machine-made paper of better quality on which 2 of the illustrations appear. On the front and back covers of the Research Institute's copy is a small faded image stamped in purple ink. That on the front cover shows 2 barefoot men with 5 legs between them; that on the back, a fish peering out of a pond surrounded by flowers. Both are excerpts from the last of Pavel Filonov's illustrations for Velimir Khlebnikov's *Izbornik stikhov, 1907–1914.* (See no. 307.) There is a faded purple roman numeral "I" on the front cover. It is not clear whether these stamps were added at the time the book was produced or by a later owner. Inscribed by Kruchenykh on inside front cover to "Tat'iana Fedorovna" and dated Baku, 1920.

387. ———. *Uchites' khudogi: Stikhi* (Учитесь худоги: Стихи / Study, artists: Verse). Tbilisi: [n.p.], 1917. [26] leaves. 24 cm.

Includes illustrations by Kirill Zdanevich. Lithographed throughout, including the handwritten text.

Inscribed in pencil on front cover as follows: "P. Miturich, 21."

388. ———. *Utinoe gnezdyshko durnykh slov* (Утиное гнездышко дурных слов / A duck's nest of bad words). [St. Petersburg: EUY, 1913.] [22] leaves. 19 cm.

Poems. Kruchenykh's seventh book. Includes illustrations by Ol'ga Rozanova. Except for the letterpress cover, entire volume is lithographed, including the handwritten text.

From an edition of 500 (*Knizhnaia letopis'* 1914, no. 194). Not among the 100 copies hand-colored by Rozanova (Compton 1978, 81). A heavy, grayish-tan machine-made paper was used for all but the first and last leaves, which are of cream wove paper. Nine leaves are full-page illustrations, 7 are purely text, and 5 combine text and drawings.

389. ———. *Vozropshchem* (Возропщем / Let's grumble). [St. Petersburg]: EUY, 1913. 12 pp., [3] plates. 19 cm.

Contains a poem, an essay, and a brief play. Tipped in at p. 1 are 2 lithographs by Kazimir Malevich, signed and titled on the stone *Arifmetika* (Arithmetic) and *Krest'ianka idet po vodu* (A peasant woman goes for water), and 1 lithograph by Ol'ga Rozanova, untitled and unsigned. On p. [7] there is a black-and-white halftone of a painting by Rozanova, *Priiut* (Refuge).

The lithographs are printed in black on white machine-made paper that contrasts with the now-yellowish, coarser, machine-made paper of the text. They are also smaller than the text pages, measuring 17.6 × 11.7 cm. The inside front cover is stamped in blue-green ink with the letters "АБ" surrounded by a circle, presumably an owner's mark.

390. ———. *Vzorval'* (Взорваль / Explodity). [St. Petersburg: EUY, 1913.] [31] leaves. 18 cm.

Cover by Nikolai Kul'bin.

Kruchenykh's ninth book. Includes a portrait of Kruchenykh by Kul'bin. Of the full-page illustrations not combined with text, 2 are signed on the stone by Ol'ga Rozanova (leaves [11] and [12]) and 2 by Kazimir Malevich (leaves [17] and [22]). A standing devil by Nataliia Goncharova is signed with initials and occupies a half-leaf preceding the section "Novye stseny iz *Igry v adu*" (New scenes from *A Game in Hell*). According to Nikolai Khardzhiev, Kruchenykh informed him that Natan Al'tman did the tailpiece that consists of the Russian word *shish* (fico), written in letters designed to look like Hebrew; if true, this would be the only instance of Al'tman's collaboration on a Futurist collection (1976, 95).

From an edition of 350 (*Knizhnaia letopis'* 1913, no. 14411). Of 31 leaves, 20 are lithographed in black. Some have either a handwritten poem or a drawing, but others combine both. The remaining 11 leaves consist of poems stamped in small capital letters in black (9) or purple (2) ink. A cream-colored, machine-made paper predominates and is used for the cover as well, but there are 3 leaves of thin, green, machine-made paper. Two of these leaves are used for what would seem to be less important purposes (publisher's announcements and the caption to Kruchenykh's portrait), although leaf [27], the third, has the short text, "Iz neumolimogo prezreniia k zhenshchine i detiam v nashem iazyke budet tol'ko muzhskoi rod" (From implacable scorn for women and children, our language shall admit only the masculine gender).

391. ———. *Vzorval'* (Взорваль / Explodity). 2nd ed., enl. [St. Petersburg: EUY, 1913]. [29] leaves. 18 cm.

Cover by Ol'ga Rozanova.

Includes illustrations by Nataliia Goncharova, Nikolai Kul'bin, Kazimir Malevich, Rozanova, and possibly Natan Al'tman. A comparison of the Research Institute's copy of the second edition to its copy of the first reveals various alterations, substitutions, and omissions. Leaf [27] of the first edition has been relithographed with slightly different wording ("implacable" scorn for women and children has become "base" scorn), and the text has been reoriented to read from the bottom to the top of the page. There are 7 stamped leaves in Research Institute's copy of the second edition, 4 of them in black ink, 3 in purple, and 1 in brown. Four of the stamped leaves of the first edition ([6], [8], [10], [13]) have been replaced with lithographed versions, with [13] replaced by a stamped version. Leaves [16] and [29] of the first edition remain stamped in the second, but their texts are new. Three other stamped leaves of the first edition ([9], [14], [21]), together with the final leaf of publisher's announcements, have been omitted entirely, and 2 new stamped leaves have been added. The result is an "enlarged" edition that is shorter than the original by 2 leaves. Although the foliation of the copies reproduced in Compton (1977) agrees with that of the Research Institute's copies, Golubeva (1977, 11:380) gives [30] and [33] leaves for the first and second editions and Tarasenkov (1966, 197) gives 31 and 32.

From an edition of 450 (*Knizhnaia letopis'* 1914, no. 192). Cover is of a heavy, gray machine-made paper. Ivory or buff machine-made paper is used throughout the text.

392. ———. *Zaumnyi iazyk u Seifullinoi, Vs. Ivanova, Leonova, Babelia, I. Sel'vinskogo, A. Veselogo, i dr.* (Заумный язык у Сейфуллиной, Вс. Иванова, Леонова, Бабеля, И. Сельвинского, А. Веселого, и др. / Transrational language in Seifullina, Vsevolod Ivanov, Leonov, Babel', Il'ia Sel'vinskii, A. Veselyi, and others). Moscow: Vseros. soiuz poetov, 1925. 59 pp. 18 cm.

Cover and tailpieces by Valentina Kulagina.

Kruchenykh's 127th book.

393. [———]. *Zhiv Kruchenykh!: Sbornik statei* (Жив Крученых!: Сборник статей / Kruchenykh lives!: A collection of essays). Moscow: Izd. Vseros. soiuza poetov, 1925. 44 pp. 19 cm.

Cover by Gustav Klutsis.

Includes contributions by David Burliuk, Boris Pasternak, Sergei Rafalovich, Tat'iana Vechorka, and Sergei Tret'iakov.

394. ———. *Zudesnik* (Зудесник / Magitchan). Moscow: [n.p.], 1922. [19] pp. 19 cm.

Poems. Kruchenykh's 119th book. Includes poetry by Igor' Terent'ev as well as Kruchenykh.

Two partially effaced stamps in purple ink may read "Valerii Briusov."

395. [———]. *Buka russkoi literatury* (Бука русской литературы / The bogeyman of Russian literature). Moscow: 41°, 1923. 44 pp. 19 cm.

Cover by Natal'ia Nagorskaia. Tailpieces by Ivan Kliun.

Four essays on Aleksei Kruchenykh by David Burliuk, Sergei Rafalovich, Sergei Tret'iakov, and Tat'iana Vechorka.

396. **Kruchenykh, Aleksei, and Roman Jakobson.** *Zaumnaia gniga* (Заумная гнига / Transrational boog). [Moscow: n.p., 1915 (cover date 1916).] [21] leaves. 22 cm.

Includes brief poems and phrases by Kruchenykh stamped in red ink (leaves [2], [3], [5], [6], [8], [10], [12], [13], [15], [17], [19]), poems by "Aliagrov" (Jakobson) in letterpress (leaf [21]), and colored linoleum cuts based on playing cards by Ol'ga Rozanova. Each linoleum cut is printed in a single color. Leaves printed in red ([4], [11], [18]) and black ([9], [14], [15]) represent cards from suits of those colors, as they are indentified in captions that form part of each image. The captions of the 2 leaves printed in yellow read "Odnovremennoe izobrazhenie chetyrekh tuzov" (Simultaneous representation of the four aces) and "Pikovaia i chervonnaia damy, odnovremennoe izobrazhenie" (The queen of spades and the queen of hearts, a simultaneous representation). Leaf [20], depicting the jack of spades, is printed in dark blue.

From an edition of 140 (*Knizhnaia letopis'* 1915, no. 19058). Research Institute's copy has a collage of light green paper on leaf [2]; in the copy reproduced in Compton (1977) it is pink. It retains a button on the red paper heart of Rozanova's cover collage, but the button has been affixed with glue rather than sewn on, as originally done (Compton 1978, 86). A dedication inscribed in ink on the inside front cover is signed "Maurevich" and dated 21 August 1915. Annotations in purple pencil on leaves [3], [5], and [6] are parodies of Kruchenykh's transrational verse. These have 3 "signatures," Zaverchenykh, Zavertykhchir, and "S. N. T. D." (the latter in roman characters), as well as 2 dates (25 and 26 August 1915). There are additional, incompletely erased annotations in the same purple pencil on leaves [8], [10], and [12].

397. **Kruchenykh, Aleksei, and Velimir Khlebnikov.** *Bukh lesinnyi* (Бух лесинный / A forest boom). St. Petersburg: EUY, [1913]. [22] leaves. 15 cm.

Front and back covers by Ol'ga Rozanova. Headpieces and tailpieces by Kruchenykh.

Kruchenykh's "8th book." Includes all of the poems from his *Starinnaia liubov'* (see no. 402) and a few other poems by him and Khlebnikov. Includes a portrait of Kruchenykh by Nikolai Kul'bin. The notice on the back cover mentions 2 illustrations by Rozanova but in fact there are 3: those on leaves [1] and [16] are signed "O. R." and that on leaf [10] is signed "O. Rozanova."

Edition size given in *Knizhnaia letopis'* (1913, no. 14412) as 4000, presumably for 400. Entire volume is reproduced by lithography in black ink on light green paper.

398. ———. *Igra v adu: Poema* (Игра в аду: Поэма / A game in hell: A poem). [Moscow: G. Kuz'min i S. Dolinskii, 1912]. 14 leaves. 19 cm.

Front cover by Nataliia Goncharova.

Includes 15 illustrations by Goncharova and handwritten text.

From an edition of 300 (*Knizhnaia letopis'* 1912, no. 27432). Entire volume is reproduced by lithography.

399. ———. *Igra v adu: Poema* (Игра в аду: Поэма / A game in hell: A poem). 2nd ed., enl. [Moscow: EUY, 1914.] [40] leaves. 19 cm.

Front and back covers by Kazimir Malevich.

Includes 3 illustrations by Malevich and 23 by Ol'ga Rozanova.

From an edition of 800 (*Knizhnaia letopis'* 1914, no. 4452). Entire volume is reproduced by lithography.

400. ———. *Mirskontsa* (Мирсконца / Worldbackward). [Moscow: G. L. Kuz'min i S. D. Dolinskii, 1912.] [39] leaves. 19 cm.

Cover collage by Nataliia Goncharova.

Poems. Includes 13 illustrations by Goncharova, 9 by Mikhail Larionov, 4 by Nikolai Rogovin, and 1 by Vladimir Tatlin (not 11, 6, 3, and 1 as stated in the list of illustrations on leaf [38]).

From an edition of 220. The text is handwritten and lithographed in black ink, except for 7 leaves with typescript-like letters stamped in green ink. These 7 leaves have 6 additional larger and cruder letters, which Compton suggests may have been added using "a rough stencil or potato-cut" (1978, 72). In the Research Institute's copy they appear to have been printed using green and black ink mixed together. Leaves [29] and [36] are slight double strikes. Research Institute's copy belongs to the group in which the cover collage by Goncharova takes the form of a large green (rather than black) plant on buff paper. It is positioned above a mounted slip that provides the title and authors. Research Institute's copy lacks the guard tissues that occur before illustrations in some copies (Janecek 1984, 79–80).

401. ———. *Slovo kak takovoe* (Слово как таковое / The word as such). [Moscow: EUY, 1913.] 15 pp. 24 cm.

Cover lithograph by Kazimir Malevich.

Literary theory. Includes a lithograph by Ol'ga Rozanova tipped in at p. 3. It is on light green machine-made paper, untitled, and signed "O. R." Malevich's lithograph is printed on light green paper and mounted on cover.

From an edition of 500 (*Knizhnaia letopis'* 1913, no. 27034).

402. ———. *Starinnaia liubov'; Bukh lesinyi* (Старинная любовь; Бух лесиный / Old-fashioned love; Forest boom). 2nd ed., enl. [St. Petersburg]: EUY, [1914]. 40 pp. 18 cm.

Contains a few more poems than the booklet previously published as *Bukh lesinnyi,* which in turn had incorporated all those in Kruchenykh's *Starinnaia liubov'*. Includes illustrations by Kruchenykh, Nikolai Kul'bin, Mikhail Larionov, and Ol'ga Rozanova.

From an edition of 600 (*Knizhnaia letopis'* 1914, no. 6165).

403. ———. *Te li le* (Тэ ли лэ). [St. Petersburg]: EUY, 1914. [14] leaves. 24 cm.

Poems. The book consists of color hectographs. Most are by Ol'ga Rozanova, but leaf [11] is signed in the hectograph with "NK" for Nikolai Kul'bin, and leaf [10] is attributed to him by Kovtun (1989, 161). Four leaves are purely drawings, one leaf is purely text handwritten in block letters, and the remaining leaves combine text and drawing.

Copy 12 of 50 available for sale. The covers and all leaves but 2 of the Research Institute's copy show different drawing and in part different coloring from the copy reproduced in Compton (1977). Only leaves [8] and [10] appear to be identical, although in both cases the impressions in the Research Institute's copy are fainter, presumably because they were pulled later. Compared to the 6 leaves from *Te li le* reproduced in Kovtun (1989, 157–62), leaves [8] and [10] again appear to be identical to the Research Institute's copy. Leaves [3] and [13] and the front cover differ from the Research Institute's copy but are identical to the copy reproduced in Compton (1977). Leaf [4] is different in all 3 copies. The explanation for these differences may be the low number of copies that the hectograph process allows from one inking, so that most leaves had to be drawn 2 or 3 times to attain the edition size of 50 (plus an undetermined number of additional copies not for sale). Research Institute's copy is missing the final letterpress leaf [15] of the Compton (1977) copy.

404. **Kruchenykh, Aleksei, Velimir Khlebnikov, and Grigorii Petnikov.** *Zaumniki* (Заумники / Transrationalists). [Moscow]: EUY, 1922. 24 pp. 21 cm.

Cover linoleum cut by Aleksandr Rodchenko.

Includes poems by all 3 authors, a letter by Khlebnikov addressed to Petnikov, a critical-polemical essay by Kruchenykh, and, on pp. [23]–24, a description of Futurist-Transrationalist activity in Tbilisi, signed "E. L."

Research Institute has 2 copies. The cover of the first is printed in black on tan paper, the cover of the second on pink paper. The first copy is inscribed by Kruchenykh to Sergei Gorodetskii and dated 30 November 1921. The publication date of 1922 therefore cannot be the date of production.

405. **Kruchenykh, Aleksei, Velimir Khlebnikov, and Tat'iana Vechorka.** *Mir i ostal'noe* (Мир и остальное / The world and the rest). Baku: [n.p.], 1920. [85] pp. 24 cm.

Each of the 3 sections is devoted to poems by 1 of the authors. The first consists of 24 poems by Kruchenykh. Of these the first 3 are in French; their texts are identical to those of the last 3, though it is clear from minor differences in spacing and punctuation that they were typed separately. The second section consists of a numbered sequence of 4 short poems by Khlebnikov together with his longer poems *Khodiat sinie kotory* (Blue who's are walking) and *3 sestry* (3 sisters). The third section consists of 15 short poems by Vechorka. Includes a Cubist portrait of Kruchenykh by Solomon Telingater (Parnis 1985, 169).

Printed on buff, machine-made paper in heavier buff wrappers. The front cover is decorated with purple and red ink in a vertically striped wallpaper-like pattern by Khlebnikov (Parnis 1985, 168–69). Telingater's portrait of Kruchenykh is reproduced in purple hectograph and laid in on p. [2]. The text is variously typescript, carbon typescript, typescript reproduced by purple hectograph, handwriting reproduced by hectograph, and handwriting reproduced by carbon paper. Research Institute's copy has emendations by several hands in the first and third sections. Those in the third section are largely limited to correcting letters that did not reproduce clearly, but in the first, some additional words are supplied. Telingater remembers 3, 4, or 5 copies being made, but Vechorka remembers 20. Parnis mentions copies in the Russian National Library in Saint Petersburg (formerly the Saltykov-Shchedrin Public Library) and the Pushkin Museum in Moscow, as well as a third copy "whose trail was lost in the United States" (Parnis 1985, 169).

406. **Kruchenykh, Aleksei, and Zina V.** *Porosiata* (Поросята / Piglets). 2nd ed., enl. [Petrograd: EUY, 1914.] 16 pp. 23 cm.

Poems and brief prose pieces. Zina is identified as an 11-year-old girl, although her "motifs (WC, garbage, pigs) make one slightly suspicious of

[her] authenticity, since they are so typical of Kruchenykh's own work" (Markov 1968, 203).

Cover is a gray pasteboard. The text is printed on light green paper.

407. ***Kryl'ia kholopa*** (Крылья холопа / Wings of a serf). Moscow: Kinopechat', [1926]. 7 pp. 17 × 26 cm.

Pamphlet on the film of 1926 directed by Iurii Tarich.

408. **Kudreiko, Anatolii.** *Osada: 1927–1928* (Осада, 1927–1928 / Siege, 1927–1928). Moscow and Leningrad: Molodaia gvardiia, 1929. 94 pp. 18 cm.

Poems.

409. **Kukryniksy** (Mikhail Kupriianov, Porfirii Krylov, Nikolai Sokolov). *Otchetnaia vystavka za 6 let: Karikatura, politplakat, kniga, zhurnal, gazeta, zhivopis', teatr* (Отчетная выставка за 6 лет: Карикатура, политплакат, книга, журнал, газета, живопись, театр / Retrospective exhibition of six years' work: Caricature, political poster, book, journal, newspaper, painting, theater). [Moscow]: Izogiz, 1932. [16] pp. 26 cm.

The exhibition, poster, prospectus, and catalog were designed by Solomon Telingater.

Includes a caricature of the 3 "Kukryniksy" by Aminadav Kanevskii.

410. ***Kul'bin.*** St. Petersburg: Ob-vo intimnogo teatra, 1912. 69 pp. 18 cm.

Essays and a poem in honor of Nikolai Kul'bin. The illustrations are tipped-in gravures of paintings and drawings by him.

411. **Kushner, Boris.** *Miting dvortsov: Alliterovannaia proza* (Митинг дворцов: Аллитерованная проза / A rally of palaces: Alliterative prose). Petrograd: Aventiura, 1918. 7 pp. 22 cm.

412. ———. *Semafory, I: Stikhi* (Семафоры, I: Стихи / Semaphores, I: Verse). Moscow: [n.p.], 1914. 44 pp. 18 cm.

Cover by M. V. Libakov.

Cover is a relief print. On p. [12] of Research Institute's copy is an 11-line poem that is not listed in the contents. It is printed in purple ink apparently from a wooden block, the central area of which did not register legibly.

413. **Kusikov, Aleksandr.** *Al'-Barrak: Oktiabr'skie poemy* (Аль-Баррах: Октябрьские поэмы / Al'-Barrak: October poems). 2nd ed., enl. Berlin and Moscow: Nakanune, 1923. 79 pp. 19 cm.

Cover by Aleksandr Arnshtam.

414. ———. *Iskandar Name* (Искандар Намэ / The book of Alexander). Moscow: Imazhinisty, 1921–1922. [16] pp. 33 cm.

Cover by Vera Aleksandrova.

Poem. Includes illustrations and a portrait of the author by Aleksandrova. Copy 59 of 500.

415. ———. *Koevangelieran* (Коевангелиеран / Kogospelran). Moscow: Pleiada, 1920. [31] pp. 27 cm.
Cover by Boris Erdman.
Poem. Title is a blend of the Russian words for *Koran* and *Gospel.* Includes illustrations by Erdman.

416. ———. *Poema poem* (Поэма поэм / Poem of poems). 2nd ed. Moscow: Imazhinisty, 1920. [29] pp. 22 cm.
Cover by Boris Erdman.
Includes illustrations by Erdman.

417. ———. *Ptitsa bezymiannaia: Izbrannye stikhi, 1917–1921* (Птица безымянная: Избранные стихи, 1917–1921 / Bird without a name: Selected verse, 1917–1921). Berlin: Skify, 1922. 62 pp. 21 cm.
Cover by El Lissitzky.

418. ———. *V nikuda: Vtoraia kniga strok* (В никуда: Вторая книга строк / Into nowhere: Second book of verse). Moscow: Imazhinisty, 1920. 80 pp. 27 cm.
Cover by S. A. Zalshupin (Hellyer 1994, no. 273). Cover vignette by Georgii Iakulov.
Includes a portrait of Kusikov by Iakulov.
Pp. 1, 2, 7–10, 73, 74, and 77–80 are missing.

419. **Kusikov, Aleksandr, and Sergei Esenin.** *Zvezdnyi byk* (Звездный бык / Starry bull). Moscow: Imazhinisty, 1921. 15 pp. 26 cm.
Poems.

420. **Kusikov, Aleksandr, and Vadim Shershenevich.** *Korobeiniki schast'ia* (Коробейники счастья / Peddlers of happiness). Kiev: Imazhinisty, 1920. [38] pp. 18 cm.
Poems.
The front cover illustrations by Boris Erdman take the form of 2 roundels with Cubist portraits of Kusikov and Shershenevich. That with Kusikov's portrait appears in a larger version on the cover of the collection *Koevangelieran.* (See no. 415.) There the roundel is 73 rather than 51 mm in diameter.

421. **[Kustodiev, Boris].** Vsevolod Voinov. *B. M. Kustodiev* (Б.М. Кустодиев / B. M. Kustodiev). Leningrad: Gos. izd-vo, 1925. 95 pp., lv, iv, [3] plates. 31 cm.
Includes 3 black-and-white lithographs by Kustodiev.

422. **Kuzmin, Mikhail.** *Forel' razbivaet led: Stikhi, 1925–1928* (Форель разбивает лед: Стихи, 1925–1928 / The trout breaks the ice: Verse, 1925–1928).

Leningrad: Izd-vo pisatelei v Leningrade, 1929. 93 pp. 18 cm.
Cover by Valentina Khodasevich.

423. ———. *Lesok: Liricheskaia poema dlia muzyki s ob"iasnitel'noi prozoi v trekh chastiakh* (Лесок: Лирическая поэма для музыки с объяснительной прозой в трех частях / The copse: Lyrical poem for music with explanatory prose in three parts). Petrograd: Neopalimaia kupina, 1922. [7]–33 pp. 26 cm.
Book ornament by Aleksandr Bozherianov.
From an edition of 500.

424. ———. *Nezdeshnie vechera* (Нездешние вечера / Otherworldly evenings). St. Petersburg: Petropolis, 1921. 134 pp. 18 cm.
Cover by Mstislav Dobuzhinskii.
Poems.

425. ———. *Seti: Pervaia kniga stikhov* (Сети: Первая книга стихов / Nets: First book of verse). 3rd ed. St. Petersburg and Berlin: Petropolis, 1923. 206 pp. 20 cm.
Cover by Natan Al'tman.

426. ———. *Vtornik Meri: Predstavlenie v trekh chastiakh dlia kukol zhivykh ili dereviannykh* (Вторник Мери: Представление в трех частях для кукол живых или деревянных / Mary's Tuesday: A performance in three parts for live or wooden puppets). Petrograd: Petropolis, 1921. 36 pp. 13 cm.
Cover by Mstislav Dobuzhinskii.
Copy 66 of 100 numbered copies from a total edition of 1000.

427. **Kuznetsova, A. D., Adriana Magidson, and Iurii Shchukin.** *Oformlenie goroda v dni revoliutsionnykh prazdnestv* (Оформление города в дни революционных празднеств / Decorating the city for revolutionary celebrations). Moscow and Leningrad: Ogiz-Izogiz, 1932. 140 pp., [2] plates. 28 cm.
Cover by Kuznetsova, Magidson, and Shchukin.
The cover incorporates a photograph by M. Iarmush of a model for a temporary festival tower on Sverdlovsk Square in Moscow, 1932.

428. **Larionov, Mikhail.** *Luchizm* (Лучизм / Rayonism). Moscow: Izd. K. i K., 1913. 21 pp., [6] plates. 15 cm.
Artistic theory. Includes relief halftones of illustrations by Nataliia Goncharova and Larionov.
Research Institute's copy has a pencil drawing by an unknown hand on the verso of plate [5]. Its caption reads "Luchistyi portret Iashi" (Rayonist portrait of Iasha). There is also a crude profile head in pencil on the verso of plate [6].

429. **Latsis, Anna, and L. Keilina.** *Deti i kino* (Дети и кино / Children and cinema). [Moscow]: Tea-Kino-Pechat', 1928. 85 pp. 18 cm.
Cover signed "S. V.," for Varavara Stepanova (Lavrent'ev 1989, 150).

430. **Lavrov, Leonid.** *Uplotnenie zhizni: Stikhi* (Уплотнение жизни: Стихи / Compression of life: Verse). Moscow: Federatsiia, 1931. 94 pp. 18 cm.
Cover by Boris Titov.
Poems.

431. **Lebedev, Vladimir.** *Okhota* (Охота / Hunting). Moscow: Raduga, 1925. 12 pp. 28 cm.
Children's book. Composed entirely of color illustrations.

432. ———. Posters produced for the Petrograd Okna ROSTA office.
Three posters produced in 1920 and 1921 for the Petrograd office of the Display Windows of the Russian Telegraph Agency (ROSTA). In his posters Lebedev drew on the folk imagery of the Russian *lubok* (popular broadsheet). Each is printed in 6 colors (various combinations of yellow, green, orange, red, blue, and black) and accompanied by a text or caption, printed in black, as follows:
(1) "Sprosi esera / Kakova ego vera? / Skazhet zemlia krest'ianam! / A krest'iane komy? / —Anglichanam!" (Ask a member of the Social Revolutionary Party what his religion is? He will say, "Land for the peasants!" And who should get the peasants? He will say, "The Englishmen!"). Printed in yellow, green, orange, and black on brownish paper. 59 × 41 cm.
(2) "Krest'ianin / Esli ty vez khleb / gosudarstvu i u tebia / Slomalas' cheka / Beda ne velika / Esli ty zakhochesh' / Im spekul'nit',-to / popadesh' v 'che-ka' / vot togda beda." (Peasant, if you were hauling grain for the state and you broke your linchpin, no big trouble. But if you decided to sell it for profit, then you would be hauled in by the Cheka [predecessor of the KGB], and that's a big trouble). Printed in red, black, yellow, and green on brownish paper. 71 × 41 cm.
(3) "Sport—eto lovkost' / sila i krasota!" (Sport—This is skill, strength, and beauty!). Printed in yellow, orange, blue, and black on brownish paper. 58 × 43 cm.

433. ———. *V. Lebedev*. Leningrad: Gos. russkogii muzei, 1928. 71 pp. 17 cm.
Exhibition catalog.

434. [———]. *Russkii plakat, 1917–1922: Vypusk pervyi, V. V. Lebedev* (Русский плакат, 1917–1922: Выпуск первый, В. В. Лебедев / The Russian poster, 1917–1922: First issue, V. V. Lebedev). St. Petersburg: Strelets, 1922. 36 pp., xxiii color plates. 21 cm.
Includes text by Nikolai Punin.
Copy 426 of 500.

435. **Le Corbusier.** *Planirovka goroda* (Планировка города / City planning). Moscow: Ogiz-Izogiz, 1933. xvi, 207 pp., 1 plate. 25 cm.
Translation of *Urbanisme.*

436. ***Lef: Zhurnal levogo fronta iskusstv*** (Леф: Журнал левого фронта искусств / Lef: Journal of the Left Front of the Arts). Moscow: Gosizdat, 1923–1925. 24 cm.

Edited by Vladimir Mayakovsky. Editorial committee included Boris Arvatov, Nikolai Aseev, Osip Brik, Nikolai Chuzhak, Boris Kushner, and Sergei Tret'iakov.

Covers by Aleksandr Rodchenko.

Contains Constructivist illustrations, including kiosk designs by Anton Lavinskii, geometric textile designs by Liubov' Popova, advertising posters by Rodchenko, and sports clothing by Varvara Stepanova. Features theoretical articles, programmatic statements about the Left Front of the Arts (LEF), and prose and poetry by Aseev, Brik, Vasilii Kamenskii, Aleksei Kruchenykh, Mayakovsky, and Boris Pasternak and literary criticism by Boris Eikhenbaum, Viktor Shklovskii, and Boris Tomashevskii. Some of the early stories of Isaak Babel' appeared here for the first time.

Irregularly published. A total of 7 issues published. Revived as *Novyi Lef.* (See no. 593.)

437. ***Leningrad, obraztsovyi sotsialisticheskii gorod: Novostroiki 1932 goda, vypusk pervyi*** (Ленинград, образцовый социалистический город: Новостройки 1932 года, выпуск первый / Leningrad, model socialist city: New building projects of 1932, first issue). [Leningrad]: Ogiz-Izogiz, 1932. 23 pp. 18 × 27 cm.

Design and cover by Aleksandr Leo.

Includes projects by Iakov Chernikhov and others.

438. **Lentulov, Aristarkh.** *Vystavka kartin A. V. Lentulova: Organizovannaia k 25-letiiu khudozhestvennoi deiatel'nosti, 1908–1933* (Выставка картин А. В. Лентулова: Организованная к 25-летию художественной деятельности, 1908–1933 / Exhibition of paintings by A. V. Lentulov: Organized on the occasion of his twenty-fifth year of artistic activity, 1908–1933). Moscow: Vsekokhudozhnik, 1933. 33 pp., [15] plates. 18 cm.

439. ***Lët: Sbornik stikhov*** (Лёт: Сборник стихов / Flight: Collection of verse). Edited by Nikolai Aseev. Moscow: Krasnaia nov', 1923. 60 pp. 23 cm.

Cover by Aleksandr Rodchenko.

Includes work by Aseev and 27 other contributors.

440. **Liashko, Nikolai.** *Domennaia pech'* (Доменная печь / Blast furnace). 3rd ed. Moscow and Leningrad: Zemlia i fabrika, 1929. 143 pp. 21 cm.

Cover by L. Voronov.

Novella. First published in its final form in 1926 (Akimov 1959–1972, 3:810).

441. ———. *Minuchaia smert'* (Минучая смерть / Death that passes by). Vol. 7 of *Polnoe sobranie sochinenii* (Полное собрание сочинений / Complete works). Moscow and Leningrad: Zemlia i fabrika, 1928. 21 cm.
Cover by 2-Stenberg-2 (Georgii and Vladimir Stenberg).
Vols. 1 and 2 of the 7-volume *Polnoe sobranie sochinenii* were not published (Akimov 1959–1972, 3:797).

442. **Libedinskii, Iurii.** *Zavtra* (Завтра / Tomorrow). Moscow and Leningrad: Molodaia gvardiia, 1924. 88 pp., [8] plates. 26 cm.
Cover by Sergei Sen'kin. Cover photomontage by Gustav Klutsis and Sen'kin.
Novel. The cover is in red and black, as are 3 of the 4 photomontage plates by Klutsis. The remaining 4 are by Sen'kin.

443. ***Liren'*** (Лирень / Lyroon). [Moscow]: Liren', 1920. 40 pp. 16 cm.
Includes works by Nikolai Aseev, Elena Guro, Velimir Khlebnikov, Vladimir Mayakovsky, Boris Pasternak, and Grigorii Petnikov.

444. ***Lirika, stikhi: II-oi sbornik*** (Лирика, стихи: II-ой сборник / Lyrics, verse: Second miscellany). Moscow: Neoklassiki, 1922. 32 pp. 18 cm.
Cover by Georgii Echeistov.
Includes poems by 15 authors.

445. **Lissitzky, El.** *Figurinen: Die plastische Gestaltung der elektro-mechanischen Schau "Sieg über die Sonne"*; *Opera gedichtet von A. Krutschonjch, Moskau, 1913* (Costume designs: The three-dimensional plan for the electromechanical show *Victory over the Sun;* libretto by A. Kruchenykh, Moscow, 1913). Hannover: Rob. Leunis und Chapman, 1923. Title sheet, 10 colored lithographs. In portfolio. 47 × 55 cm (portfolio); 46 × 53 cm (lithographs).
Costume designs for an unrealized electromechanical theater in which a single console would control all the elements of a performance—light, sound, and the mechanical figures that would replace actors. As a sample production Lissitzky chose the Futurist opera of 1913 *Pobeda nad solntsem* (Victory over the sun). The lithographs derive from gouaches preserved in the Tretyakov Gallery in Moscow that Lissitzky traced to create the versions now in the Van Abbe Museum in Eindhoven. The latter were then transferred to stone (Lissitzky 1987, 182).
Copy 67 of 75, signed and numbered by Lissitzky.

446. [———]. Miscellaneous publications that include design work by El Lissitzky.
Issues of 3 periodicals for which Lissitzky contributed graphic design work. Vol. 2, no. 3 (1922); vol. 4, no. 3 (1922); and vol. 5, no. 3 (1923) of *Broom* and vol. 4, no. 11 (November 1921) of the Dutch architectural journal *Wendingen* (Turns) feature covers by El Lissitzky. No. 8/9 (1924) of *Merz* includes typography and layout by Lissitzky.

447. ———. *Pro dva kvadrata: Suprematicheskii skaz v 6-ti postroikakh* (Про два квадрата: Супрематический сказ в 6-ти постройках / Concerning two squares: A Suprematist tale in six constructions). Berlin: Skify, 1922. [10] leaves. 28 cm.

Children's book.

Leaf [9] has the words "Postroeno 1920 Vitebsk" (Built 1920 Vitebsk) and the UNOVIS device. Research Institute's copy is from the regular, soft-bound edition, rather than the 50-copy hardcover edition that was signed and numbered by Lissitzky (Lissitzky 1987, 184). A Dutch translation, *Van twee kwadraten,* appeared in the same year in *De stijl* 5, nos. 10–11 and also as an additional 50-copy edition signed and numbered by Lissitzky.

448. ———. *Russland: Die Rekonstruktion der Architektur in der Sowjetunion* (Russia: The reconstruction of architecture in the Soviet Union). Neues Bauen in der Welt, vol. 1. Vienna: A. Schroll, 1930. 103 pp. 29 cm.

Cover and dust jacket by Lissitzky.

Research Institute's copy is missing the dust jacket.

449. **Lissitzky, El.** Archive. Correspondence, photographs of graphic design work, and miscellaneous documents and personal items.

Includes 126 detailed letters written by El Lissitzky to his wife, Sophie Lissitzky, between 1922 and 1941. More than two-thirds of these letters are handwritten and about one-third are on Lissitzky's letterhead, many with drawings. The largest number of these letters were written in Germany, Switzerland, and Moscow during the years 1922 through 1930. Written in German, they contain rich, evocative descriptions of Lissitzky's ongoing projects (articles, architectural competitions, book designs, typography work). In addition the archive contains 2 address books that show the range of Lissitzky's international contacts; an original inventory containing the list of Lissitzky's Prouns—an acronym for Project for the Affirmation of the New—(70 entries—paintings, prints, works on paper, and typographical material—were recorded in 1924 in Sophie's hand, to which Lissitzky added 28 items); official documents, including a typewritten contract for a series of 4 lectures to be delivered at INKhUK and a typewritten contract with Yiddisher-Folks-Farlag regarding Lissitzky's illustrations for 11 children's books; Lissitzky's library card issued 12 June 1931; Lissitzky's employment history filed with the Central Park of Culture and Leisure in the late 1929 when he took the job as an architect (the history covers Lissitzky's activities from 1911 until he took this job); and documentary photographs of Lissitzky's designs for major international and Russian trade exhibitions (120); architectural projects (28); and artistic works, especially Prouns (28), as well as commercial and typographical designs.

450. **Lissitzky, El.** Archive of Jan Tschichold. Articles.

Four articles. One copy of Lissitzky's aphorisms, "Topographie der typographie" (Topography of typography [*Merz,* July 1923]), signed by Lissitzky; 1 copy of Lissitzky's German article "SSSR's Architektur" (n.p.); 1 copy of Lissitzky's article "K. und Pangeometrie" (K. and pan-geometry [*Almanach Europa*, 1925]); and 1 typewritten copy of Lissitzky's German article "Unser Buch" (Our book) dated Moscow 1927 with handwritten signature and editorial notations. The latter article concerns the Modernist theory of typography and book art, its historical development, and its contemporary social and aesthetic significance.

451. ———. Archive of Jan Tschichold. Correspondence.

Letters, postcards, a birth announcement, and photographic materials. Eleven letters from Lissitzky to Tschichold (2 handwritten and 9 typewritten) dated from January 1925 to 29 September 1932. This correspondence, all of which is in German, concerns the exchange of graphic designs and provides a critical discussion of Soviet art journals, Tschichold's writings, Franz Roh's book *Nach-Expressionismus* (Post-expressionism [1915]), and Lissitzky's book *Foto und Typofoto in USSR* (Photography and typophoto in the USSR). Lissitzky primarily recounts their joint endeavors in publishing and the exchange of materials and also provides detailed descriptions of his artistic activities and personal thoughts on politics. He repeatedly mentions his "preoccupation with" or "concentration on" architecture and his work for the Association of New Architects (ASNOVA).

Three handwritten letters from Sophie Lissitzky to Edith Tschichold dated from 26 September 1930 to 30 October 1930. This more personal correspondence discusses the Lissitzkys' life in Moscow, the lack of basic foodstuffs, the exorbitant prices of household items, food lines, personal illness, and family matters. She also asks about news from Germany, expresses her frustrated desire to return home to Germany, and describes Lissitzky's design work on exhibitions, publications, and Gorky Park and her own work on photomontages using images of mothers and children.

A birth announcement in the form of a photomontage incorporating a photograph of the artist's son, "Klein el 12. Oktober 1930 Moskau" (Small El, 12 October 1930, Moscow [1 photo negative and 2 positive prints]); and 1 typewritten description of the Lissitzkys' birth announcement design and Lissitzky's illustrations for Pelikan drawing ink.

452. ———. Graphic design work and related items.

Copies and documentation of lithographic work and graphic design projects. Twenty-three assorted copies of Lissitzky's lithographic work *Proun* (1923) with handwritten notations and editorial instructions in German. Ten printed copies (in assorted sizes) of Lissitzky's work *Proun 93 Spirale.*

Twenty-three assorted printed copies of Lissitzky's graphic designs, including 1 copy of the cover and title page to the children's book *Pro dva kvadrata* (see no. 447); 1 copy of the double-sided page designs from Vladimir Mayakovsky's work *Dlia golosa* (see no. 504); 5 copies of the cover to the magazine *Veshch', Gegenstand, Objet,* 1922 (see no. 818); 1 copy of the cover to the brochure *Proun 1 Kestnermappe* (Proun 1 Kestner portfolio [Hannover, 1923]); 1 copy of the cover to the magazine *Russland. Neues Bauen in der Welt* (Russian modern architecture in the world [no. 1, 1929]); 5 copies of the stationery letterhead for *Veshch', Gegenstand, Objet* (1922); 1 copy of the cover to the children's book *4 Teyashim* (Four billy goats) using Hebrew letters; 1 copy of the double-page designs for the journal *Merz* (no. 8/9, 1924 [see no. 446]); 3 copies of a pen-and-ink drawing; 2 examples of the cover design for *Dlia golosa* with handwritten notations in German; 1 photo of *Proun GK;* and 4 photographic copies of book cover designs, including Alexander Tairoff's *Das entfesselte Theater* (Theater unbound [1923]).

Three glass negatives of Lissitzky's designs, including those for Pelikan ink (1924), with handwritten description; *Proun 93 Spirale* (this negative is broken); and a slide depicting a page of recommended typefaces for typewriters.

Sixteen photographic enlargements of Lissitzky's advertisement designs for Pelikan ink, typewriter ribbons, and carbon paper (circa 1924); 2 photographic negatives of these works, 2 typewritten descriptions of them; 13 printed copies of Lissitzky's advertisement designs for Pelikan ink, typewriter ribbons, and carbon paper (circa 1924); and 12 printed copies of another of Lissitzky's advertisement designs for Pelikan ink, typewriter ribbons, and carbon paper (circa 1924).

Twenty-six examples of Lissitzky's printed designs mounted on cardboard sheets and partially labeled with the name of the artist and title; 26 unmounted examples of Lissitzky's printed designs; 10 magazine clippings of Lissitzky's printed designs with handwritten editorial and design notations; 1 handwritten list of Lissitzky's published works; 1 tracing paper sketch of Lissitzky's design for the cover of the journal *Broom* from 1922 (see no. 446); Lissitzky's design for a speaker's podium on a public square (also known as the Lenin Tribune), dated "1920, UNOVIS"; 1 fragmented text in Czech with handwritten German notations concerning Lissitzky's designs for the Futurist opera *Pobeda nad solntsem* (Victory over the sun); 26 assorted printed examples of Lissitzky's designs with occasional handwritten notations; 1 mounted photograph of the Russian exhibit designed by Lissitzky for the *Internationale Presse-Ausstellung* (International press exhibition) held in Cologne in 1928; 1 article from the Russian journal *Vesch', Gegenstand, Objet* (no. 1, 1922); and 11 clippings of articles on Lissitzky, largely from German newspapers.

Two small vertical storyboards with images from Lissitzky's children's book *Pro dva kvadrata.* Each storyboard (33 × 11 cm) contains 4 images (5 × 6.5 cm). Two copies of *Pro dva kvadrata,* 1 with a glossy cover and 1 with a matte cover.

453. ———. Miscellaneous photographic items.

One color photograph of Lissitzky's signature; 1 copy of Lissitzky's self-portrait, *Der Konstrukteur,* with a handwritten dedication to Jan Tschichold dated Moscow, July 1925; 1 photographic negative of the self-portrait with 1 photographic enlargement and 11 assorted, printed copies; 3 self-portraits (including 1 stereoplate photogram) of Lissitzky, *El Lissitzky: Der Konstrukteur* (1923); 1 photograph of Lissitzky's work *Proun 93 Spirale;* and 1 photograph of his work *Proun* (1923).

454. ———. Miscellaneous publications and related items.

One copy of Lissitzky's exhibition pamphlet *El Lissitzky. Moscow. Schau der Arbeit, 1919–1923* (El Lissitzky. Moscow. Display of work, 1919–1923) with black letters on silver paper; 1 typewritten description by Jan Tschichold of Lissitzky's designs for the exhibition; 4 mounted photographs of Lissitzky's illustrations in Vladimir Mayakovsky's book *Dlia golosa* (see no. 504) with a photo laboratory delivery notice; 1 photograph and 4 printed copies of Lissitzky's Russian title page for *Dlia golosa;* 1 copy of *Dlia golosa;* 20 photographs taken from the same text; 1 copy of Lissitzky's guidebook for the All-Union Exhibition of the Printing Trades (see no. 840) with handwritten dedication to Tschichold; 1 color pencil sketch for the cover of the guidebook carrying the initials *VPV* (Vsesoiuznaia poligraficheskaia vystavka); 1 copy of Lissitzky's bulletin for the All-Union Exhibition of the Printing Trades (see no. 839); 1 copy of Lissitzky's and Hans Arp's book *Die Kunstismen* (see no. 455); and 2 copies of the publisher's announcement for it.

455. **Lissitzky, El, and Hans Arp.** *Die Kunstismen* (Art isms). Zurich, Munich, and Leipzig: E. Rentsch, 1925. xi pp., 48 pp. of ill. 26 cm.

Cover and layout by Lissitzky.

456. ***Literatura fakta: Pervyi sbornik materialov rabotnikov Lefa*** (Литература факта: Первый сборник материалов работников Лефа / The literature of fact: First collection by contributors to *Lef*). Moscow: Federatsiia, 1929. 268 pp. 20 cm.

Includes contributions by Osip Brik, Nikolai Chuzhak, Teodor Grits, Petr Neznamov, Viktor Pertsov, Viktor Shklovskii, Vladimir Trenin, and Sergei Tret'iakov.

457. ***Literatura i iskusstvo: Zhurnal marksistskoi kritiki i metodiki*** (Литература и искусство: Журнал марксистской критики и методики / Literature and art: Journal of Marxist criticism and methodology). Moscow: Khudozhestvennaia lit-ra, 1930–1931. 25 cm.

Organ of the Communist Academy's Institute of Literature, Art, and Language.

No. 9/10 (1931) features examples of John Heartfield's photomontages; Gustav Klutsis's article "Fotomontazh, kak novaia problema agitatsionnogo iskusstva" (Photomontage as a new issue of the propaganda art), which is supplemented by some of his posters such as the one that marks the thirteenth anniversary of the October Revolution; and David Arkin's article " O khudozhestvennoi promyshlennosti voobshche i o farfore v chastnosti" (On artistic production in general and on porcelain in particular), which discusses porcelain production from various Soviet factories.

Irregularly published. Publisher varies. Continuation of *Pechat' i revoliutsiia* (Press and revolution [1921–1930]). Continued by *Marksistko-leninskoe iskusstvoznanie* (Marxist-Leninist aesthetics [1932]).

Research Institute's holdings: scattered issues.

458. ***Literatura mirovoi revoliutsii: Tsentral'nyi organ Mezhdunarodnogo ob"edineniia revoliutsionnykh pisatelei*** (Литература мировой революции: Центральный орган Международного объединения революционных писателей / Literature of the world revolution: Central organ of the International Union of Revolutionary Writers). Edited by L. Averbakh, A. Gidash, and Bruno Jasieński. Moscow and Leningrad: Khudozhestvennaia literatura, 1931–1932. 24 cm.

Monthly publication of the International Union of Revolutionary Writers. Jasieński was one of a number of international communists who lived in Moscow at the time. Includes works by socially conscious artists from abroad, such as William Gropper, John Heartfield, and Louis Lozowick and an international chronicle of literary events and publications, essays by Isaac Deutscher, Edward Fitzgerald, and Sergei Tret'iakov. Editions also published in Chinese, English, French, German, and Spanish.

Continuation of *Vestnik inostrannoi literatury.* (See no. 819.) Continued by *Internatsional'naia literatura* (International literature [1933–1944]).

Research Institute's holdings: scattered issues.

459. ***Literaturnye shushu(t)ki: Literaturnye sekrety*** (Литературные шушу(т)ки: Литературные секреты / Literary jokes: Literary secrets). Edited by Aleksei Kruchenykh. Moscow: Leningradskii teatr Doma pechati, 1928. 20 leaves. 17 × 21 cm.

Cover design by Igor' Terent'ev.

Humorous verses, epigrams, and other ephemera not originally intended for publication, mostly handwritten by their authors, Nikolai Aseev, Il'ia Il'f, Vera Inber, Valentin Kataev, Vasilii Kazin, Semen Kirsanov, Leonid Leonov, Vladimir Mayakovsky, Petr Neznamov, Lev Nikulin, Iurii Olesha, Evgenii Petrov, Il'ia Sel'vinskii, and Terent'ev. The contributions by Il'f, Leonov, and Nikulin include small drawings.

Copy 21 of 100. Cover is printed in green on buff paper. In the Research Institute's copy, imperfections in reproduction by lithography on glass have occasionally been corrected in pencil.

460. **Livshits, Benedikt.** *Polutoraglazyi strelets* (Полутораглазый стрелец / One-and-a-half-eyed archer). Leningrad: Izd-vo pisatelei v Leningrade, 1933. 295 pp., [1] plate. 20 cm.

Cover illustration by Vladimir Burliuk.

Memoirs.

Research Institute's copy is missing the dust jacket by Mark Kirnarskii and David Burliuk.

461. ———. *Volch'e solntse: Kniga stikhov vtoraia* (Волчье солнце: Книга стихов вторая / Wolves' sun: Second book of verse). Moscow: Futuristy "Gileia," 1914. 64 pp., [5] plates. 18 cm.

Includes a color relief halftone of a painting by Vasil'eva, a black-and-white photolithographic halftone of a painting by Alexandra Exter, and an appended sequence of 4 line blocks by David Burliuk printed in blue, *Chetyre zhenshchiny* (Four women).

462. **Lugovskoi, Vladimir.** *Evropa: Stikhi* (Европа: Стихи / Europe: Verse). Edited by Eduard Bagritskii. Moscow: Federatsiia, 1932. 71 pp. 18 cm.

Cover and dust jacket by Boris Titov.

463. ———. *Stradaniia moikh druzei: Tret'ia kniga stikhov, 1928–1929* (Страдания моих друзей: Третья книга стихов, 1928–1929 / The sufferings of my friends: Third book of verse, 1928–1929). Moscow: Izd-vo "Federatsiia," 1930. 123 pp. 18 cm.

Cover and dust jacket by Boris Titov.

464. **Lukhmanov, Nikolai.** *Arkhitektura kluba* (Архитектура клуба / Architecture of the club). [Moscow]: Teakinopechat', 1930. 102 pp. 23 cm.

Discussion of trends in club design in the 1920s. Many of the examples discussed are by Konstantin Mel'nikov.

465. ———. *Nol' tselykh, nol' v periode: Puteshestvie v stranu simvolov* (Ноль целых, ноль в периоде: Путешествие в страну символов / Zero point zero: A journey to the land of symbols). [Smolensk]: Izd. SGOVSRPP, 1923. 50 pp. 17 cm.

Cover and decorations by M. N. Volchanetskii.

Literary theory.

466. **Lunacharsky, Anatoly.** *Iskusstvo i molodezh'* (Искусство и молодежь / Art and youth). [Moscow]: Molodaia gvardiia, 1929. 132 pp. 20 cm.

Cover's wood engraving signed "AS," for Anatolii Suvorov.

Essays.

467. **Lunts, Leonid.** *Parki kul'tury i otdykha* (Парки культуры и отдыха / Parks of culture and rest). Moscow and Leningrad: Gosstroiizdat, [1934] (cover date 1935). 518 pp., [11] folded leaves of plates. 28 cm.

Cover and dust jacket by Boris Titov.

468. **Lur'e, Artur.** *Chetki: Desiat' pesen iz Anny Akhmatovoi* (Четки: Десять песен из Анны Ахматовой / Rosary: Ten songs from Anna Akhmatova). Pervaia tetrad'. Petrograd and Moscow: Gos. muzykal'noe izd-vo, 1919. 19 pp. 36 cm.

This "first notebook" contains settings for soprano and piano of 5 poems from Akhmatova's collection of verse of the same title (1913). The lithographed cover is unsigned, but it is stylistically similar to that by Georgii Iakulov for the following item.

469. ———. *Dnevnoi uzor* (Дневной узор / Daylight pattern). Petrograd and Moscow: Gos. muzykal'noe izd-vo, 1918. 19 pp. 36 cm.

Cover lithograph by Georgii Iakulov.

Five piano pieces.

470. ———. *Roial' v detskoi* (Рояль в детской / Piano in the nursery). St. Petersburg: Gos. muzykal'noe izd-vo, 1920. 3, 7, 3, 5, 3, 3, 7, 3 pp. 31 cm.

Cover lithograph by Petr Miturich.

Includes 8 illustrations printed in black and red by Miturich—1 illustration to accompany each of the 8 short piano pieces.

471. ***Makovets*** (Маковец / Makovets). Moscow: Mlechnyi put', 1922. 31 cm.

Edited by A. M. Chernyshev.

The title of this journal, published by Chernyshev in editions of 650, was taken from the name of a short-lived society formed in 1922. The group Makovets, in turn, was named after the hill on which stands the Trinity-Sergius Lavra (now known as the Sergiev Posad Monastery and Museum), founded in the fifteenth century. Contains full-page, tipped-in, lithographed drawings by Vasilii Chekrygin (the most famous member of the group), N. Chernyshev, Sergei Gerasimov, Vera Pestel', Sergei Romanovich, and Aleksandr Shevchenko. No. 1 includes poetry by Nikolai Aseev, Sergei Bobrov, Konstantin Bol'shakov, Pavel Florenskii, Velimir Khlebnikov, and Boris Pasternak. Also includes an address by Florenskii, "Khramovoe deistvo, kak sintez iskusstva" (The church ritual as a synthesis of art), delivered in October 1918 at the Trinity-Sergius Lavra for the Commission for the Preservation of Artistic Monuments and Antiquity.

Irregularly published. A total of 2 issues published.

Research Institute's holdings: scattered issues.

472. **Malevich, Kazimir.** *Blinde Architektur.* 9.2 × 15 cm.

Photograph of a drawing done by Malevich in 1923. Taken by Hannes Meyer, director of the Bauhaus from 1928 to 1930. From 1930 to 1936 Meyer lived and worked in the Soviet Union, taking part in various architectural projects.

473. ———. *Bog ne skinut: Iskusstvo, tserkov', fabrika* (Бог не скинут: Искусство, церковь, фабрика / God is not overthrown: Art, church,

factory). Vitebsk: UNOVIS, 1922. 40 pp. 17 cm.

Artistic theory.

474. ———. *Die gegenstandslose Welt* (The abstract world). Bauhausbücher, 11. Munich: A. Langen, 1927. 104 pp. 24 cm.

Typography, binding, and cover by László Moholy-Nagy.

German-language translation of the then-unpublished Russian text *Vvedenie v teoriiu pribavochnogo elementa v zhivopisi* (Introduction to the theory of the added element in painting).

475. ———. *K voprosu izobrazitel'nogo iskusstva* (К вопросу изобразительного искусства / On representational art). [S.l.]: Gos. izd-vo, 1921. 15 pp. 27 cm.

Cover has an open square enclosing a smaller open square, both printed in black. Not in Karshan 1975.

Front cover of Research Institute's copy has faint impression in red ink of the Affirmers of the New Art (UNOVIS) stamp (a circle 38 mm in diameter containing a solid square over the word *UNOVIS*. Research Institute's copy also has a pencil sketch in the Suprematist style on the back cover.

476. ———. *O novykh sistemakh v iskusstve: Statika i skorost', ustanovlenie A* (О новых системах в искусстве: Статика и скорость, установление А. / On new systems in art: Statics and speed, statute A). Vitebsk: Artel' khudozhestvennogo truda pri Vitsvomase, 1919. 32 pp., [3] plates. 22 cm.

Tipped in at the title page are 3 Cubist plates by Malevich.

Text is written in small capital letters and longhand and is interspersed with Suprematist squares, rectangles, and circles. Reproduced by lithography, presumably under the supervision of El Lissitzky (Karshan 1975, no. 27). Khardzhiev asserts that Lissitzky was responsible for the cover as well (1976, 95).

477. ———. *Ot kubizma i futurizma k suprematizmu: Novyi zhivopisnyi realizm* (От кубизма и футуризма к супрематизму: Новый живописный реализм / From Cubism and Futurism to Suprematism: The new realism in painting). 3rd ed. Moscow: K. Malevich, 1916. 31 pp., [2] plates. 18 cm.

Revised and expanded version of *Ot kubizma k suprematizmu,* now with halftone plates of a black circle and a black square, the latter repeated as the front cover illustration. (See no. 478.)

478. ———. *Ot kubizma k suprematizmu: Novyi zhivopisnyi realizm* (От кубизма к супрематизму: Новый живописный реализм / From Cubism to Suprematism: The new realism in painting). 2nd ed. Petrograd: [Zhuravl'], 1916. 14 pp. 18 cm.

From the second of 2 identical editions published by Zhuravl' in 1916 (Karshan 1975, no. 24).

479. ———. *Ot Sezanna do suprematizma: Kriticheskii ocherk* (От Сезанна до супрематизма: Критический очерк / From Cézanne to Suprematism: A critical sketch). [Petrograd]: Otdel izobrazitel'nykh iskusstv Narkomprosa, [1920]. 16 pp. 18 cm.

480. ———. *Suprematizm: 34 risunka* (Супрематизм: 34 рисунка / Suprematism: Thirty-four drawings). Vitebsk: UNOVIS, [1921 (Khardzhiev 1976, 96)] (cover date 1920). 3 pp., [34] plates (2 folded). 22 cm.
Plates were lithographed by Lissitzky (Khardzhiev 1976, 96).

481. [———]. *Vystavka proizvedenii K. S. Malevicha* (Выставка произведений К.С. Малевича / Exhibition of works by K. S. Malevich). Moscow: Izd. Gos. Tret'iakovskoi gallerei, 1929. 10 pp. 18 cm.
Exhibition catalog. Text by Aleksei Fedorov-Davydov.

482. **Malyi teatr SSSR.** *Desiat' let raboty Malogo teatra, 1917–1927* (Десять лет работы Малого театра, 1917–1927 / Ten years' work of the Maly Theater, 1917–1927). Moscow: Muzei Malogo teatra, 1927. 103 pp. 18 cm.
Cover by Sergei Chekhonin.

483. **Malyshkin, Aleksandr.** *Padenie Daira: Povest'* (Падение Даира: Повесть / The fall of Dair: A tale). Moscow: Krug, 1926. 72 pp. 15 cm.

484. **Mandel'shtam, Osip.** *Stikhotvoreniia* (Стихотворения / Poems). Moscow and Leningrad: Gos. izd-vo, 1928. 194 pp. 18 cm.
Slipcase by Dmitrii Mitrokhin.
Research Institute's copy has a verse inscription dated 6 November and is missing the slipcase.

485. **Mantel', Aleksandr.** *Risunki dlia tkanei* (Рисунки для тканей / Designs for textiles). Moscow and Leningrad: Gos. izd-vo, 1930. 61 pp. 19 cm.

486. **Margolin, Samuil.** *Khudozhnik teatra za 15 let* (Художник театра за 15 лет / The theater artist over the last fifteen years). Biblioteka zhurnala iskusstvo. [Moscow]: Ogiz-Izogiz, 1933. 126 pp., [1] plate. 13 cm.

487. **Mariengof, Anatolii.** *Buian-ostrov: Imazhinizm* (Буян-остров: Имажинизм / The island Buian: Imagism). Moscow: Imazhinisty, 1920. 32 pp. 17 cm.
Poetic theory.

488. ———. *Razocharovanie* (Разочарование / Disappointment). [Moscow]: Imazhinisty, 1922. [16] pp. 18 cm.
Cover signed "G. E.," possibly for Georgii Echeistov.
Poems.

489. ———. *Razvratnichaiu s vdokhnoven'em: Poema* (Развратничаю с вдохновеньем: Поэма / My inspired debauchery: A poem). Moscow: Imazhinisty, 1921. [15] pp. 22 cm.

490. ———. *Ruki galstukom* (Руки галстуком / Arms like a necktie). Moscow: Imazhinisty, 1920. [15] pp. 36 cm.

Cover by Georgii Iakulov.
Poem. Includes illustrations by Iakulov.

491. ———. *Tuchelët: Kniga poem* (Тучелёт: Книга поэм / Cloud flier: A book of poems). Moscow: Imazhinisty, 1921. [31] pp. 17 cm.
Cover with portrait of Anatolii Mariengof by Georgii Iakulov.

492. **Markov, Lev, and Aleksandr Durov.** *Kabluk futurista* (Каблук футуриста / The Futurist's high heel). Moscow: [n.p.], 1914. 20 pp. 23 cm.
Poems likely intended as a parody of Futurist works (Markov 1968, 215).

493. **Markov, Vladimir.** *Faktura: Printsipy tvorchestva v plasticheskikh iskusstvakh* (Фактура: Принципы творчества в пластических искусствах / Texture: Creative principles in the visual arts). St. Petersburg: Soiuz molodezhi, 1914. 70 pp. 19 cm.
Inscribed "I. Pouni" (Ivan Puni) in black ink in roman characters.

494. **Maslenikov, Nikolai.** *Izo-rabota v izbe-chital'ne* (Изо-работа в избе-читальне / Artwork in the recreation room). Moscow: Doloi negramotnost', 1925. 55 pp. 23 cm.
Includes illustrations by Isaak Leizerov.

495. ***Massovye prazdnestva: Sbornik Komiteta sotsiologicheskogo izucheniia iskusstv*** (Массовые празднества: Сборник Комитета социологического изучения искусств / Mass festivals: A collection of essays by the Committee for the Sociological Study of the Arts). Leningrad: Academia, 1926. 204 pp., [1] plate. 22 cm.

496. **Matsa, Ivan.** *Besedy ob arkhitekture* (Беседы об архитектуре / Conversations about architecture). Nauchno-populiarnaia seriia knig po arkhitekture, no. 1. Moscow: Vses. akademiia arkhitektury, 1936. 95 pp. 23 cm.
Cover by N. M. Lobanov.

497. ———. *Iskusstvo epokhi zrelogo kapitalizma na Zapade* (Искусство эпохи зрелого капитализма на Западе / Western art of the era of mature capitalism). Moscow: Izd-vo Kommunisticheskoi akademii, 1929. 256 pp., [47] plates. 22 cm.

498. ———. *Leningradskii IZORAM* (Ленинградский ИЗОРАМ / Leningrad IZORAM). Moscow and Leningrad: Ogiz-Izogiz, 1932. 42 pp. 21 cm.

499. ———. *Tvorcheskii metod i khudozhestvennoe nasledstvo* (Творческий метод и художественное наследство / Creative method and artistic heritage). Moscow: Komakademiia i Izogiz, 1933. 335 pp. 21 cm.
Cover and title engraved in wood by Mikhail Pikov.
Inscribed by Matsa to the artist Louis Lozowick.

500. **Matsa, Ivan, Lidiia Reingardt, and Lazar' Rempel'.** *Sovetskoe iskusstvo za 15 let: Materialy i dokumentatsiia* (Советское искусство за 15 лет: Материалы и документация / Fifteen years of Soviet art: Source materials and documentation). Moscow and Leningrad: Ogiz-Izogiz, 1933. 663 pp., [16] plates. 26 cm.

501. **Mayakovsky, Vladimir.** *Bania: Drama v 6-ti deistviiakh, s tsirkom i feierverkom* (Баня: Драма в 6-ти действиях, с цирком и фейерверком / The bathhouse: A drama in six acts with circus and fireworks). Moscow and Leningrad: Gos. izd-vo, 1930. 77 pp. 20 cm.

Cover by A. Surikov.

502. ———. *Bez doklada ne vkhodit'* (Без доклада не входить / No admittance without being announced). Moscow and Leningrad: Gos. izd-vo, 1930. 110 pp. 20 cm.

Cover by Sergei Sen'kin.

Poems.

503. ———. *Chelovek: Veshch'* (Человек: Вещь / Man: Thing). [Moscow]: ASIS, [1918]. 60 pp. 18 cm.

Cover by Mayakovsky (Golubeva 1977, 14/1:18).

Poems.

504. ———. *Dlia golosa* (Для голоса / For voice). Berlin: Gos. izd-vo RSFSR, 1923. 61 pp. 18 cm.

Design by El Lissitzky.

Poems.

505. ———. *255 stranits Maiakovskogo: Kniga 1* (255 страниц Маяковского: Книга 1 / 255 pages of Mayakovsky: Book one). Moscow and Petrograd: Gos. izd-vo, 1923. 255 pp., [1] plate. 18 cm.

Contains Mayakovsky's brief autobiography and 4 long poems.

A second volume was planned but never published.

506. ———. *Fleita pozvonochnik* (Флейта позвоночник / Backbone flute). Petrograd: [Osip Brik], 1916. 16 pp. 24 cm.

Poem.

The mark of the publisher Vzial appears on the cover.

507. ———. *Geroi i zhertvy Revoliutsii* (Герои и жертвы Революции / Heroes and victims of the Revolution). Petrograd: Otdel izobrazitel'nykh iskusstv Komissariata narodnogo prosveshcheniia, [1918]. [19] leaves. In portfolio. 35 cm.

Includes 9 lithographs of heroes of the Revolution (such as the worker and the Red Army soldier) and 9 lithographs of its victims (such as the factory owner and the banker). The artists represented are Kseniia Boguslavskaia, Vladimir Kozlinskii, S. Makletsov, and Ivan Puni, and the captions are by Mayakovsky.

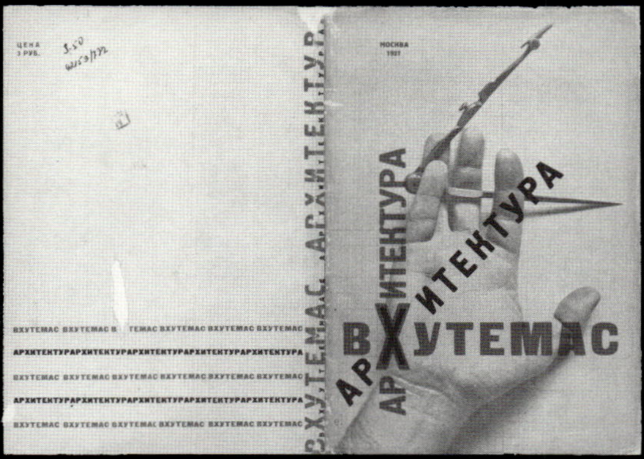

1

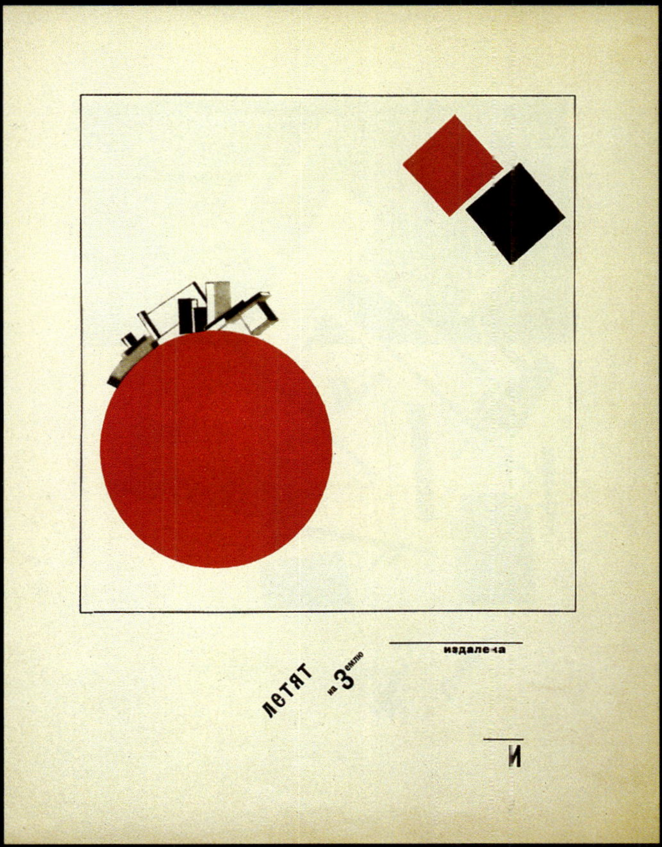

2

Fig. 1. *Arkhitektura.*
Cover by El Lissitzky. See no. 23.

Fig. 2. *Pro dva kvadrata.* by El Lissitzky.
See no. 447.

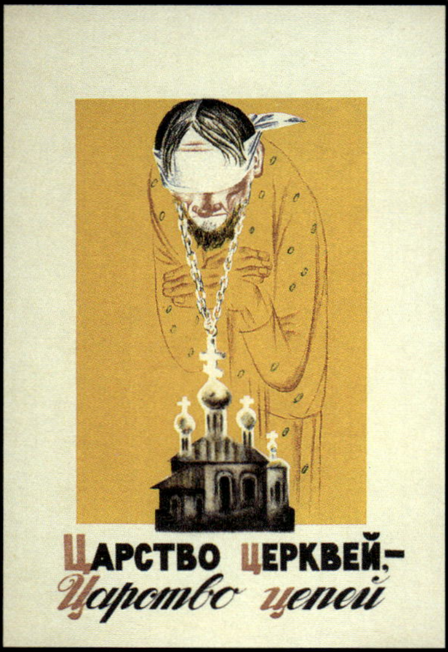

4

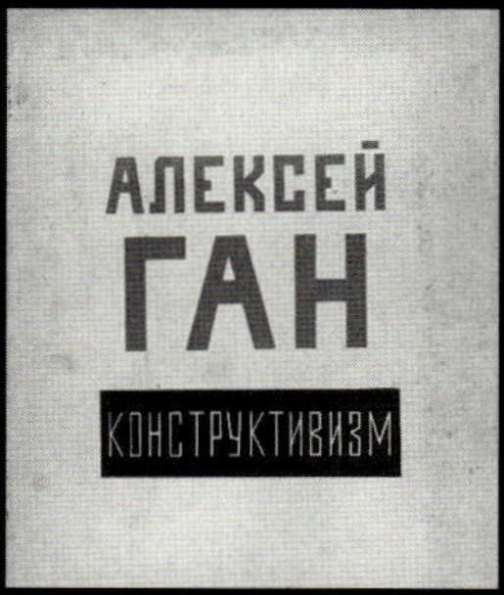

3

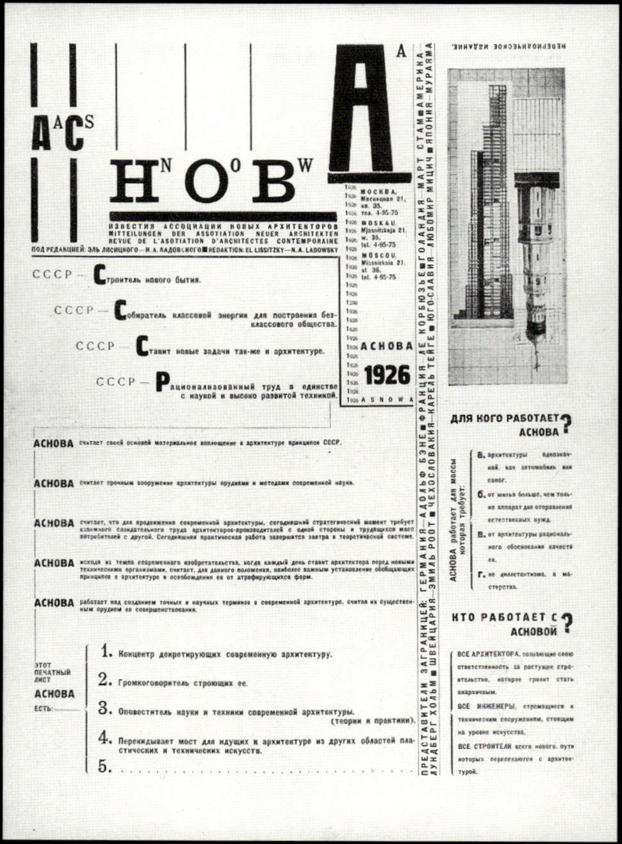

5

Fig. 3. ***Konstruktivizm,*** **by Aleksei Gan.**
Cover attributed to Aleksandr Rodchenko. See no. 201.

Fig. 4. ***Antireligioznaia azbuka,*** **by Mikhail Cheremnykh.**
See no. 122.

Fig. 5. ***Asnova,*** **no. 1 (1926).**
Cover by El Lissitzky. See no. 52.

25.)

E L

20. 10. 24

~~EL LISSITZKY~~

LOCARNO. BELVEDERE.

LIEBE MUTTI, es war sehr dum, dass wir nicht Postlagernd München, sondern Tihes verabredet haben, jetzt glaube ich nicht dass du mein Brief kriegst Es freut mich dass du in Hannover nicht alles Hofnungslos wieder findest. Zuerst deine Fragen:

1/ Arp habe ich das Material für Kunsthaus geschickt und gestern eine Antwort von im erchalten, das er es übergeben hat.
2/ Nach Venedig habe ich noch nicht geschrieben: habe bis Heute immer wegen meinen Aufentchalt rumgelaufen.
3/ Habe Malewitsch geschrieben wie im die Sachen zu schicken, aber habe noch keine Antwort. Habe ein Brief von im bekommen, aber es ist nicht Antwort auf meins.
4/ Für die Bücher dancke ich dir sehr, aber gebrauchen kann ich wenig davon. Lass dass, es kostet nur viell Porto.
5/ Frau Ermolajeff geht es besser, aber dass arme Mädel ist nicht in Ordnung; auch Lungen.

Wenn mann mir die Aufenthalt weiter gibt (ich habe sehr Angst dass die werden bei mir 2000 Fr. Kaution verlangen), dann müss ich mich Privat unterbringen. Ich darf jetzt nicht zuviell Geld ausgeben und ich müss mehr Raum zum arbeiten haben. Hier im Hotel ist nicht unser Häuschen und Garten in Ambri. Es ist alles schön für kurze Zeit. Es fängt mich an zu drücken.
Die Leute die ich hier kännen gelernt habe gecheren zu einer kleiner Gemeinschaft, es sind von dem Landauer Kreis , ein Tolstojaner usw. Du weist wie ich skeptisch bin zu so was, aber ein Paar (deutsche), er ein guter Tischler, die Frau schon viel durchgelebt, intelligent, mit 57 weisse Hüner, jetzt in einem eigenem Haus, denn mann mit eigene Hände wider aufgerichtet hat, die Leute finden meine Achtung und haben sich auch für mich bemüht. Die suchen jetzt für mir wass passendes und in der Nähe von Ihnen um wenn notwendig mich zu versorgen. Aber vorläufig ist dass ales problematisch, wegen meiner Unstabilitet.
Wenn Dicki gut untergebracht werden kann wird es vielleicht auch im dort Freude machen.
Von den Hausbau kann ich noch nichts mitteilen. Die Leute sind reich gewordene geizige Spieser. Die Frau hat den armen Ermolajeff nicht gut behandelt. Ich glaube nicht das es so einfach mit dem Bau wird.
Es ist bei mir jetzt eine Gelegencheit ein Atelier für mich Selbst 5 mal 5 Meter gross für 2000 Fr. auszubauen. Aber dass ist jetzt auch Merchen.
Mit Geld schicken eile nicht. Arp hat von Rentsch nur 100 Fr. erchalten, also die 25 bin ich noch im schuldig, den 50 fallen auf die Schreibmaschine. Überhaupt die ganze Geschichte geht schief: mit seinem Buch hat vorläufig Rentsch nur Unannämlichkeiten und der Schaten fält auf mich und unser Buch. Das ist schon Blödismus. <u>Ich brauche unbedingt DIK.</u>
Eben ist angekommen Kunstblatt mit Lenin. Bei mir ist ein Gefühl dass der armer Malewitsch in einem WC zu Worte kommt. Die Korrektur ist nicht erfolgt, die redaktionelle Notiz ist nicht richtig. Immer derselbe Blödsinn. Zu Teufel. Jetzt fühlt nur, dass Malewitsch an die Wand geschlept wird.

Ich schicke dir das Heft.

Das Wetter ist noch immer gut. Sonne. Nach dem Untergang wird kühl.

Diese Woche muss ich mich wieder pixen.

Habe ein Spaziergang nach Ascona gemacht. Unten im Dorf ist ganz Blöde, oben war ich nicht.

G ist bei die oben erwehnte Leute untergebracht will sich hier mit Kunsthandel bescheftigen. Vielleicht mache ich was mit dem Tieschler zusammen dafür.

Also schau dass alles bei dir gut geht wünsche dir viel Erfolg in deinem Grosbetrieb. Grosz hat schönem Dada-Material geschickt leider zu spät.

Sage Hani er soll braw sein sage Dicki er soll braw sein sage Mutti sie soll braw sein ich werde braw sein

und
allgemeine
küsserei
und
grüsserei

euer

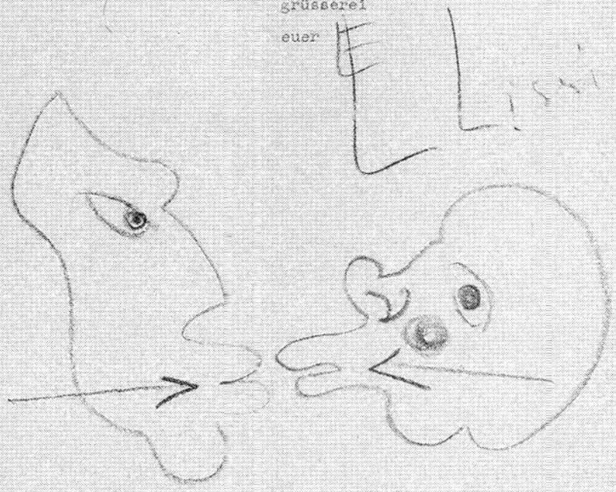

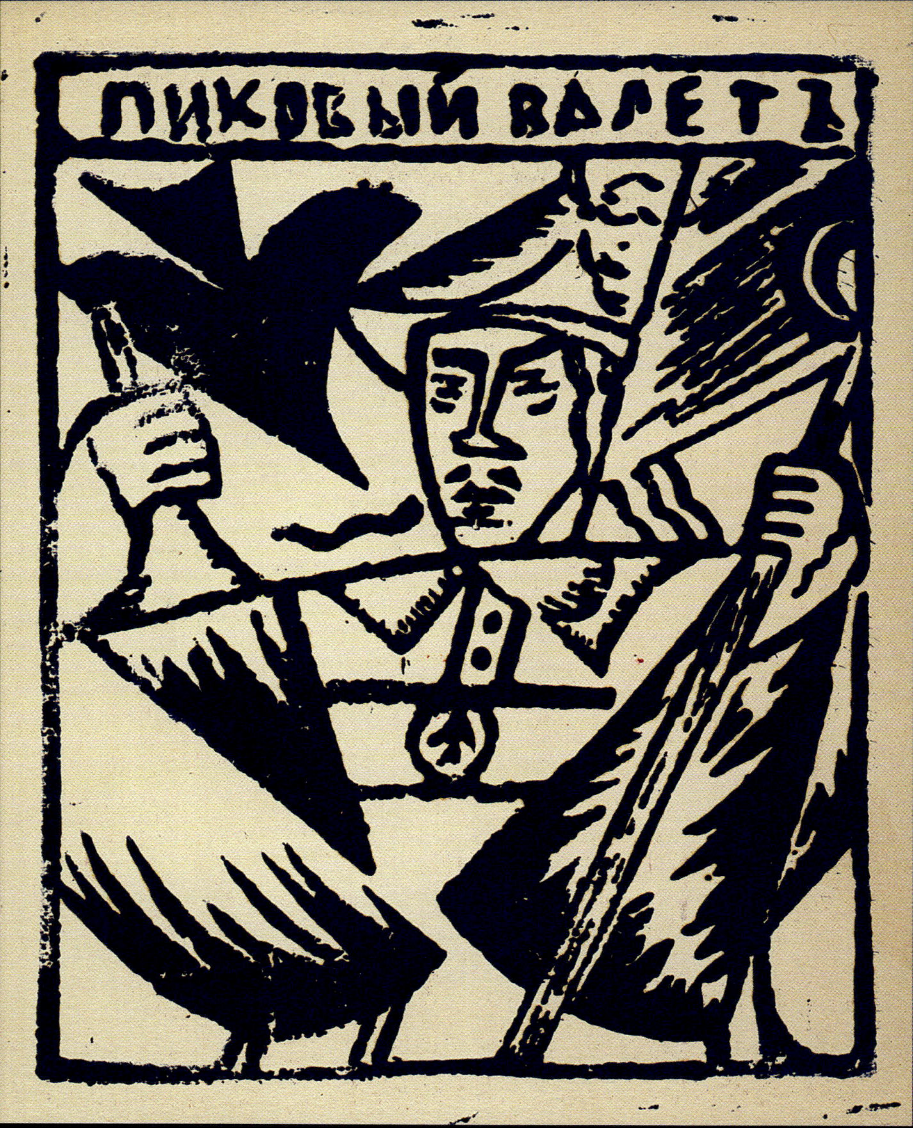

Fig. 7. ***Zaumnaia gniga,*** **by Aleksei Kruchenykh and Roman Jakobson.**
Illustration by Ol'ga Rozanova. See no. 396.

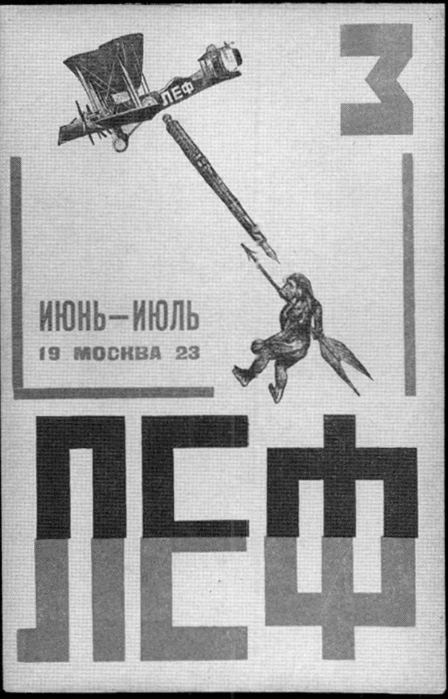

9

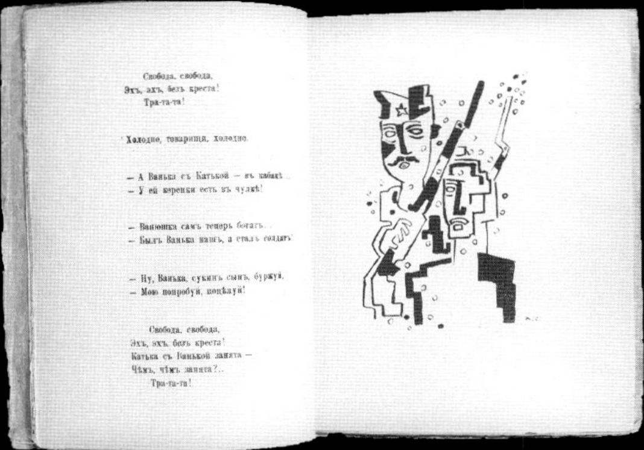

8

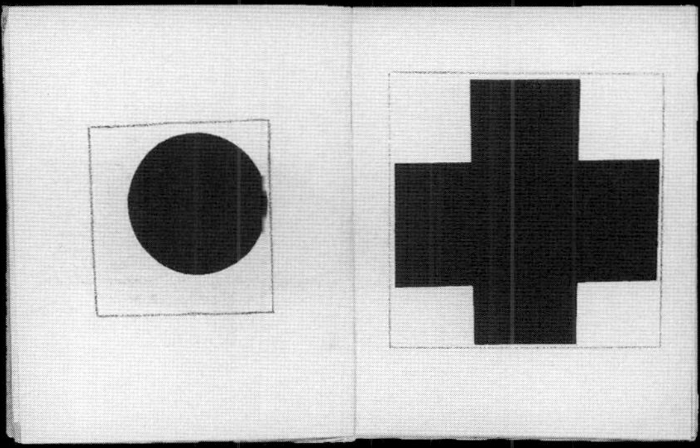

Fig. 8. *Dvenadtsat'*, by Alexander Blok.
Illustration by M. Larionov. See no. 84.

Fig. 9. *Lef*, no. 3 (1923).
Cover by Aleksandr Rodchenko. See no. 436.

Fig. 10. *Suprematizm*. by Kazimir Malevich.
See no. 480.

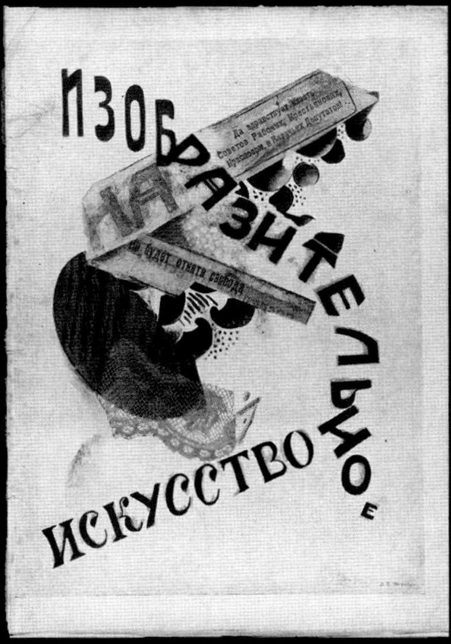

11

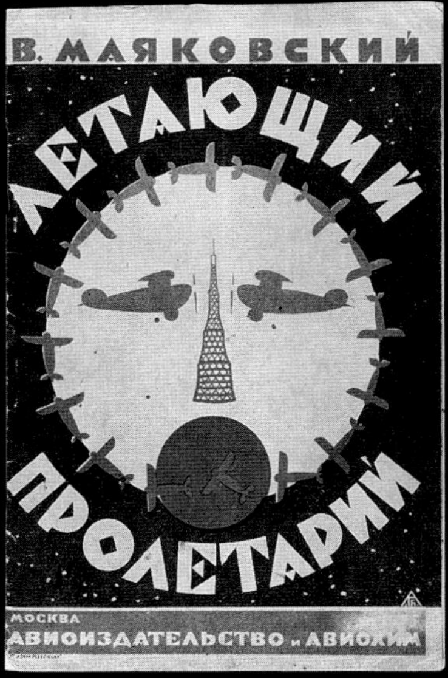

12

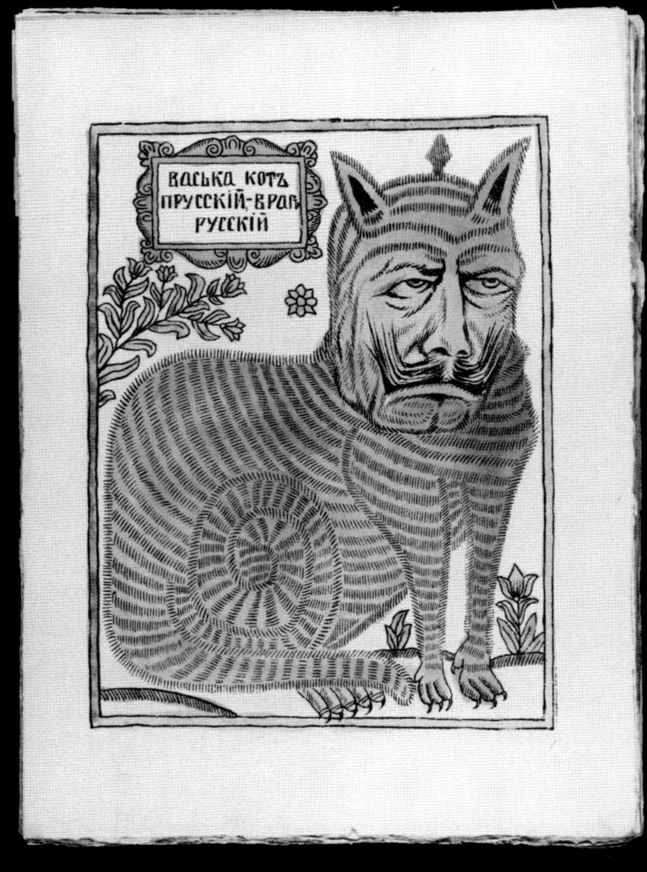

13

Fig. 11. ***Izobrazitel'noe isskusstvo*, no. 1 (1919).**
Cover by David Shterenberg. See no. 276.

Fig. 12. ***Letaiushchii proletarii*, by Vladimir Mayakovsky.**
Cover by Grigorii Bershadskii. See no. 515.

Fig. 13. ***Kartinki—voina russkikh s nemtsami.***
See no. 297

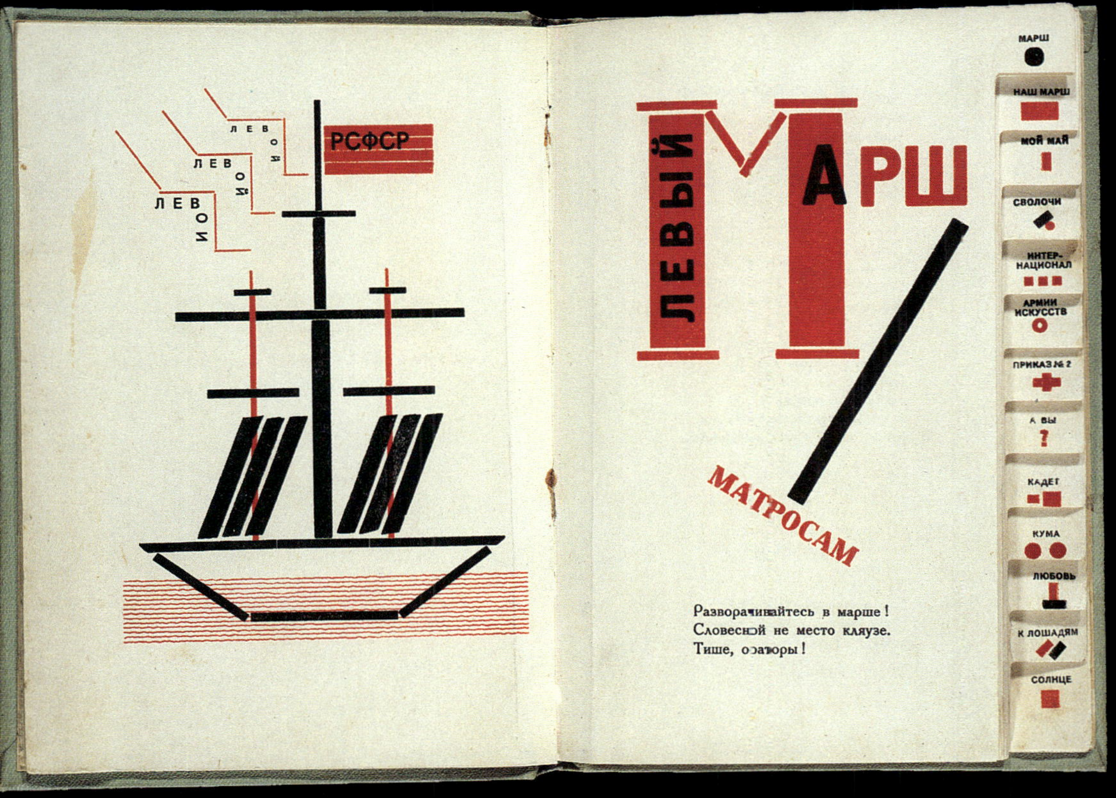

14

Fig. 14. ***Dlia golosa,*** **by Vladimir Mayakovsky.**
Design by El Lissitzky. See no. 504.

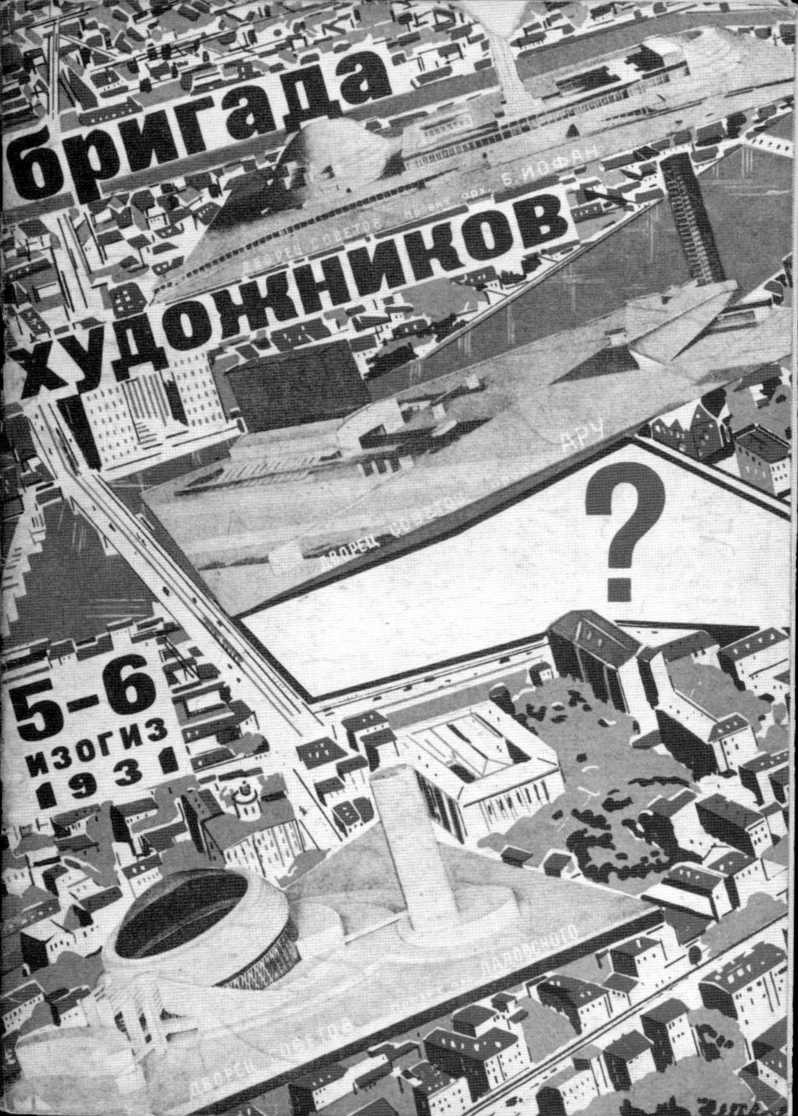
бригада
художников
?
5–6
ИЗОГИЗ
1931
ДВОРЕЦ СОВЕТОВ
Б. ИОФАН
АРУ

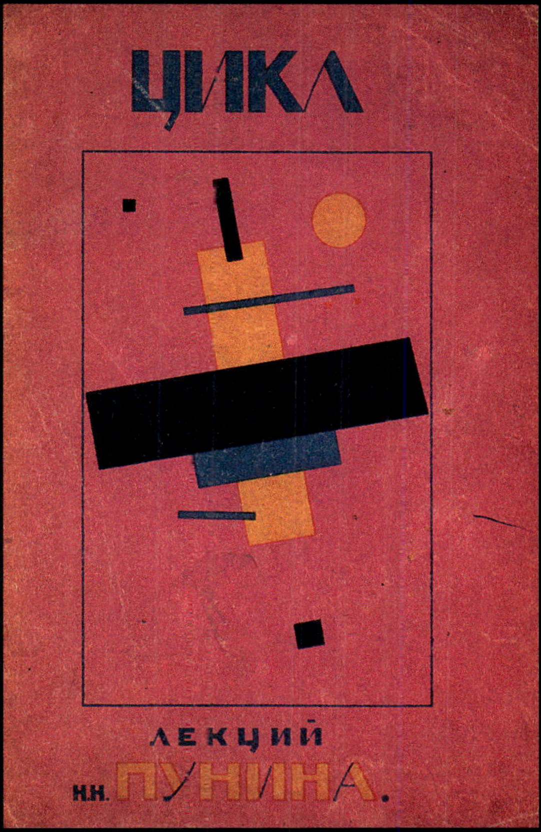

17

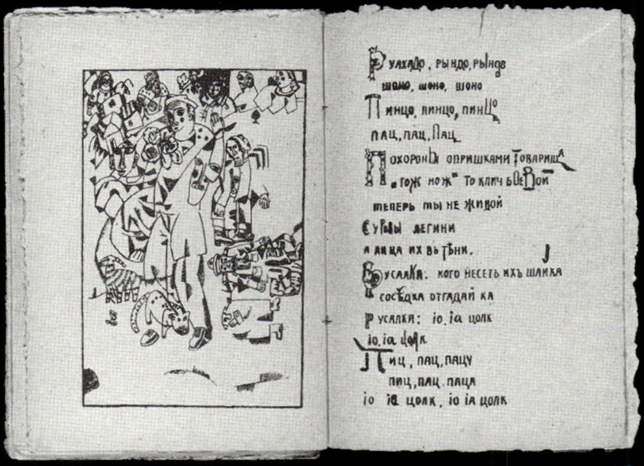

16

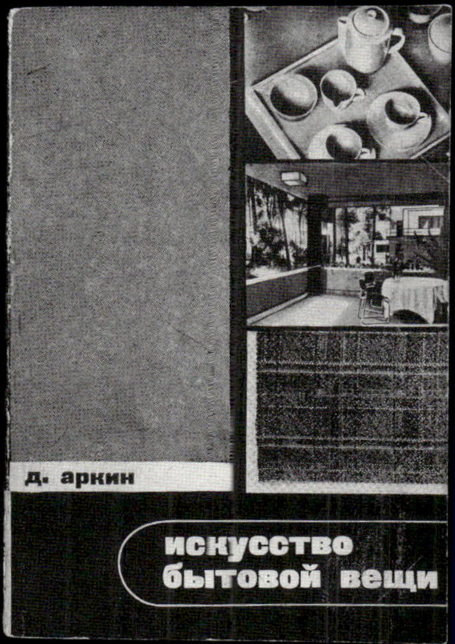

18

Fig. 16. ***Izbornik stikhov,*** **1907–1914, by Velimir Khlebnikov.**
Illustration by Pavel Filonov. See no. 307.

Fig. 17. ***Pervyi tsikl lektsii,*** **by Nikolai Punin.**
Cover illustration by Kazimir Malevich. See no. 656

Fig. 18. ***Iskusstvo bytovoi veshchi,*** **by David Arkin.**
Cover by Solomon Telingater. See no. 29.

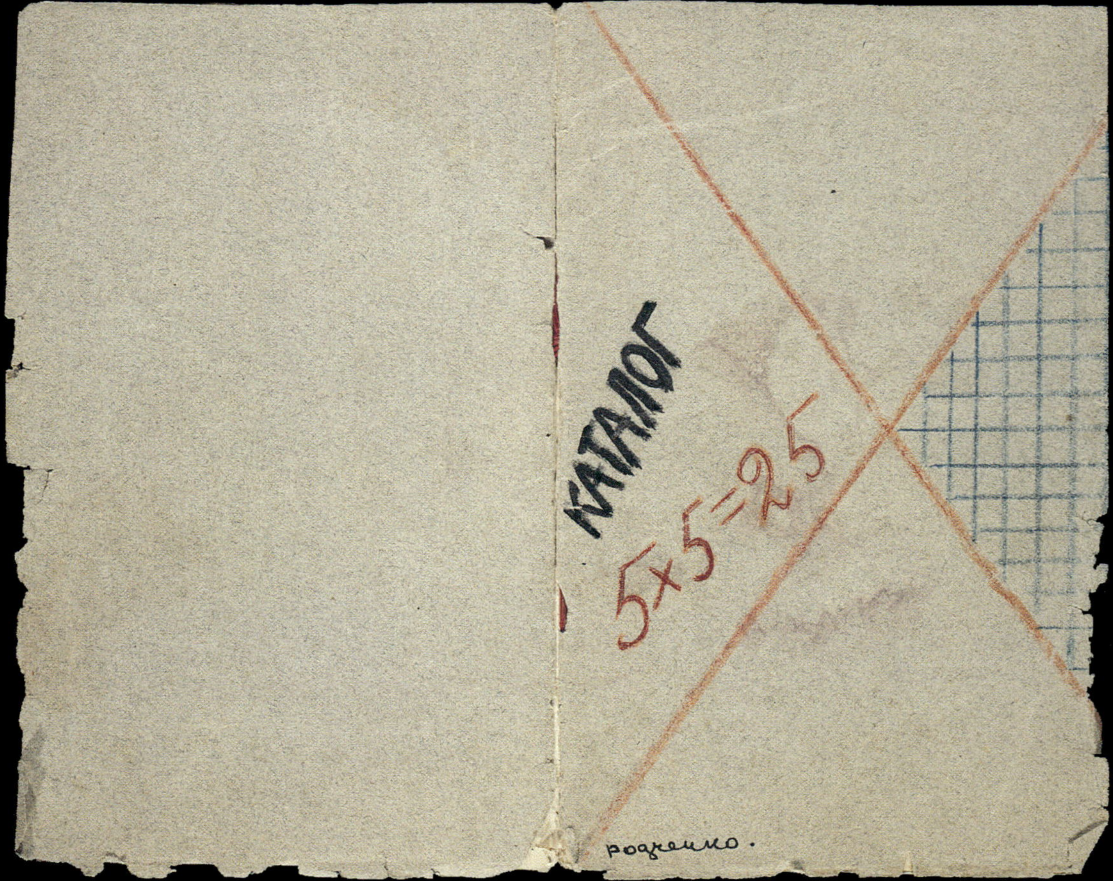

19a

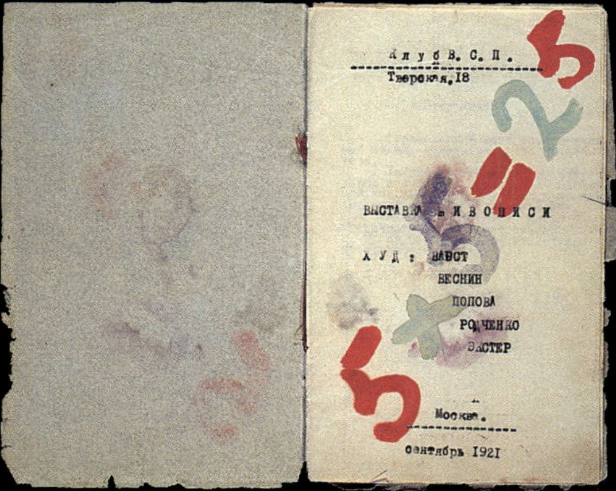
Клуб В. С. П.
Тверская, 18
ВЫСТАВКА ЖИВОПИСИ
ХУД: ВАРСТ
ВЕСНИН
ПОПОВА
РОДЧЕНКО
ЭКСТЕР
Москва.
Сентябрь 1921

19b

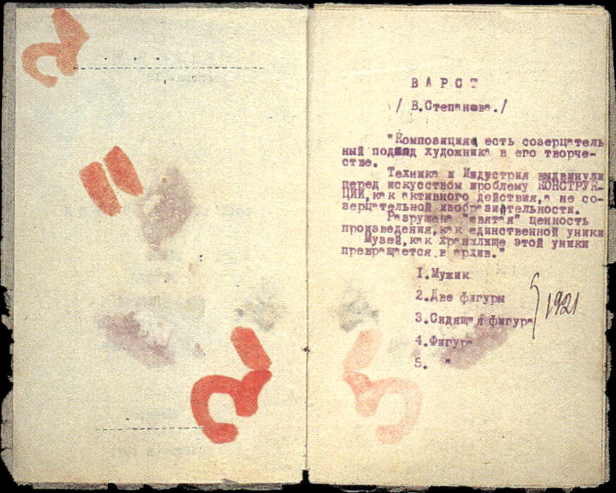
ВАРСТ
/ В. Степанова. /

"Композиция есть созерцательный подход художника в его творчестве.
Техника и Индустрия выдвинули перед искусством проблему КОНСТРУКЦИИ, как активного действия, а не созерцательной изобразительности.
Разрушена "святая" ценность произведения, как единственной уники.
Музей, как хранилище этой уники превращается в архив."

I. Мужик
2. Две фигуры
3. Сидящая фигура
4. Фигура
5. "

1921

19c

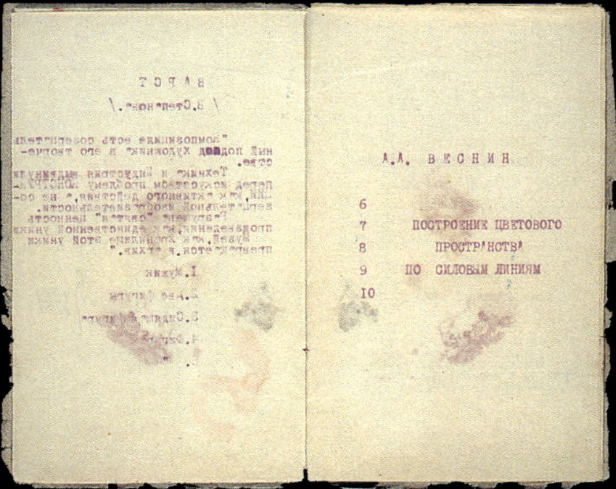
А.А. ВЕСНИН
6
7 ПОСТРОЕНИЕ ЦВЕТОВОГО
8 ПРОСТРАНСТВА
9 ПО СИЛОВЫМ ЛИНИЯМ
10

19d

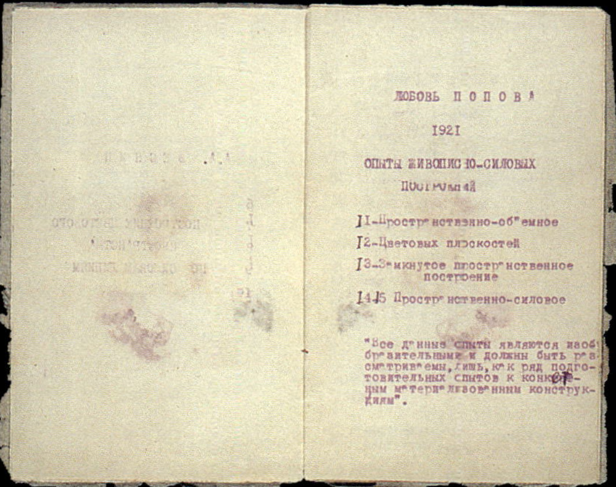
ЛЮБОВЬ ПОПОВА
1921
ОПЫТЫ ЖИВОПИСНО-СИЛОВЫХ
ПОСТРОЕНИЙ

II-Пространственно-об"емное
I2-Цветовых плоскостей
I3-Замкнутое пространственное построение
I4-I5 Пространственно-силовое

"Все данные опыты являются изобразительными и должны быть рассматриваемы, лишь, как ряд подготовительных опытов к конкретным материализованным конструкциям".

19e

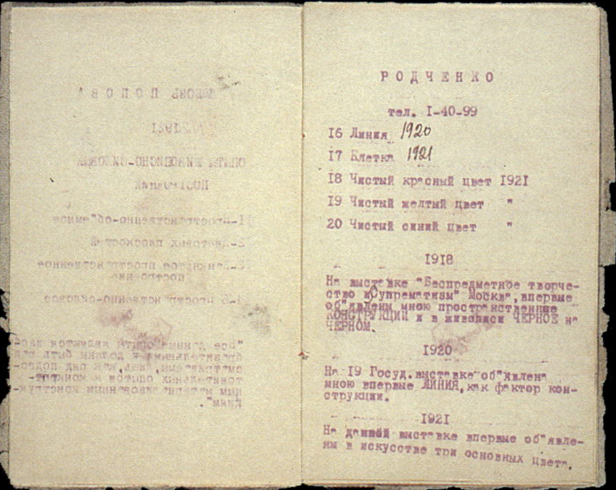
РОДЧЕНКО
тел. I-40-99
I6 Линия 1920
I7 Клетка 1921
I8 Чистый красный цвет 1921
I9 Чистый желтый цвет "
20 Чистый синий цвет "

1918
На выставке "Беспредметное творчество и Супрематизм" Москва, впервые об"явлены мною пространственные КОНСТРУКЦИИ и в живописи ЧЕРНОЕ на ЧЕРНОМ.

1920
На I9 Госуд. выставке об"явлена мною впервые ЛИНИЯ, как фактор конструкции.

1921
На данной выставке впервые об"явлены в искусстве три основных цвета.

19f

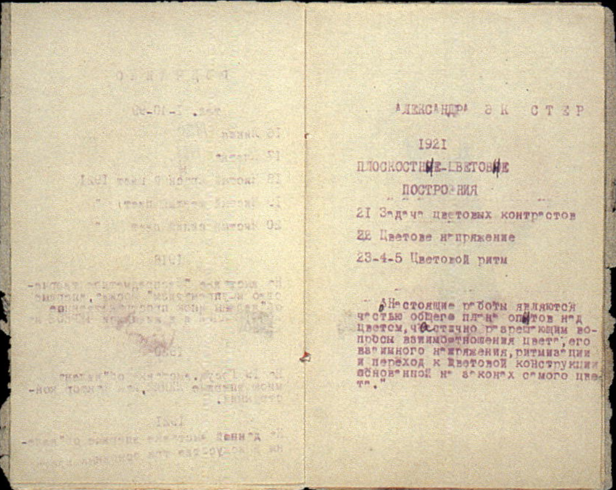
АЛЕКСАНДРА ЭКСТЕР
1921
ПЛОСКОСТНЫЕ-ЦВЕТОВЫЕ
ПОСТРОЕНИЯ
2I Задача цветовых контрастов
22 Цветове напряжение
23-4-5 Цветовой ритм

"Настоящие работы являются частью общего плана опытов над цветом, частично разрешающим вопросы взаимоотношения цвета, его взаимного напряжения, ритмизации и переход к цветовой конструкции основанной на законах самого цвета."

19g

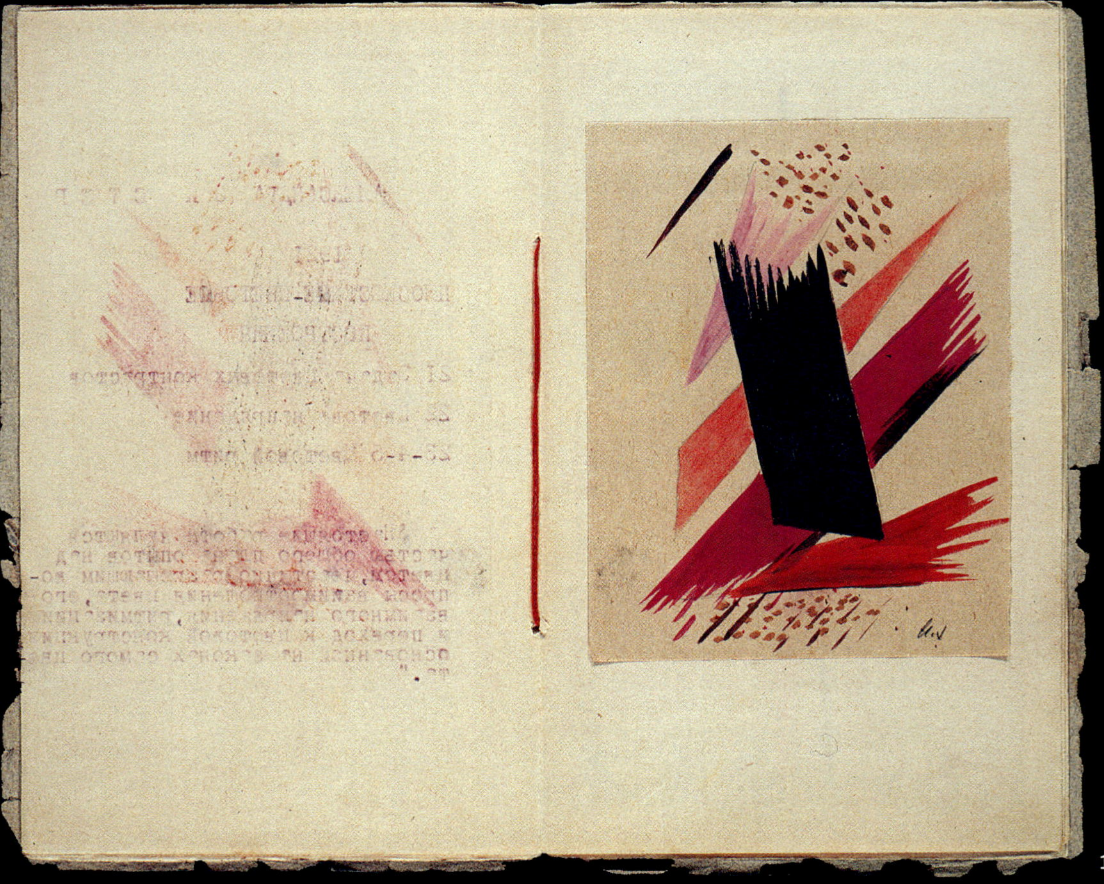

19h

Fig. 19. ***5 x 5 = 25*****, by Alexandra Exter et al.**
continued.

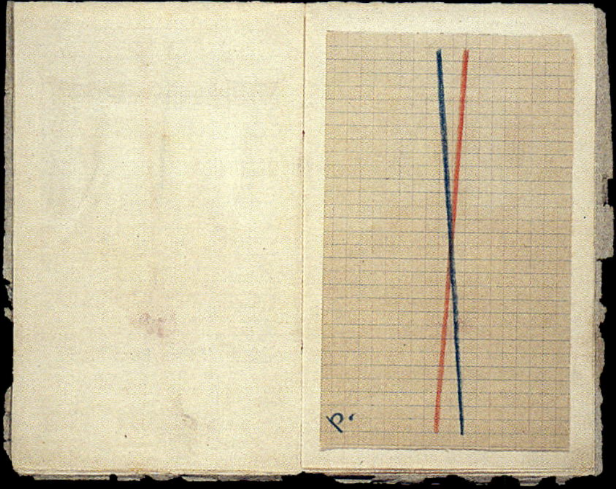
19i

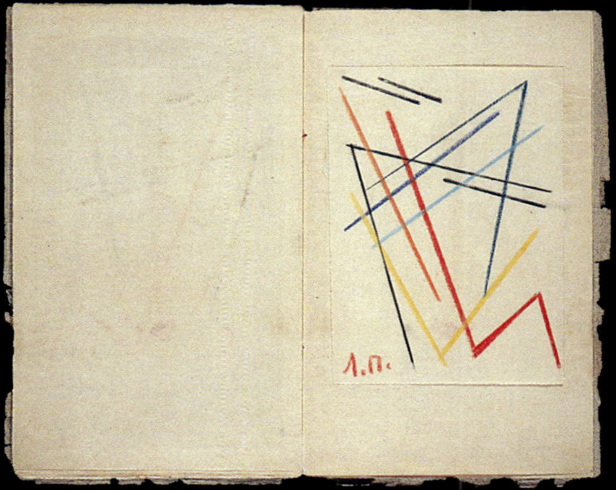
19j

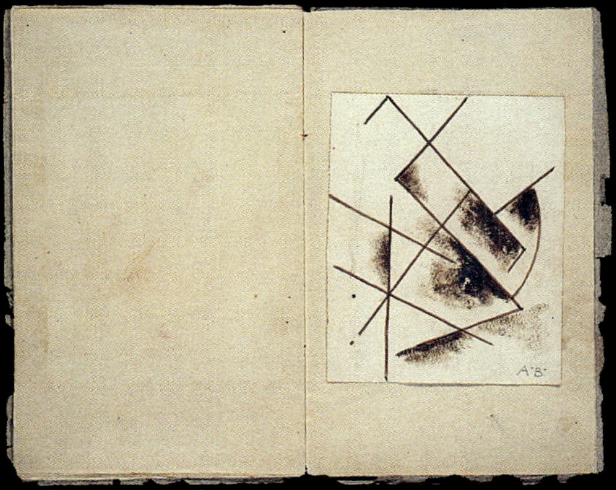
19k

19l

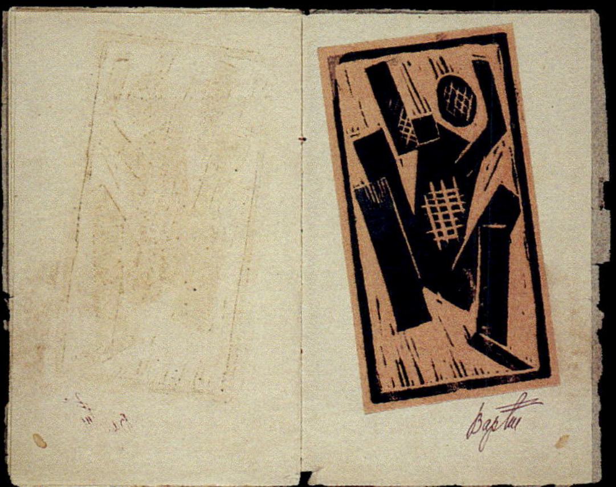
19m

19n

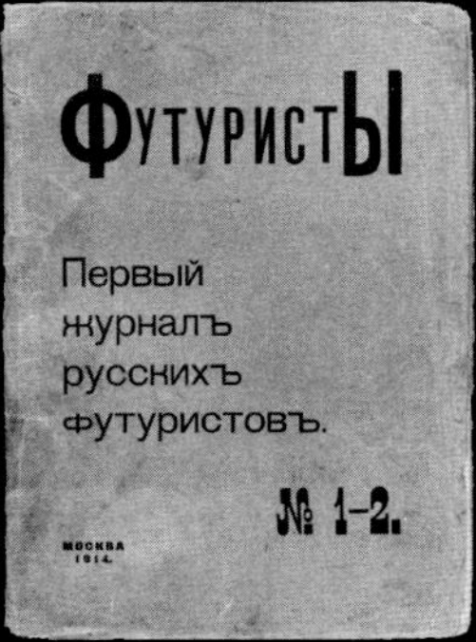
Футуристы
Первый журналъ русскихъ футуристовъ.
№ 1–2.
МОСКВА 1914.

20

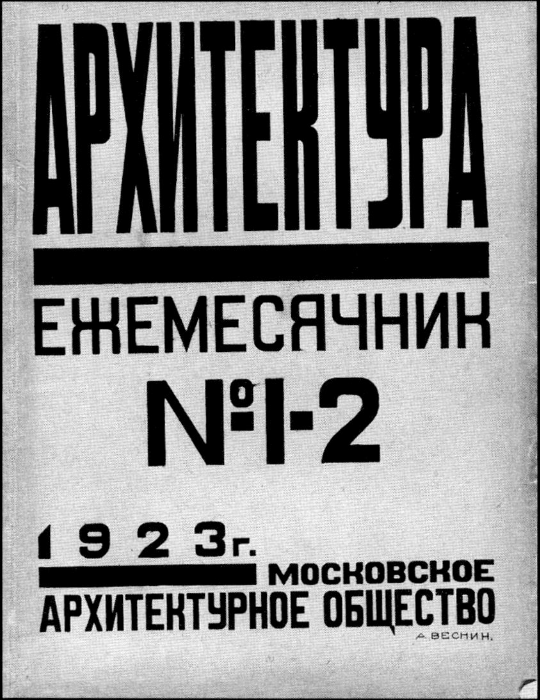
АРХИТЕКТУРА
ЕЖЕМЕСЯЧНИК
№ 1-2
1923 г.
МОСКОВСКОЕ АРХИТЕКТУРНОЕ ОБЩЕСТВО
А. ВЕСНИН.

21

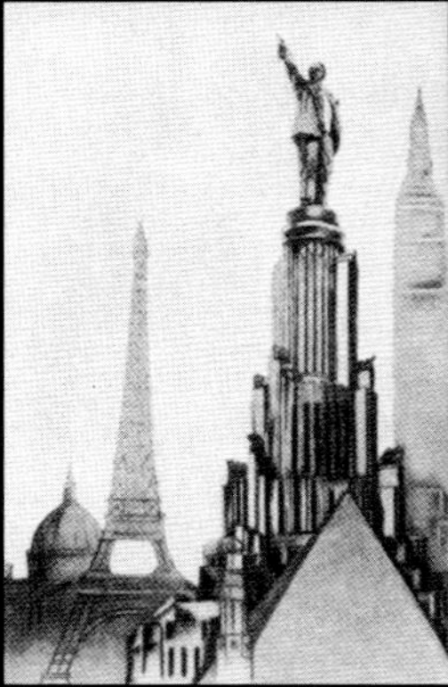

22

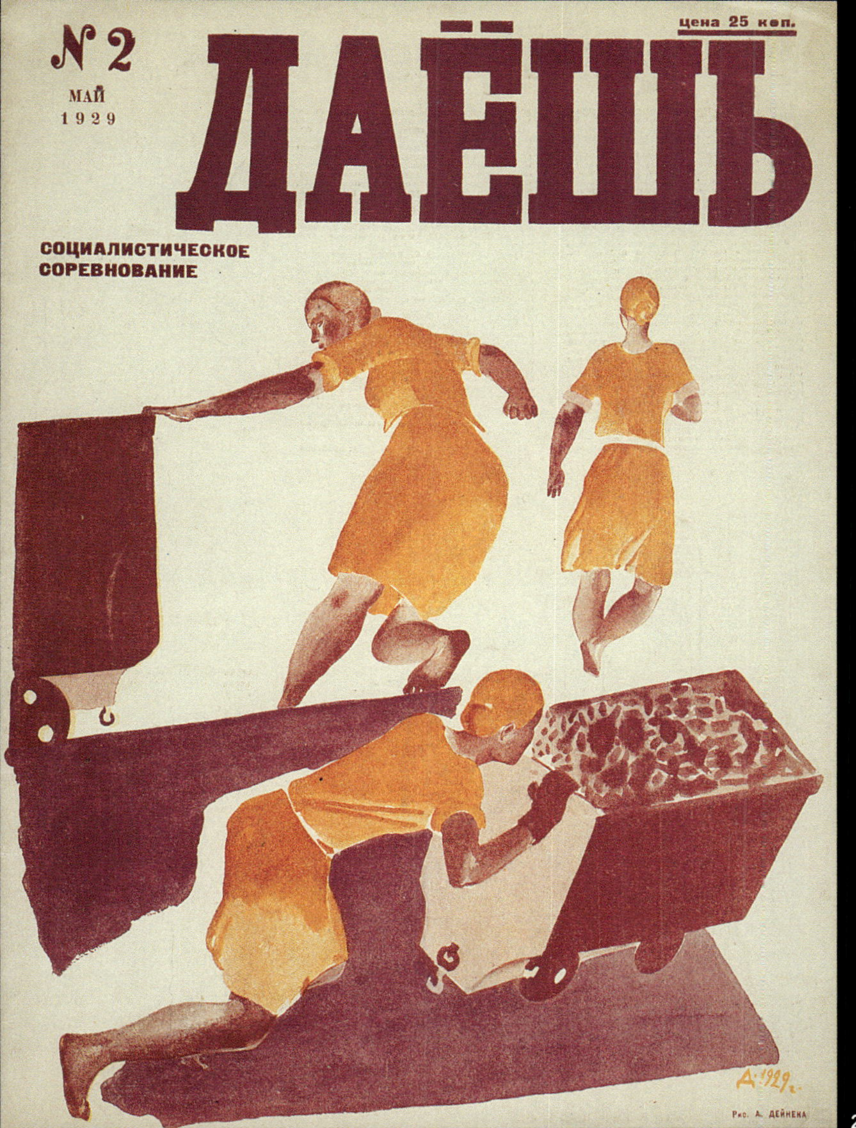
№ 2
МАЙ
1929
цена 25 коп.
ДАЁШЬ
СОЦИАЛИСТИЧЕСКОЕ
СОРЕВНОВАНИЕ
Д. 1929 г.
Рис. А. ДЕЙНЕКА

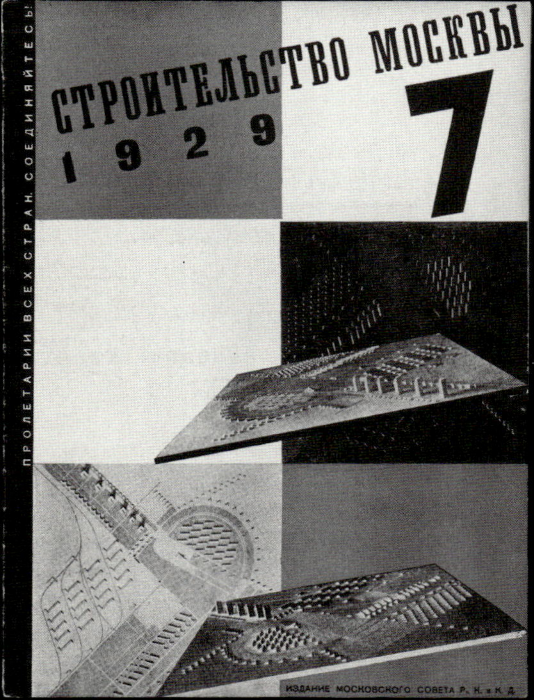
СТРОИТЕЛЬСТВО МОСКВЫ
1929
7
ПРОЛЕТАРИИ ВСЕХ СТРАН, СОЕДИНЯЙТЕСЬ!
ИЗДАНИЕ МОСКОВСКОГО СОВЕТА Р., К. и К. Д.

24

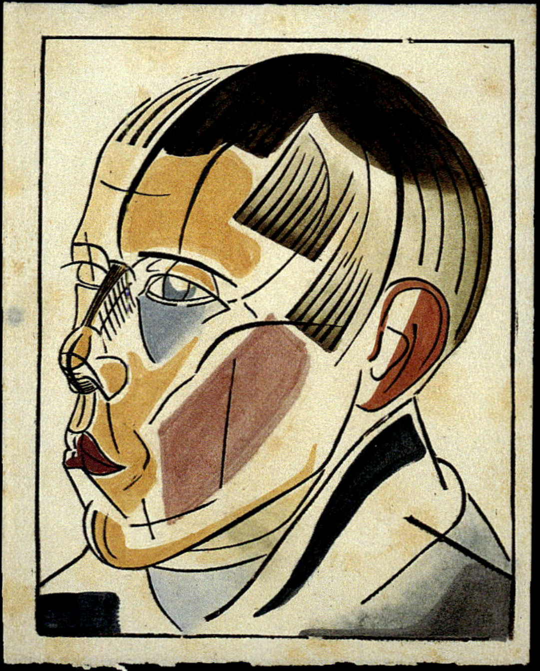

25

508. ———. *Groznyi smekh: Okna ROSTA* (Грозный смех: Окна РОСТА / Menacing laughter: The ROSTA windows). Moscow and Leningrad: Khudozhestvennaia lit-ra, 1932. 79 pp. 25 cm.

Design and cover by Varvara Stepanova.

Stenciled propaganda sheets from the Russian Telegraph Agency (ROSTA) windows with some of Mayakovsky's captions. In some cases Mayakovsky did the illustrations as well.

509. ———. *Ia!* (Я! / Me!). Moscow: G. L Kuz'min i S. D. Dolinskii, [1913]. 15 leaves. 24 cm.

Cover by Mayakovsky (Golubeva 1977, 14/1:18).

Poems. Includes 4 lithographs by Vasilii Chekrygin and 3 lithographs by Lev Zhegin (signed with the roman letters "L. S."). The lithographed text was handwritten by Chekrygin (Khardzhiev 1976, 60).

510. ———. *Ispaniia, okean, Gavanna, Meksika, Amerika* (Испания, океан, Гаванна, Мексика, Америка / Spain, ocean, Havanna, Mexico, America). Moscow and Leningrad: Gos. izd-vo, 1926. 89 pp. 17 cm.

Cover by Aleksandr Rodchenko.

Poems.

511. ———. *Izbrannyi Maiakovskii* (Избранный Маяковский / Mayakovsky: Selections). Berlin and Moscow: Nakanune, 1923. 259 pp., [1] leaf of plates. 19 cm.

Cover by Ioel' (Golubeva 1977, 14/1:19).

512. ———. *Kak delat' stikhi* (Как делать стихи / How to make poetry). Za bol'shoe iskusstvo bol'shevizma. Moscow: Ogiz, Molodaia gvardiia, 1931. 127 pp. 20 cm.

Poetic technique.

First published 1927.

513. ———. *Khorosho! Oktiabr'skaia poema* (Хорошо! Октябрьская поэма / Good! An October poem). Moscow and Leningrad: Gos. izd-vo, 1927. 104 pp. 21 cm.

Cover by El Lissitzky.

514. ———. *Klop: Feericheskaia komediia* (Клоп: Феерическая комедия / Bedbug: A fairy-tale comedy). Moscow and Leningrad: Gos. izd-vo, 1929. 69 pp. 20 cm.

Cover by Aleksandr Rodchenko (Khan-Magomedov 1986, 139).

515. ———. *Letaiushchii proletarii* (Летающий пролетарий / Flying proletariat). Moscow: Avioizd-vo i Aviokhim, [1925]. 64 pp. 23 cm.

Cover by Grigorii Bershadskii.

Poems.

516. ———. *Lirika* (Лирика / Lyrics). Moscow and St. Petersburg: Krug, 1923. 91 pp. 19 cm.

Cover by Anton Lavinskii.

517. ———. *Liubliu* (Люблю / I love). MAF, Seria poetov, no. 1. Moscow: VKhUTEMAS, 1922. 47 pp. 17 cm.
518. ———. *Maiakovskaia gallereia: Te kogo ia nikogda ne videl—Puankare, Mussolini, Kerzon, Pilsudskii, Stines, Gompers, Vandervel'de* (Маяковская галлерея: Те кого я никогда не видел—Пуанкарэ, Муссолини, Керзон, Пилсудский, Стинес, Гомперс, Вандервельде / Mayakovsky's gallery: People I have never seen—Poincaré, Mussolini, Curson, Piłsudski, Stinnes, Gompers, Van der Velde). Moscow: Krasnaia nov', 1923. 63 pp. 20 cm.
   Cover by Mayakovsky.
   Includes illustrations by Mayakovsky.
519. ———. *Maiakovskii izdevaetsia: Pervaia knizhitsa satiry* (Маяковский издевается: Первая книжица сатиры / Mayakovsky jeers: First booklet of satire). MAF, Seriia poetov, no. 3. Moscow: VKhUTEMAS, 1922. 48 pp. 18 cm.
520. ———. *Maiakovskii ulybaetsia, Maiakovskii smeetsia, Maiakovskii izdevaetsia* (Маяковский улыбается, Маяковский смеется, Маяковский издевается / Mayakovsky smiles, Mayakovsky laughs, Mayakovsky jeers). Moscow and St. Petersburg: Krug, 1923. 109 pp. 17 cm.
   Cover by Aleksandr Rodchenko.
   Poems.
521. ———. *Misteriia-buff: Geroicheskoe epicheskoe i satiricheskoe izobrazhenie nashei epokhi* (Мистерия-буфф: Героическое эпическое и сатирическое изображение нашей эпохи / Mystery bouffe: A heroical, epical, and satirical representation of our times). Petrograd: [IMO], 1918. 78 pp. 27 cm.
   Cover by Mayakovsky (Golubeva 1977, 14/1:43).
   Play.
522. ———. *Misteriia-buff: Geroicheskoe epicheskoe i satiricheskoe izobrazhenie nashei epokhi* (Мистерия-буфф: Героическое эпическое и сатирическое изображение нашей эпохи / Mystery bouffe: A heroical, epical, and satirical representation of our times). 2nd ed. Petrograd: IMO, [1919]. 71 pp. 22 cm.
523. ———. *MIuD* (МЮД). Moscow and Leningrad: Gos. izd-vo, 1930. 16 pp. 17 cm.
   Cover by Vera Ivanova.
   Children's poem. Includes illustrations by Ivanova. MIuD is the acronym for *Mezhdunarodnyi iunosheskii den'* (International youth day).
524. ———. *Moe otkrytie Ameriki* (Мое открытие Америки / My discovery of America). Moscow and Leningrad: Gos. izd-vo, 1926. 142 pp. 18 cm.
   Cover by Aleksandr Rodchenko.
   Travel notes.
525. ———. *My i pradedy: Stikhi* (Мы и прадеды: Стихи / We and our ancestors: Verse). Moscow: Molodaia gvardiia, 1927. 34 pp. 20 cm.
   Cover by Nikolai Il'in (Golubeva 1977, 14/1:24).

526. ———. *My vas zhdem, tovarishch ptitsa, otchego vam ne letitsia?* (Мы вас ждем, товарищ птица, отчего вам не летится? / We're waiting for you, comrade bird, why don't you fly?). Moscow and Leningrad: Ogiz, Molodaia gvardiia, 1931. 15 p. 17 cm.
Cover by Tat'iana Mavrina.
Children's book in verse. Includes illustrations by Mavrina.

527. ———. *Ni znakhar', ni bog, ni angely boga—krest'ianstvu ne podmoga* (Ни знахарь, ни бог, ни ангелы бога—крестьянству не подмога / Neither healer nor god nor the angels of god are a help to the peasantry). Moscow: Krasnaia nov', 1923. 35 pp. 17 cm.
Cover by Mayakovsky (Golubeva 1977, 14/1:19).
A story in verse. Includes illustrations by Mayakovsky.

528. ———. *NO.S: Novye stikhi* (НО.С: Новые стихи / NO.S: New verse). Moscow: Federatsiia, [1928]. 107 pp., [1] plate. 18 cm.
Cover by Aleksandr Rodchenko.

529. ———. *Oblako v shtanakh: Tetraptikh* (Облако в штанах: Тетраптих / A cloud in trousers: Tetraptych). 2nd ed., uncensored. [Moscow]: ASIS, [1918]. 61 pp. 18 cm.
Design and cover by Mayakovsky.
Poem.
Edition statement appears on the cover label.

530. ———. *O Kurske, o komsomole, o mae, o polete, o Chapline, o Germanii, o nefti, o 5 Internatsionale i o proch.* (О Курске, о комсомоле, о мае, о полете, о Чаплине, о Германии, о нефти, о 5 Интернационале и о проч. / About Kursk, about the Komsomol, about May, about flight, about Chaplin, about Germany, about oil, about the Fifth International, etcetera). Moscow: Krasnaia nov', 1924. 90 pp. 18 cm.
Cover by Ruvim Mazel'.
Poems.

531. ———. *Parizh* (Париж / Paris). Moscow: Moskovskii rabochii, 1925. 40 pp. 17 cm.
Cover by Aleksandr Rodchenko.
Poems.

532. ———. *Pesni rabochim* (Песни рабочим / Songs for workers). Moscow: Doloi negramotnost', 1925. 97 pp. 18 cm.
Cover by Samuil Adlivankin (Golubeva 1977, 14/1:22).
Includes illustrations by Adlivankin.

533. ———. *Pro eto* (Про это / About this). Moscow and Petrograd: Gos. izd-vo, 1923. 43 pp., [8] plates. 23 cm.
Poem. The cover and plates are photomontages by Aleksandr Rodchenko and incorporate photographs by B. Kapustianskii, Abram Shterenberg, and E. Vasserman.

534. ———. *Prostoe kak mychanie* (Простое как мычание / Simple as mooing). Petrograd: Parus, 1916. 116 pp. 22 cm.
Poems.
Inscribed "Veidman" and dated January 1918 on title page. What appears to be the same hand has supplied in purple ink the censored lines of *Oblako v shtanakh*. (See no. 529.) A newspaper notice of Mayakovsky's appearance at a poetry reading has been mounted on p. [3] and dated February 1918, again apparently by Veidman.

535. ———. *Rasskaz o dezertire* (Рассказ о дезертире / Story about a deserter). Moscow: Gos. izd-vo, 1921. 15 pp. 21 cm.
Includes text and illustrations by Mayakovsky.

536. ———. *Razgovor s fininspektorom o poezii* (Разговор с фининспектором о поэзии / Conversation with a finance inspector about poetry). [Tbilisi]: Zakkniga, 1926. 14 pp., 1 plate. 17 cm.
Design and photomontage covers by Aleksandr Rodchenko.
Includes an illustration by Rodchenko.

537. ———. *Sergeiu Eseninu* (Сергею Есенину / To Sergei Esenin). [Tbilisi]: Zakkniga, 1926. 15 pp. 18 cm.
Front and back covers by Aleksandr Rodchenko.
Poem. Includes 2 photomontage illustrations by Rodchenko.

538. ———. *Sifilis* (Сифилис / Syphilis). [Tbilisi]: Zakkniga, 1926. 15 pp. 17 cm.
Cover by Aleksandr Rodchenko.
Poem. Includes photomontages by Rodchenko.
Research Institute's copy bears the ownership stamp "V. T." in purple ink.

539. ———. *Slony v komsomole* (Слоны в комсомоле / Elephants in the Komsomol). [Moscow]: Molodaia gvardiia, 1929. 94 pp. 18 cm.
Cover by Nikolai Il'in (Golubeva 1977, 14/1:28).
Poems.

540. ———. *Solntse: Poema* (Солнце: Поэма / Sun: A poem). Moscow and St. Petersburg: Krug, 1923. [28] pp. 16 cm.
Cover by Mikhail Larionov.
Includes illustrations by Larionov.

541. ———. *Stikhi revoliutsii: Oktiabr', fevral', golod, Evropa, iskusstvo, smeshnoe* (Стихи революции: Октябрь, февраль, голод, Европа, искусство, смешное / Poetry of the revolution: October, February, famine, Europe, art, laughs). Moscow: Krasnaia nov', 1923. 98 pp. 17 cm.

542. ———. *150.000.000.* [Moscow]: Gos. izd-vo, 1921. 70 pp. 18 cm.
Poem.

543. ———. *Tol'ko novoe* (Только новое / Only new things). Leningrad and Moscow: Gos. izd-vo, 1925. 55 pp. 17 cm.
Cover by Vladimir Izenberg.
Poems.

544. ———. *13 let raboty* (13 лет работы / Thirteen years' work). 2 vols. Moscow: VKhUTEMAS, 1922. 19 cm.

Cover by Anton Lavinskii.

Poems.

545. ———. *Tuda i obratno* (Туда и обратно / There and back). Moscow: Federatsiia, 1930. 93 pp. 18 cm.

Cover by Aleksandr Rodchenko.

Poems.

546. ———. *Veshchi etogo goda: Do 1 avgusta 1923 g.* (Вещи этого года: До 1 августа 1923 г. / Works of this year: To 1 August 1923). Berlin: Nakanune, [1923 (Golubeva 1977, 14/1:20)]. 108 pp. 18 cm.

Poems.

The date printed on the volume is 1924.

547. ———. *Vladimir Il'ich Lenin.* Leningrad and Moscow: Gos. izd-vo, 1925. 94 pp. 17 cm.

Cover by E. Shol'te.

Poem.

548. ———. *Vladimir Maiakovskii: Tragediia* (Владимир Маяковский: Трагедия / Vladimir Mayakovsky: A tragedy). Moscow: Izd. 1-go zhurnala russkikh futuristov, 1914. 44 pp., [7] plates. 18 cm.

The 7 plates are by David and Vladimir Burliuk. Mayakovsky's tragedy was produced along with Aleksei Kruchenykh's *Pobeda nad solntsem* (Victory over the sun) at the Luna Park Theater in St. Petersburg in December 1913.

From an edition of 500 (*Knizhnaia letopis'* 1914, no. 8655). Research Institute's copy is missing the last plate.

549. ———. *Voina i mir* (Война и мир / War and the universe). Petrograd: Parus, 1917. 47 pp. 22 cm.

Poem.

Mayakovsky spelled the third word of the title "мiр" rather than "мир" in the pre-1918 orthography. By so doing he transformed the traditional opposition of "war" and "peace," familiar from the title of Leo Tolstoy's novel, to the characteristically hyperbolic "War and the universe." This distinction was lost in subsequent editions printed in the new orthography, in accordance with which both words are written "мир."

550. [———]. *Voina i mir* (Война и мир / War and the universe). 3rd ed. Leningrad: Gos. izd-vo, 1924. 54 pp. 18 cm.

Cover by Vladimir Izenberg.

551. ———. *Vo ves' golos: Pervoe vstuplenie v poemu* (Во весь голос: Первое вступление в поэму / At the top of his lungs: First introduction to a poem). Moscow: Gosizdat RSFSR, Moskovskii rabochii, 1930. 21 pp. 18 cm.

552. ———. *Vo ves' golos: Pervoe vstuplenie v poemu* (Во весь голос: Первое вступление в поэму / At the top of his lungs: First introduction to a poem).

2nd ed. Novinki proletarskoi literatury. Moscow: Khudozhestvennaia lit-ra, 1931. 12 pp. 19 cm.

Design and cover by Solomon Telingater.

553. ———. *Vse, sochinennoe Vladimirom Maiakovskim, 1909–1919* (Все, сочиненное Владимиром Маяковским, 1909–1919 / Everything written by Vladimir Mayakovsky, 1909–1919). [Petrograd]: IMO, [1920]. 280 pp. 22 cm.

554. [———]. *Zhivoi Maiakovskii: Razgovory Maiakovskogo* (Живой Маяковский: Разговоры Маяковского / Mayakovsky alive: Mayakovsky's conversations). Compiled by Aleksei Kruchenykh. Nos. 1 and 2 of 3. Moscow: Izd. "Gruppy druzei Maiakovskogo," 1930. 23 cm.

Design of no. 2 by Ivan Kliun. Cover of no. 1 by Igor' Terent'ev. Cover of no. 3 by Kliun.

Covers of all 3 numbers have a portrait of Mayakovsky (Golubeva 1977, 11:382). Cover portrait of no. 2 is from a portrait by David Burliuk that appeared in *Trebnik troikh* facing p. [34]. (See no. 775.)

No. 1 from an edition of 200. No. 2 from an edition of 300. No. 3 from an edition of 100 (Bowlt and Hernad 1993, 163). Reproduced by lithography on glass.

555. [———]. Isaak Eventov. *Maiakovskii-plakatist: Kriticheskii ocherk* (Маяковский-плакатист: Критический очерк / Mayakovsky as poster artist: A critical essay). Leningrad and Moscow: Iskusstvo, 1940. 72 pp. 23 cm.

556. [———]. R. V. Ivanov-Razumnik. *Vladimir Maiakovskii: "Misteriia" ili "Buff"* (Владимир Маяковский: «Мистерия» или «буфф» / Vladimir Mayakovsky: "Mystery" or "Buffo"). Berlin: Skify, 1922. 55 pp. 22 cm.

Cover by El Lissitzky.

557. [———]. Vasilii Katanian. *Kratkaia letopis' zhizni i raboty V. V. Maiakovskogo* (Краткая летопись жизни и работы В. В. Маяковского / Short chronicle of the life and work of V. V. Mayakovsky). Moscow: Sov. pisatel', 1939. 71 pp. 18 cm.

558. [———]. Vasilii Katanian. *Maiakovskomu: Sbornik vospominanii i statei* (Маяковскому: Сборник воспоминаний и статей / To Mayakovsky: A collection of reminiscences and articles). Leningrad: Khudozhestvennaia lit-ra, 1940. 345 pp., [5] plates. 22 cm.

Discussion of Mayakovsky as a visual artist.

Plates and pp. 3–14 are missing.

559. [———]. Aleksei Kruchenykh. *Stikhi V. Maiakovskago: Vypyt* (Стихи В. Маяковскаго: Выпыт / The poetry of V. Mayakovsky: An inquiry). [St. Petersburg]: EUY, 1914. 29 pp. 21 cm.

Cover by David Burliuk.

The cover is a portrait of Mayakovsky that appeared previously in *Trebnik troikh*. (See no. 775.)

Research Institute has 2 copies, 1 in which the lithograph tipped in at the title page is by Ol'ga Rozanova and 1 by Kazimir Malevich. Both title pages, however, credit Rozanova. The lithograph by Malevich is not in Karshan (1975) as part of this publication, but is apparently identical to his no. 8.

560. [———]. *Vladimir Maiakovskii.* Edited by Vasilii Katanian. [Moscow]: Gos. izd-vo izobrazitel'nykh iskusstv, [1931]. 287 pp. 24 cm.

561. [———]. *Vladimir Maiakovskii: Odnodnevnaia gazeta Leningradskogo otdela Federatsii ob"edinenii sovetskikh pisatelei* (Владимир Маяковский: Однодневная газета Ленинградского отдела Федерации объединений советских писателей / Vladimir Mayakovsky: Single-issue newspaper of the Leningrad section of the Federation of Soviet Writers' Organizations). [Leningrad]: Krasnaia gazeta, 1930. 4 pp. 56 cm.

Special issue published 24 April 1930 on the occasion of Mayakovsky's death.

562. **Mayakovsky, Vladimir, and Sergei Tret'iakov.** *Rasskaz pro to, kak uznal Fadei zakon, zashchishchaiushchii rabochikh liudei: Kodeks zakonov pro trud* (Рассказ про то, как узнал Фадей закон, защищающий рабочих людей: Кодекс законов про труд / Story of how Fadei found out about the law that protects working people: The labor code). Moscow: Trud i kniga, 1924. 47 pp. 17 cm.

Includes illustrations by Samuil Adlivankin.

563. **Meyerhold, Vsevolod.** *V. E. Meierkhol'd: Sbornik k 20-ti letiiu rezhisserskoi i 25-ti letiiu akterskoi deiatel'nosti* (В. Э. Мейерхольд: Сборник к 20-ти летию режиссерской и 25-ти летию актерской деятельности / V. E. Meyerhold: A collection to honor his twenty years as a director and twenty-five as an actor). Tver: Oktiabr', 1923. 28 pp. 30 cm.

564. **Mezonin poezii** (The mezzanine of poetry). *Krematorii zdravomysliia* (Крематорий здравомыслия / Crematorium of common sense). Mezonin poezii, nos. 3–4. Moscow: Mezonin poezii, 1913. [48] pp. 22 cm.

Cover by Boris Fridenson.

Poems by Sofiia Beketova, Konstantin Bol'shakov, Konstantin Chaikin, Riurik Ivnev, Khrisanf (Léon Zack), Boris Lavrenev, Mariia Moravskaia, Nelli, Petr Pogodin, Mikhail Sandomirskii, Igor' Severianin, Vadim Shershenevich, Pavel Shirokov, and Sergei Tret'iakov. Fiction by Shershenevich and Khrisanf. Criticism by "the abbot Fanferliush" (Shershenevich) and M. Rossiianskii (Zack). The poem credited to "Nelli" may have been written by Valerii Briusov or Nadezhda L'vova (Markov 1968, 114–15).

565. ———. *Pir vo vremia chumy* (Пир во время чумы / Feast in time of plague). Mezonin poezii, no. 2. Moscow: Mezonin poezii, 1913. [32] pp. 21 cm.

Cover by Léon Zack.

Poems by Graal'-Arel'skii, Riurik Ivnev, Khrisanf (Zack), Nadezhda L'vova, Petr Pogodin, Igor' Severianin, Vadim Shershenevich, Pavel Shirokov, and Sergei Tret'iakov. Criticism by "the abbot Fanferliush" (Shershenevich) and M. Rossiianskii (Zack).

566. ———. *Vernissazh* (Вернисcаж / Vernissage). Mezonin poezii, no. 1. Moscow: Mezonin poezii, 1913. 32 pp. 21 cm.

Cover by Léon Zack.

Poems by N. Benediktova, Valerii Briusov, Konstantin Chaikin, Riurik Ivnev, Khrisanf (Zack), Boris Lavrenev, Vadim Shershenevich, Pavel Shirokov, and Aleksei Sidorov. Criticism by "the abbot Fanferliush" (Shershenevich) and M. Rossiianskii (Zack).

567. **Mikhailov, Aleksei.** *Gruppirovki sovetskoi arkhitektury* (Группировки советской архитектуры / Groupings in Soviet architecture). Edited by Iu. Ianel'. Moscow and Leningrad: Ogiz-Izogiz, 1932. 133 pp. 21 cm.

Collection of articles written 1930–1931 by an associate of the artists' group October.

568. [———]. *Izoiskusstvo rekonstruktivnogo perioda* (Изоискусство реконструктивного периода / The visual arts in the period of reconstruction). Edited by Iu. Ianel'. Moscow and Leningrad: Ogiz-Izogiz, 1932. 207 pp. 22 cm.

Collection of articles written 1928–1931.

569. **Miklashevskii, Konstantin.** *Gipertrofiia iskusstva* (Гипертрофия искусства / Hypertrophy of art). Petrograd: [n.p.], 1924. 80 pp. 20 cm.

570. **Miliutin, Nikolai.** *Problema stroitel'stva sotsialisticheskikh gorodov: Osnovnye voprosy ratsional'noi planirovki i stroitel'stva naselennykh mest SSSR* (Проблема строительства социалистических городов: Основные вопросы рациональной планировки и строительства населенных мест СССР / The problem of building socialist cities: Fundamental questions of rational urban planning and construction in the USSR). Moscow: Gos. izd-vo, 1930. 82 pp., [1] plate. 24 × 27 cm.

Cover title is *Sotsgorod* (The socialist city).

571. ***Mnogogrannik*** (Многогранник / Polyhedron). Baku: Izd-vo D. I. pri B. S., 1927. 30 pp. 18 cm.

Cover by Viktor Gorin.

Miscellany includes contributions by F. Baranovskii, D. Bugoslavskii, S. Erlikh, Gorin, and Viktor Vitkovich.

From an edition of 500. Handwritten poems reproduced by lithography on glass.

572. ***Moi zhurnal—Vasiliia Kamenskogo*** (Мой журнал—Василия Каменского / My journal—by Vasilii Kamenskii). Moscow: Vasilii Kamenskii, 1922. 16 pp. 33 cm.

Edited by S. Frid.

Cover by E. Bebutova and Pavel Kuznetsov.

Semimonthly journal. Includes an introductory statement about the origin of the journal; an interview with various poets and artists (such as L. Kamenev, Kuznetsov, Vladimir Mayakovsky, and Aleksandr Tairov), "Chto uvlekaet vas segodnia?" (What fascinates you today?); an article by Frid, "Pushkin—Lermontov, Mayakovsky—Kamenskii"; a prose poem by Kamenskii addressed to the professors and students of the Higher State Artistic and Technical Workshops (VKhUTEMAS); poems and theoretical articles by Kamenskii; and 2 pages (pp. 15–16) of humorous advertisements extolling Kamenskii's virtues and talents.

A total of 1 issue published.

573. **Molchanov, Ivan.** *Traktorostroi: Stikhi* (Тракторострой: Стихи / Tractor factory: Verse). Edited by M. Brodskii (Krasnov). Saratov: Ogiz RSFSR, N.-V. kraevoe otd-nie, 1931. 64 pp. 17 cm.

574. ***Moloko kobylits: Sbornik—risunki, stikhi, proza*** (Молоко кобылиц: Сборник—рисунки, стихи, проза / The milk of mares: A collection—drawings, verse, prose). Moscow: Futuristy "Gileia," 1914. 89 pp., [12] plates. 19 cm.

Includes black-and-white photographs of 2 paintings by Alexandra Exter, 2 lithographs in black ink on blue paper by David Burliuk and 6 by Vladimir Burliuk, as well as 1 watercolor by David Burliuk, 1 watercolor by Vladimir Burliuk, and poems by David and Nikolai Burliuk; Vasilii Kamenskii; Velimir Khlebnikov; Aleksei Kruchenykh; Benedikt Livshits; Vladimir Mayakovsky; and Igor' Severianin.

From an edition of 400. Research Institute's copy has *mirīstei'* written on the cover in black ink. This neologism of Khlebnikov's was originally intended to be the title of the collection (Markov 1968, 165–66). Research Institute's copy is stamped in red on original cover (retained when copy was rebound) as follows: "Biblioteka Glavnogo [upravleniia] po delam pechati" (Library of the chief [directorate] for press matters).

575. **Moskovskaia assotsiatsiia khudozhnikov dekoratorov** (Moscow Association of Scene Designers). *Pervaia teatral'no-dekorativnaia vystavka* (Первая театрально-декоративная выставка / First exhibition of theatrical scenery design). Moscow: Moskovskaia assotsiatsiia khudozhnikov dekoratorov, 1929. 32 pp. 17 cm.

Exhibition catalog.

576. ***Moskovskie mastera*** (Московские мастера / Moscow masters). Moscow: [n.p.], 1916. 100 pp. 26 cm.

Covers by Aristarkh Lentulov.

Artistic journal dedicated to poetry, prose, theater, music, painting, and bibliography. Includes a musical poem (with French notations by Nikolai Roslavets), a theoretical essay on theater by Samuil Vermel', works by Vladimir and David Burliuk, Petr Konchalovskii, Pavel Kuznetsov, Lentulov, and Il'ia Mashkov, and poetry by Konstantin Bol'shakov, David and Nikolai Burliuk, Vasilii Kamenskii, Velimir Khlebnikov, and Benedikt Livshits.

A total of 1 issue published.

577. **Moskovskii rabochii** (Moscow worker). *Polnyi annotirovannyi ukazatel' knig izdannykh s 1922 g. po 1928 g.* (Полный аннотированный указатель книг изданных с 1922 г. по 1928 г. / A complete annotated guide to books published from 1922 to 1928). Moscow and Leningrad: Moskovskii rabochii, 1928. 306 pp., 14 pp. of publisher's advertising. 22 cm.

Typographical design by Solomon Telingater.

The index lists books issued by Moscow Worker and New Moscow from 1922 to 1928. These 2 publishing houses merged in 1927 under the name of Moscow Worker. Includes lists of journals published from 1926 to 1927 and reproductions of most of their covers.

578. ***Moskovskii teatr revoliutsii, 1922–1932: Sbornik statei*** (Московский театр революции, 1922–1932: Сборник статей / Moscow theater of the Revolution, 1922–1932: Collection of essays). [Moscow]: Izd-vo Mosoblispolkoma, 1933. 221 pp., [10] plates. 26 cm.

Includes illustrations by Vladimir Favorskii, Andrei Goncharov, Boris Grozevskii, Pavel Pavlinov, Mikhail Pikov, and Mikhail Tarkhanov.

579. **Mur, Leo.** *Fabrika serykh tenei: Den' kino-fabriki* (Фабрика серых теней: День кино-фабрики / Factory of gray shadows: A movie studio's day). Moscow and Leningrad: Kinopechat', 1927. 154 pp. 21 cm.

580. ***My*** (Мы / We). Moscow: Kn-vo pri Vseros. soiuze poetov "Chikhi-Pikhi," 1920. 63 pp. 18 cm.

Includes poetry by Konstantin Bal'mont, Viacheslav Ivanov, Riurik Ivnev, Velimir Khlebnikov, Aleksandr Kusikov, Lev Nikulin, Boris Pasternak, Semen Rubanovich, Ivan Rukavishnikov, Vadim Shershenevich, and Sergei Tret'iakov.

581. **Narbut, Heorhii.** *Ukrains'ka abetka* (Українська абетка / Ukrainian alphabet). St. Petersburg: Vyd. Drukarni T-vo Golike i Vil'borg, 1917. 14 sheets. 33 cm.

Narbut started work on *Ukrainsk'ka abetka* for the publishers Golike & Vil'borg in 1917. Due to the revolutionary events of that year, that edition was not published as planned. However in 1921, soon after Narbut's death, 14 of the original 15 drawings were published by friends of the artist in a small edition of black-and-white lithographs. The date of 1917 on the title sheet and the publisher's name Golike & Vil'borg are those of the original, unrealized edition (Biletskyi 1985, 140–50).

582. ***Navigator's Log Book, Airplane NO25: First Non-Stop Flight Moscow–North Pole–United States of America.*** 2 vols. Moscow: State Arts Publishers, 1939. In portfolio. 28 cm.
Design by Solomon Telingater.

583. ***Nebokopy*** (Небокопы / Sky Miners). Ego-Futuristy, 8. Edited by Ivan Ignat'ev. St. Petersburg: Peterburgskii glashatai, 1913. 16 pp. 22 cm.
Poems and prose. Includes poems by Vasilisk Gnedov and articles on contemporary poetry by Anastasiia Chebotarevskaia and Viktor Khovin. The cover has a photograph of Ignat'ev. A photograph of Gnedov appears on p. 16.

584. ***Neo-futurizm*** (Нео-футуризм / Neofuturism). Kazan: Futurum, 1913. 29, [82] pp. 28 cm.
Parodies of Futurist poetry and art by a group of journalists (Khardzhiev 1976, 80 n. 112). Contains a polemical introduction by A. Gribatnikov.

585. **Neutra, Richard.** *Amerika, die Stilbildung des neuen Bauens in den Vereinigten Staaten* (America, the development of style in new building in the United States). Neues Bauen in der Welt, vol. 2. Vienna: Anton Schroll, 1930. 163 pp. 29 cm.
Cover and dust jacket by El Lissitzky.

586. ———. *Kak stroit Amerika?* (Как строит Америка? / How does America build?). Moscow: Makiz, 1929. 177 pp. 23 cm.
Translation of *Wie baut Amerika?* Includes an introduction by Aleksei Shchusev.

587. ***Neva: Almanakh stikhov*** (Нева: Альманах стихов / Neva: A miscellany of verse). Tbilisi: Feniks, 1919. 15 pp. 20 cm.
Includes contributions by Iurii Degen, Riurik Ivnev, Boris Korneev, Mikhail Kuzmin, Nikolai Semeiko, and Mikhail Struve.

588. **Neznamov, Petr.** *Khorosho na ulitse: Stikhi* (Хорошо на улице: Стихи / It's nice outside: Verse). Moscow: Federatsiia, 1929. 95 pp. 18 cm.
Cover by Aleksandr Rodchenko.

589. ***No. 4: Vystavka kartin—futuristy, luchisty, primitiv*** (N° 4: Выставка картин—футуристы, лучисты, примитив / Number four: An exhibition of paintings—Futurists, Rayonists, Primitives). Moscow: [n.p.], 1914. 12 pp., [15] plates. 20 cm.

Catalog of an exhibition held at the Society of Lovers of the Arts, beginning 23 March 1914. Participants listed in the catalog include Sergei Baidin, A. A. Baryshnikov, Ivan Bobkov, Timofei Bogomazov, Vasilii Chekrygin, Alexandra Exter, I. M. Firsov, Georgii Gol'ts, Nataliia Goncharova, Stanislav Gurvits-Gurskii, N. P. Iankin, Vasilii Kamenskii, G. V. Labunskaia, Mikhail Larionov, Mikhail Le-Dantiu, Viacheslav Levkievskii, Nikolai Lopatin, Lev Shekhtel' (under the psuedonym Ostof'ev), N. D. Pavliuchenko, Sergei Podgaevskii, Sergei Romanovich, Vera Shekhtel', Aleksandr Shevchenko, and Kirill Zdanevich. On a printed insert in Research Institute's copy, the names Nikolai Lapshin and Nikolai Rogovin have been substituted for Lopatin and Pavliuchenko. The exhibition was the fourth organized by Larionov and his associates.

Research Institute's copy inscribed on the title page in black ink "Ot budushchego—proshlomu" (From the future—to the past).

590. ***Nova generatsiia: Zhurnal Levoï formatsiï mistetstv*** (Нова генерация: Журнал Левої формації мистецтв / New generation: Journal of the Left Front of the Arts). Kharkov: [n.p.], 1927–1930. 25 cm.

The Ukrainian version of *Lef* (see no. 436), this monthly journal presented source material and criticism on modern Ukrainian, Russian, and Western European art and literature. Includes examples of Suprematist porcelain and Bauhaus furniture and porcelain; many articles by Kazimir Malevich setting forth his views on contemporary art; and poems, prose, and criticism by Nikolai Aseev, Osip Brik, Nikolai Chuzhak, Sergei Kirsanov, Vladimir Mayakovsky, Viktor Pertsov, Grigorii Petnikov, Viktor Shklovskii, and Sergei Tret'iakov.

A total of 3 issues published in 1927, after which *Nova generatsiia* became a monthly.

Research Institute's holdings: scattered issues.

591. ***Novaia rampa*** (Новая рампа / New footlights). Moscow: Rosfil', 1924. 26 cm.

Weekly organ of the State Academic Theaters and the concert company Russian Philharmony (ROSFIL).

A total of 25 issues published.

Research Institute's holdings: scattered issues.

592. **Nove mystetstvo** (Нове мистецтво / New art). Kharkov: Otdel iskusstva UPP USSR, 1925–1928. 26 cm.

Covers by Vasyl' Iermilov.

Ukrainian journal devoted to theater. Includes reviews and programs for major theaters.

Research Institute's holdings: scattered issues.

593. ***Novyi Lef: Zhurnal levogo fronta iskusstv*** (Новый Леф: Журнал левого фронта искусств / New Lef: Journal of the Left Front of the Arts). Moscow: GIZ, 1927–1928. 24 cm.

Edited by Vladimir Mayakovsky and Sergei Tret'iakov (1928).

Cover photographs and typographical design by Aleksandr Rodchenko.

Monthly journal. *Novyi Lef* was devoted to prose and literary criticism with a special emphasis on photography and cinematography. Includes poetry and prose by Nikolai Aseev, Osip Brik, Sergei Eisenstein, Semen Kirsanov, Boris Kushner, A. Levinskii, Boris Pasternak, V. Petrov, Rodchenko, Viktor Shklovskii, Varvara Stepanova, Tret'iakov, and Dziga Vertov.

A total of 24 issues published. Revival of *Lef*. (See no. 436.)

Research Institute's holdings: scattered issues.

594. ***Novyi zritel': Teatral'nyi ezhenedel'nik MONO*** (Новый зритель: Театральный еженедельник МОНО / New spectator: Theatrical weekly of MONO). Moscow: Novaia Moskva, 1924–1929. 26 cm.

Edited by Vera Inber and O. K. Kameneva. Editorial committee included S. Girinis, V. Tikhonovich, and N. Tsenin.

Covers by Petr Galadzhev, Semen Gershtein, Nikolai Lukhmanov, Aleksandr Rodchenko, K. Savitskii, and Konstantin Vialov.

Organ of the Moscow Department of Public Education (MONO).

Weekly journal dedicated to theater, circus, and film. Includes short articles, reviews, programs, and librettos from productions by major Russian theaters.

Subtitle varies.

Research Institute's holdings: scattered issues.

595. **Obolenskaia, Iuliia.** *Voina korolei: Iz serii "Petrushka," Kukol'nyi teatr* (Война королей: Из серии "Петрушка," Кукольный театр / War of the kings: From the Puppet theater's Petrushka series). Moscow and Petrograd: Izd. Teatral'nogo otdela Narodnogo komissariata prosveshcheniia, 1918. [16] leaves. 26 × 35 cm.

Text by Obolenskaia. Illustrations by Konstantin Kandaurov and Obolenskaia, lithographed by R. Bakhman.

Research Institute's copy signed on front cover by Konst[antin] Tverskoi.

596. **Obshchestvo khudozhnikov moskovskoi shkoly** (Society of Artists of the Moscow School). *1-ia vystavka Obshchestva khudozhnikov moskovskoi shkoly* (1-я выставка Общества художников московской школы / First

exhibition of the Society of Artists of the Moscow School). Moscow: [n.p.], 1917. 8 pp. 17 cm.

597. **Obshchestvo khudozhnikov-stankovistov** (Society of Easel Artists). *Katalog pervoi vystavki* (Каталог первой выставки / Catalog of the first exhibition). Moscow: [OST], 1925. 8 pp. 17 cm.

598. ———. *OST: Katalog vtoroi vystavki* (ОСТ: Каталог второй выставки / OST: Catalog of the second exhibition). Moscow: Khudozhestvennyi otdel Glavnauki N.K.P., 1926. 16 pp. 17 cm.

599. **Obshchestvo moskovskikh khudozhnikov** (Society of Moscow Artists). *Katalog vystavki kartin i skul'ptury Obshchestva moskovskikh khudozhnikov* (Каталог выставки картин и скульптуры Общества московских художников / Catalog of an exhibition of pictures and sculpture by the Society of Moscow Artists). Moscow: Obshchestvo moskovskikh khudozhnikov, 1929. 31 pp., [40] plates. 15 cm.

600. **Obshchestvo russkikh skul'ptorov** (Society of Russian Sculptors). *Katalog 2-i vystavki skul'ptury Obshchestva russkikh skul'ptorov ORS* (Каталог 2-й выставки скульптуры Общества русских скульпторов ОРС / Catalog of the second sculpture exhibition of the Society of Russian Sculptors ORS). Moscow: Izd. Glavnauki, 1927. 16 pp. 17 cm.

601. ———. *Katalog 4-i vystavki skul'ptury Obshchestva russkikh skul'ptorov ORS, 1929–1931* (Каталог 4-й выстаки скульптуры Общества русских скульпторов ОРС, 1929–1931 / Catalog of the fourth sculpture exhibition of the Society of Russian Sculptors ORS, 1929–1931). Moscow: Ogiz-Izogiz, 1931. 14 pp. 19 cm.

Cover by Vladimir Favorskii.

602. ***Ocharovannyi strannik: Al'manakh intuitivnoi kritiki i poezii.*** (Очарованный странник: Альманах интуитивной критики и поэзии / The enchanted wanderer: Miscellany of intuitive criticism and poetry). St. Petersburg: Ego Futuristy, 1913–1916. 28 cm.

Edited by Viktor Khovin.

A periodical published by the Ego-Futurists, *Ocharovannyi strannik* advocated Ego-Futurism as a continuation of the decadent ideas circulating at the turn of the century. Their enthusiasm for Oscar Wilde is shown in the quotations from Wilde that appear on the covers of all issues except the final one. Includes essays by Khovin and Samuil Vermel', a bibliography of contemporary publications, and poems by Russian Symbolists such as Zinaida Hippius and Fedor Sologub, by Ego-Futurists such as Dmitrii Kriuchkov, Igor' Severianin, and Vadim Shershenevich, and by Cubo-Futurists such as Elena Guro, Vasilii Kamenskii, and Velimir Khlebnikov. No. 6 (Winter 1914/1915) features an essay by Khovin, "Futurism i voina" (Futurism and the war), which criticizes Filippo Marinetti and discusses Khovin's attitude toward the war. No. 9 (Winter 1915) includes an article by Khovin on Wilde and a portrait of Wilde by Henri Toulouse-Lautrec. No. 10 (Spring 1916) contains a review by Mikhail Matiushin of a lecture on Suprematism given in 1916 by Kazimir Malevich.

Irregularly published. A total of 10 issues published.

603. ***O Furmanove: Sbornik statei*** (О Фурманове: Сборник статей / On Furmanov: A collection of essays). Moscow: Khudozhestvennaia lit-ra, 1931. 159 pp. 21 cm.

Cover by Solomon Telingater.

Essays on the writer Dmitrii Furmanov.

604. **Okhochinskii, Vladimir.** *Plakat, I: Razvitie i primenenie* (Плакат, I: Развитие и применение / The poster, I: Development and use). Leningrad: Akademiia khudozhestv, [1926]. 91 pp., [2] color plates. 18 cm.

Inscribed by Okhochinskii to Moisei Brodskii.

605. ***Oktiabr': Bor'ba za proletarskie klassovye pozitsii na fronte prostranstvennykh iskusstv*** (Октябрь: Борьба за пролетарские классовые позиции на фронте пространственных искусств / October: Struggle for proletarian class positions on the visual arts front). Moscow: Izogiz, 1931. 28 pp. 26 cm.

Designed by El'brus Gutnov, N. Spirov, Solomon Telingater, and members of the October group.

October, founded in 1928 in Moscow, focused on the industrial and applied arts. Telingater's dynamic typography relies on the frequent use of superimposed errors, underlined segments, and varied typefaces. This is the second in a series of 5 general declarations and manifestos published by October.

606. ***Oktiabr' v iskusstve i literature, 1917–1927*** (Октябрь в искусстве и литературе, 1917–1927 / October in art and literature, 1917–1927). Leningrad: Izd. "Krasnoi gazety," [1927]. 85 pp. 24 cm.

Cover, initials, headpieces, and tailpieces are by Sergei Chekhonin. Title page vignette is by A. Fedorovskii.

Five essays by D. M. Aranovich, Evgenii Braudo, Anatoly Lunacharsky, Vsevolod Voinov, and Aleksandr Voronskii.

Research Institute's copy has been rebound, retaining the original cover.

607. **Okunev, Iakov.** *Griadushchii mir: Utopicheskii roman* (Грядущий мир: Утопический роман / The future world: A utopian novel). [Petrograd]: Dlia izd-va "Priboi" ispolneno izd-vom "Tret'ia strazha," 1923. 69 pp. 23 cm.

Cover by Nikolai Akimov.
Includes illustrations by Akimov.

608. **Olesha, Iurii.** *Spisok blagodeianii* (Список благодеяний / List of blessings). Moscow: Federatsiia, 1931. 95 pp. 17 cm.
Cover by Boris Titov.
Play.

609. ———. *Tri tolstiaka: Roman dlia detei* (Три толстяка: Роман для детей / Three fat men: A novel for children). 2nd ed. Moscow and Leningrad: Zemlia i Fabrika, 1930. 188 pp. 23 cm.
Cover by Mstislav Dobuzhinskii.
Includes 25 tipped-in color relief prints by Dobuzhinskii.

610. ———. *3 tolstiaka* (3 толстяка / Three fat men). Moscow: Sov. pisatel', 1935. 207 pp. 22 cm.
Children's book. Includes wood engravings by Vladimir Kozlinskii.

611. ***Oslinyi khvost i Mishen'*** (Ослиный хвост и Мишень / Donkey's Tail and Target). Moscow: Ts. A. Miunster, 1913. 151 pp. 30 cm.
Cover illustration by Mikhail Larionov. It is a detail from his lithograph on leaf [8] of *Mirskontsa*. (See no. 400.)
Miscellany. Includes halftones of works by Nataliia Goncharova, Ivan Larionov, Larionov, Mikhail Le-Dantiu, Viacheslav Levkievskii, Sergei Romanovich, Aleksandr Shevchenko, and Kirill Zdanevich and 12 lithographs by Larionov, 10 of them tipped in. Also contains a manifesto by Rayonists and Futurists, S. Khudakov's article "Literatura, khudozhestvennaia kritika i doklady" (Literature, art criticism, debates and speeches), Larionov's article "Luchistaia zhivopis'" (Rayonist painting), and Varsanofii Parkin's article "Oslinyi khvost i Mishen'." S. Khudakov is "evidently the pseudonym of Il'ia Zdanevich" (Kovtun 1987, 59 n. 31).
From an edition of 525.

612. ***O teatre*** (О театре / On the theater). [Tver]: Tverskoe izd-vo, [1922]. 151 pp. 19 cm.
Cover by Mikhail Sokolov.
Includes contributions by Ivan Aksenov, Boris Arvatov, Emil' Beskin, Oskar Blium, Vladimir Blium, Boris Ferdinandov, Aleksei Gan, V. Rappoport, L. Sabaneev, V. Tikhonovich, and M. Zagorskii.

613. ***Ot Moskvy kupecheskoi k Moskve sotsialisticheskoi*** (От Москвы купеческой к Москве социалистической / From merchant Moscow to socialist Moscow). Moscow: Ogiz-Izogiz, 1932. Title leaf, 22 plates. In portfolio. 20 × 34 cm.
Design by Varvara Stepanova.

Plates include brief excerpts from a speech given in 1931 by Lazar' Kaganovich, "Za sotsialisticheskuiu rekonstruktsiiu Moskvy i gorodov SSSR" (In support of the socialist reconstruction of Moscow and other cities of the USSR). The design incorporates photographs by Boris Ignatovich, Kazachinskii, Eleazar Langman, Aleksandr Rodchenko, and V. Savel'ev and photographs from institutional sources.

614. **Pakhomov, Aleksei.** *Leto* (Лето / Summer). Leningrad: Ogiz, 1927. [8] pp. 29 cm.

Children's book composed entirely of color illustrations.

615. **Pamphlets on early Soviet film.** Pamphlets published by Roskino. Moscow: Roskino, 1932–1933. 15 cm.

Research Institute has 31 pamphlets in this series. Each is devoted to a single film and provides a brief statement of the theme, a longer synopsis, a social and political discussion of the film, and suggestions for group activities (e.g., meetings, exhibitions, wall newspapers, and slogans and themes for posters).

616. ———. *Populiarnaia kino-bibliotechka. Bibliotechka kino-akterov* (Популярная кино-библиотечка. Библиотечка кино-актеров / Popular film library. Library of film actors). Moscow: Kinopechat', [1926–1928?]. 16 pp. 16 cm.

Covers by Petr Galadzhev, Mikhail Getmanskii, Mark Kirnarskii, E. Semenova, N. S. Sokolik, and Konstantin Vialov.

Research Institute has 62 pamphlets in this series, all of which are illustrated. Each is devoted to a single actor or actress, Soviet or foreign. Sergei Eisenstein and Viktor Shklovskii wrote the issue on Aleksandra Khokhlova.

617. ———. *V pomoshch' kino-zriteliu* (В помощь кино-зрителю / An aid for the filmgoer). Moscow: Tea-Kino-Pechat', [1926–1929?]. 8 pp., including cover. 13 cm.

Covers by Iakov Guminer and others.

Research Institute has 242 pamphlets in this series, most of which are illustrated. Each is devoted to a single film or, in a few cases, to 2 films. Both Soviet and foreign films are represented. Each pamphlet consists primarily of a plot synopsis, but cast and production credits also are given.

618. **Parnakh, Valentin.** *Gontcharova, Larionow: L'art décoratif théâtral moderne.* Paris: La Cible, 1919. 18 pp., [14] plates. In portfolio. 33 cm.

The plates include 2 *pochoirs* by Nataliia Goncharova and 4 by Mikhail Larionov, all but 1 of them on folded double sheets, 33 × 50 cm., folded to 33 × 25.

Copy 304 of 515. Inscribed by Jacques Povolozky, the publisher, to André Salmon and dated 2 September 1919.

619. ———. *Motdinamo* (Worddynamo). Paris: La Cible, 1920. 25, [1] leaf, [15] plates. 18 cm.

Cover by Nataliia Goncharova.

Poems. Includes 8 lithographs by Goncharova and 7 by Mikhail Larionov. The Russian title *Slovodvig* (an invented term suggesting "words set in motion") and imprint appear on leaf [26].

620. ———. *Samum* (Самум / Dynamic word). Paris: Kvo Nah, 1919. 43 pp., [3] plates. 23 cm.

Poems. Includes 3 illustrations by Nataliia Goncharova.

621. **Pasternak, Boris.** *Poverkh bar'erov: Stikhi raznykh let* (Поверх барьеров: Стихи разных лет / Above the barriers: Verse of various years). Moscow and Leningrad: Gos. izd-vo, 1929. 159 pp. 20 cm.

622. ———. *Spektorskii* (Спекторский). Moscow and Leningrad: Khudozhestvennaia lit-ra, 1931. 62 pp. 15 cm.

Poem.

623. [———]. *Gruzinskie liriki* (Грузинские лирики / Georgian poets). Translated by Boris Pasternak. Moscow: Sov. pisatel', [1937]. 72 pp. 18 cm.

Cover by A. Sokolov.

Translated from the Georgian.

624. ***Pedagogicheskii teatr*** (Педагогический театр / Pedagogical theater). Moscow: Gos. masterskaia Pedagogicheskogo teatra Glavsotsvosa Narkomprosa, 1925–1926. 27 cm.

Design supervised by L. R. Svirskii.

Pedagogicheskii teatr, published in editions of 2,000, was the first miscellany in this series published by the Central Studio of the Pedagogical Theater of the People's Commissariat for Education (Narkompros).

A total of 2 issues published.

Research Institute's holdings: scattered issues.

625. **Pereleshin, Boris, Aleksandr Rakitnikov, and Ippolit Sokolov.** *A.* [Moscow]: RSFSR, 1921. 14 pp. 17 cm.

Poems.

626. ***Perevoz DaDa—Transbordeur DaDa*** (Перевоз ДаДа—/ Transportation DaDa—). Berlin and Paris: Izd. Gomeopat, 1922–1949. 25 cm.

Pamphlets of Dada poetry and prose written and published by the artist and poet Serge Charchoune. The first 3 pamphlets in the series were published in Berlin, and the remainder were published in Paris. Contains text in French and Russian. No. 6 is described as part of the series *Pressovannaia kniga* (A pressed book).

A total of 13 issues published.

Research Institute's holdings: scattered issues.

627. **Pertsov, Viktor.** *Literatura zavtrashnego dnia* (Литература завтрашнего дня / The literature of tomorrow). Moscow: Izd-vo "Federatsiia," 1929. 173 pp. 21 cm.

Cover by Aleksandr Rodchenko.

628. ***Pervaia Konnaia*** (Первая Конная / First Cavalry Army). Moscow: Ogiz-Izogiz, 1938. [235] pp. 36 cm.

Book design by Aleksandr Rodchenko and Varvara Stepanova.

A volume commemorating the exploits of Marshal Budennyi's forces during the civil war. Includes photographs by M. G. Prekhter, Rodchenko, I. M. Shagin, Arkadii Shaikhet, and the photo laboratory of the State Publishing House for the Fine Arts (Izogiz) and text by Oleg Leonidov.

Research Institute's copy is missing the illustrated folding slipcase.

629. ***1 Olimpiada teatrov i iskusstv narodov SSSR: Iiun'–iiul', Moskva*** (1 Олимпиада театров и искусств народов СССР: Июнь-июль, Москва / First olympiad of the theaters and arts of the peoples of the USSR: June–July, Moscow). [Moscow]: Orgkomitet Olimpiady and Gosizdat RSFSR, 1930. [40] pp. 23 cm.

Layout and cover by Solomon Telingater.

Contains text in English, German, and Russian.

630. ***1-aia vseobshchaia germanskaia khudozhestvennaia vystavka*** (1-ая всеобщая германская художественная выставка / First general German art exhibition). Moscow and Leningrad: Mezhrabpom, 1924. 36 pp. 22 cm.

631. ***Pervaia Vsesoiuznaia spartakiada, Moskva 1928 g., i Zimniaia rabochaia spartakiada, Oslo*** (Первая Всесоюзная спартакиада, Москва 1928 г., и Зимняя рабочая спартакиада, Осло / First All-Union Spartakiad, Moscow 1928, and Winter Workers' Spartakiad, Oslo). Edited by V. Mikhel's. Moscow: Fizkul'tura i sport, 1928. [162] pp. and 10 pp. of advertisements. 23 × 31 cm.

Cover by Avenir Chernomordik. Title page by Vsevolod Filippov. Layout by Chernomordik, Filippov, and Nikolai Shebuev.

Includes gravures printed in brown and green ink, as well as relief halftones printed in black.

Dedication on title page in German, signed by Leo Limberg in purple ink.

632. ***1-aia vystavka lubkov*** (1-ая выставка лубков / First exhibition of popular prints). Moscow: [n.p.], 1913. 32 pp. 19 cm.

Catalog of exhibition of *lubki* (popular prints) and objects, both Russian and foreign, organized by "D. N. Vinogradov" (corrected to N. D. Vinogradov in pencil on the title page) and held in Moscow 19–24 February 1913. Includes an introduction by Mikhail Larionov, who organized a similar exhibition that took place in Moscow the following month. The last section of the catalog lists 5 sketches by Nataliia Goncharova for "popular" prints, and the *lubok*-inspired cover of the catalog may be hers as well.

633. ***Peta: Pervyi sbornik*** (Пета: Первый сборник / Peta: First collection). Moscow: Peta, 1916. 48 pp., [2] plates. 23 cm.

Includes illustrations by Aleksandr Lopukhin and Fedor Platov and contributions by Nikolai Aseev, Sergei Bobrov, Konstantin Bol'shakov, Velimir Khlebnikov, Lopukhin, Platov, Evgenii Shilling, and Sergei Tret'iakov.

Copy 31 of the first 50, on heavy paper and with a special cover, from the total edition of 200.

634. **Petnikov, Grigorii.** *Kniga izbrannykh stikhotvorenii* (Книга избранных стихотворений / Book of selected poems). [Kharkov]: Gos. izd-vo Ukrainy, 1930. 100 pp. 18 cm.

Front and back covers by Kazimir Malevich.

Includes a silhouette of Petnikov by Dmitrii Mitrokhin.

635. ———. *Porosl' solntsa: 3-'ia kniga stikhov* (Поросль солнца: 3-ья книга стихов / Young shoots of the sun: Third book of verse). Moscow: Liren', 1918. 15 pp., 2 plates. 25 cm.

Includes illustrations by Mariia Siniakova.

Copy 99. Inscribed by Petnikov to Nikolai Nikolaevich Pernik (?) and dated Moscow, May 1920.

636. **Petritskii, Anatolii.** *Teatral'ni stroi* (Театральні строї / Theater design). [Kharkov]: Derzh. vyd-vo Ukrainy, 1929. 23 pp., [57] plates. 35 cm.

Includes text by Vasyl' Khmuryi.

Inscribed by Vsevolod Meyerhold.

637. ***5 × 5 = 25: Vystavka zhivopisi*** (5 × 5 = 25: Выставка живописи / 5 × 5 = 25: An exhibition of painting). Moscow: [Klub V.S.P.], 1921. [12] leaves. 18 cm.

Catalog of an exhibition that took place at the Club of the All-Russia Poets Union, Moscow, in September 1921. The 5 artists, each of whom exhibited 5 works, were Alexandra Exter, Liubov' Popova, Aleksandr Rodchenko, Varvara Stepanova, and Aleksandr Vesnin. One original work by each is tipped in.

Composed of hectographed and typescript pages. Covers for each catalog were created by Rodchenko or Stepanova. The cover of the Research Institute's copy is by Rodchenko.

638. ***Plan vtoroi piatiletki*** (План второй пятилетки / Goals of the second Five-Year Plan). Leningrad: Ogiz-Izogiz, 1935. In portfolio. 24 × 35 cm.

Sixteen color relief prints with statistical pictographs on pictorial backgrounds, of the sort recommended by Ivan Ivanitskii in *Izobrazitel'naia statistika i venskii metod.* (See no. 271.)

639. **Platov, Fedor.** *Nazad, chtoby moia istina ne razdavila vas* (Назад, чтобы моя истина не раздавила вас / Back, or my truth will crush you). Aleksandr Lopukhin. *Prorok, kotoryi govorit: 3 grafiki* (Пророк, который говорит: 3 графики. / A prophet who simply speaks: Three prints). Moscow: Peta, 1915. 24 pp., [3] plates. 21 cm.

Platov's work consists of apothegms in the spirit of Friedrich Nietzsche. Inscribed by Platov to Fedor Semenovich Bogorodskii.

640. **Polonskii, Viacheslav.** *Russkii revoliutsionnyi plakat* (Русский революционный плакат / The Russian revolutionary poster). [Moscow]: Gos. izd-vo, 1925. 192 pp., [56] plates. 35 cm.

Cover by "K. E. B."

Several pages bear the ownership stamp of Gr[igorii] Fedorov in purple ink.

641. **[Popova, Liubov'].** *Katalog posmertnoi vystavki khudozhnika konstruktora L. S. Popovoi* (Каталог посмертной выставки художника конструктора Л. С. Поповой / Catalog of the posthumous exhibition of Constructivist artist L. S. Popova). Moscow: [VKhUTEMAS], 1924. 12 pp., [12] plates. 17 cm.

Cover by Aleksandr Rodchenko (Lavrent'ev 1989, 149).

642. ***Poruganie moshchei iskusstva. Otkrytoe pis'mo Maiakovskomu*** (Поругание мощей искусства. Открытое письмо Маяковскому / Profanation of the relics of art. An open letter to Mayakovsky). [Moscow]: Kn-vo "Khobo" pri Tvorcheskom biuro Nichevokov, [1922]. iv pp. 28 cm.

Free supplement to *Sobachii iashchik.* (See no. 727.) *Poruganie moshchei iskusstva* is signed by Riurik Rok, Sergei Sadikov, and Boris Zemenkov. *Otkrytoe pis'mo Maiakovskomu* is signed by Petr Miturich.

From an edition of 75.

643. ***Poshchechina obshchestvennomu vkusu: Stikhi, proza, stat'i*** (Пощечина общественному вкусу: Стихи, проза, статьи / A slap in the face of public taste: Verse, artistic prose, essays). Moscow: G. L. Kuz'min, [1912]. 112 pp. 23 cm.

Includes contributions by David and Nikolai Burliuk, Wassily Kandinsky, Velimir Khlebnikov, Aleksei Kruchenykh, Benedikt Livshits, and Vladimir Mayakovsky.

From an edition of 600 (*Knizhnaia letopis'* 1913, no. 1776). Inscribed by Kruchenykh to Kornelii Zelinskii and dated 14 September 1962. In the inscription Kruchenykh describes himself as one of the book's few surviving contributors 50 years after its appearance, and the only one still living in the Soviet Union. He confesses to entertaining the fantastic hope of living to see the book's next 50-year anniversary. Bound in burlap (26 cm. tall).

644. ***Proektor*** (Проектор / Projector). Moscow: I. Ermol'ev, 1915–1918. 29 cm.

Edited by I. Ermol'ev.

Biweekly journal dedicated to cinematography.

Publisher varies.

Research Institute's holdings: scattered issues.

645. ***Programmy Gosudarstvennykh Akademicheskikh teatrov*** (Программы Государственных Академических театров / Programs of the State Academic Theaters). Moscow: Upravlenie gos. Akademicheskimi teatrami, 1925–1927. 26 cm.

Edited by M. Morgenshtein.

Theatrical weekly. Contains programs and librettos for productions at major Moscow theaters.

A total of 93 issues published. Continuation of *Programmy Moskovskikh gosudarstvennykh i Akademicheskikh teatrov i zrelishchnykh predpriiatii* (Programs of Moscow state and academic theaters and public entertainment [1922–1923]). Continued by *Sovremennyi teatr* (Contemporary theater [1927–1929]).

Research Institute's holdings: scattered issues.

646. ***Prohrama Mizhnarodn'oho konkursu na proiekt Derzhavnoho ukraïns'koho teatru masovoho muzychnoho diistva na 4.000 cholovika, v m. Kharkovi*** (Програма Міжнародного конкурсу на проєкт Державного українського театру масового музичного дійства на 4.000 чоловіка в м. Харкови / Prospectus for an international competition to design the 4,000-seat Ukrainian state theater for large-scale musical performances in the city of Kharkov). Kharkov: Kharkivs'kyi okruzhnyi vykonavchyi komitet; Mis'ka rada; Komitet spryiannia budivnytstvu, 1930. 183 pp. 29 cm.

Design by Adol'f Strakhov.

There are 5 sections, in Ukrainian, Russian, German, English, and French respectively. Each section is annotated in blue ink, changing the deadline for submissions to the competition from 25 December to 30 December 1930. Inserted is a folded map showing the site of the proposed theater.

647. **Prokof'ev, Boris.** *Edikt o vselennizme gorodam Peterburgu, Moskve: Vselennskoe iskusstvo* (Эдикт о вселеннизме городам Петербургу, Москве: Вселеннское искусство / Edict concerning Cosmism, addressed to the cities of St. Petersburg and Moscow: Cosmic art). St. Petersburg: Vselennskii gong, 1914. 15 pp. 27 cm.

648. ***Proletarskoe foto*** (Пролетарское фото / Proletarian photo). Moscow: Soiuzfoto i OZPKF, 1931–1933. 25 cm.

Edited by A. Ianskii.

Artistic, methodological, scientific, and technical journal. Contains photographs by Boris Ignatovich, Aleksandr Rodchenko, and Arkadii Shaikhet and a section devoted to reviews of domestic and international periodicals. No. 2 (1931) contains a review of the illustrated journal *SSSR na stroike*. (See no. 752.) No. 3 (1932) includes a section dedicated to John Heartfield and his use of photomontage.

Published monthly in 1931 and biweekly thereafter. Continuation of *Sovetskoe foto*. (See no. 747.) Continued by *Sovetskoe foto* (Soviet photo [1934–1991]).

Research Institute's holdings: scattered issues.

649. ***Proletarskoe kino*** (Пролетарское кино / Proletarian cinema). Moscow: Proletkino, 1925. [13] pp. 34 cm.

Edited by I. N. Bursak.

A total of 1 issue published.

650. ***Proletarskoe kino: Organ Assotsiatsii rabotnikov revoliutsionnoi kinematografii*** (Пролетарское кино: Орган Ассоциации работников революционной кинематографии / Proletarian cinema: Monthly journal of the Association of Workers of Revolutionary Cinematography). Moscow: GIKhL, 1931–1932. 25 cm.

Irregularly published. Continuation of *Kino i zhizn'*. (See no. 325.) Continued by *Sovetskoe kino* (1933–1935). (See no. 748.)

Research Institute's holdings: scattered issues.

651. **Pudovkin, Vsevolod.** *Kino-rezhisser i kino-material* (Кино-режиссер и кино-материал / The cinema director and cinematic material). Moscow: Kinopechat', 1926. 92 pp. 16 cm.

Front flyleaf and title page inscribed by Lubomír Linhart. Research Institute's copy rebound and heavily annotated.

652. **Puni, Ivan.** *Sovremennaia zhivopis'* (Современная живопись / Contemporary art). Berlin: L. D. Frenkel', 1923. 36 pp., [24] plates. 32 cm.

653. **Punin, Nikolai.** *Andrei Rublev*. Petrograd: Apollon, 1916. 23 pp., [5] plates. 26 cm.

Monograph on the early fifteenth-century icon painter.

654. ———. *Noveishie techeniia v russkom iskusstve* (Новейшие течения в русском искусстве / Current trends in Russian art). 2 vols. Leningrad: Gos. russkii muzei, 1927–1928. 18 cm.

Vol. 1, *Traditsii noveishego russkogo iskusstva* (Traditions of current Russian art), has a relief halftone cover illustration after Vladimir Tatlin's drawing *Rybaki* (Fishermen). Vol. 2, *Predmet i kul'tura* (Object and culture), has a relief halftone cover illustration after Lev Bruni's drawing *Les* (Forest).

655. ———. "*Pamiatnik III Internatsionala*": *Proekt khud. V. E. Tatlina* («Памятник III Интернационала»: Проект худ. В. Е. Татлина / *Monument to the Third International:* A project of the artist V. E. Tatlin). St. Petersburg: Otdel izobrazitel'nykh iskusstv N.K.P., 1920. [4] pp. 28 cm.

656. ———. *Pervyi tsikl lektsii, chitannykh na kratkosrochnykh kursakh dlia uchitelei risovaniia: Sovremennoe iskusstvo* (Первый цикл лекций, читанных на краткосрочных курсах для учителей рисования: Современное искусство / First cycle of lectures, delivered at short courses for teachers of drawing: Contemporary art). Petrograd: Otdel izobrazit. iskusstva Narkomprosa, 1920. 84 pp. 22 cm.

Front and back covers have Suprematist designs by Kazimir Malevich.

657. ———. *Tatlin: Protiv kubizma* (Татлин: Против кубизма / Tatlin: Against Cubism). St. Petersburg: Gos. izd-vo, 1921. 25 pp., [16] plates. 30 cm.

658. ***Rabis: Organ Ts.K. Vserabisa*** (Рабис: Орган Ц. К. Всерабиса / Rabis: Organ of the Central Committee of All-Union Art Workers Union). Moscow: Ts.K. Vserabis, 1927–1934. 26 cm.

Weekly organ of the Central Committee of All-Union Art Workers Union (Vserabis), which was dedicated to theater, cinema, the circus, and music. Rabis was a trade union for workers who were active in the realm of arts and was primarily concerned with issues related to education, libraries, and culture in general. The union was founded in May 1919 and was headed by Iuvenal Slavinskii, who was its first president. It was later known as Sorabis, a shortened form of Soiuz rabotnikov iskusstv (Union of Art Workers).

Irregularly published. Continuation of *Vestnik rabotnikov iskusstv* (Art workers bulletin [1920–1926]).

Research Institute's holdings: scattered issues.

659. ***Raboche Krest'ianskaia Krasnaia Armiia*** (Рабоче Крестьянская Красная Армия / Worker and Peasant Red Army). Moscow: Izogiz, 1934. [7] pp., [200] plates, including folded photomontage frontispiece. 31 × 35 cm.

Design by El Lissitzky.

Includes photographs printed in a variety of tonalities—black, blue, sepia, and purple.

Bound with attached slipcase that folds out to support the volume at an angle for display.

660. ***Rabochie zhilishcha: Primernye proekty*** (Рабочие жилища: Примерные проекты / Workers' housing: Model projects). [Leningrad]: Izd-vo N.K.T. "Voprosy truda," 1924. 17 pp., [32] plates. 30 × 39 cm.
Cover by Aleksandr Vesnin.
Includes text by E. V. Vilents-Gorovits and the architect A. K. Ivanov and projects by N. Chaikovskii, Sergei Chernyshev, K. A. Greinert, Aleksandr Ivanitskii, Ivanov, Viktor Kokorin, Nikolai Kolli, Boris Korshunov, Edgar Norvert, Leonid Vesnin.

661. ***Rabochii i teatr*** (Рабочий и театр / Worker and theater). Leningrad: Kul'totdel LGSPS i Upravlenie Gos. Akademicheskimi teatrami, 1924–1937. 27 cm.
Illustrated journal dedicated to the performing arts in Leningrad and Moscow.
Irregularly published. Publisher varies. Continued by *Iskusstvo i zhizn'* (Art and life [1938–1941]).
Research Institute's holdings: scattered issues.

662. ***Rabochii zritel'*** (Рабочий зритель / Workers' spectator). Moscow: MGSPS, 1923–1925. 26 cm.
Theatrical and artistic weekly. No. 25/26 (1924) contains a review of the first exhibition of German art in the USSR, organized by the Historical Museum in Moscow. The exhibition of German art produced from 1914 until 1924 included works by Expressionists as well as by socially conscious artists from a group called Veritas. This issue also features a painting by Otto Dix and programs and librettos from the major theaters in Moscow.
Research Institute's holdings: scattered issues.

663. ***Radio*** (Радио / Radio). [Sevastopol]: Taran, [1919?]. 12 pp., [1] plate. 30 cm.
Includes a portrait of Vadim Baian by Vladimir Mayakovsky and poems by Baian, Mariia Kalmykova, and Boris Poplavskii.

664. ***Radio slushatel'*** (Радио слушатель / Radio listener). Moscow: Izd. NKPT, 1928–? 32 cm.
Cover by Aleksandr Rodchenko.
Illustrated weekly that includes program notes of radio selections as well as current events, health tips and exercises, and advertisements. The cover design incorporates a central spiral motif through which a photograph on the first page is seen, creating a different montage for each issue.
Research Institute's holdings: scattered issues.

665. **Radishchev, Leonid.** *Svet i teni* (Свет и тени / Light and shadows). Biblioteka zhurnala "Iunyi proletarii." [Leningrad]: Krasnaia gazeta, 1929. 116 pp. 20 cm.
Cover signed "WK" (?).
Collection of previously published feuilletons.

666. **Radlov, Nikolai.** *O futurizme* (О футуризме / On Futurism). St. Petersburg: Akvilon, 1923. 68 pp. 18 cm.

667. **Radlova, Anna.** *Korabli: Vtoraia kniga stikhov* (Корабли: Вторая книга стихов / Ships: Second book of verse). St. Petersburg: Alkonost, 1920. 56 pp. 17 cm.
668. ———. *Krylatyi gost': Tret'ia kniga stikhov* (Крылатый гость: Третья книга стихов / Winged guest: Third book of verse). [Petrograd]: Petropolis, 1922. 55 pp. 17 cm.
Inscribed by Sasha Kondratov and Radlova.

669. **Rafalovich, Sergei.** *Mark Antonii: Tragediia* (Марк Антоний: Трагедия / Mark Antony: A tragedy). Berlin: Kn-vo pisatelei, 1923. 67 pp. 20 cm.
Cover by Ivan Puni.
670. ———. *Speculum animae* (Mirror of the soul). [St. Petersburg]: Shipovnik, [1911]. 98 pp. 25 cm.
Cover by Sergei Chekhonin.
Title page vignettes by Vladimir Chembers.
Poems. Includes illustrations by Boris Anisfel'd, Chekhonin, Mstislav Dobuzhinskii, D. E. Iakovlev, and Sergei Sudeikin.

671. **Remizov, Aleksei. Elektron** (Электрон / Electron). St. Petersburg: Alkonost, 1919. 32 pp. 16 cm.
Cover by Remizov.
Rhythmic prose on the end of the world, arranged on the page like verse.
672. ———. *O sud'be ognennoi* (О судьбе огненной / On fiery destiny). [Petrograd]: Segodnia, [1918]. [4] pp. 20 cm.
Cover by Elena Turova.
Retelling of a legend from Heraklitus of Ephesus. Includes illustrations by Turova.
673. ———. *Snezhok* (Снежок / Snowball). [Petrograd]: Segodnia, [1918]. [4] pp. 20 cm.
Cover by Elena Turova.
Children's story. Includes illustrations by Turova.

674. ***Repertuar Sinei bluzy*** (Репертуар Синей блузы / The repertory of the Blue Blouse). Moscow: MGSPS "Trud i kniga," 1928. 27 cm.

Edited by Boris Iuzhanin.

Monthly newspaper presenting current events in a music-hall format of songs and sketches skewed to proletarian ideology. Contains numerous articles by members of the company and costume designs by Dani, Liubov' Popova, and Varvara Stepanova. Iuzhanin was the founder of Blue Blouse workers' groups in 1923 at the Moscow Institute of Journalism. The name of these theatrical groups and their journal was derived from the loose blue smocks worn by the factory workers.

A total of 2 issues published. Continuation of *Siniaia bluza* (Blue blouse [1924–1928]).

Research Institute's holdings: scattered issues.

675. **Rodchenko, Aleksandr.** Archive of Jan Tschichold. Letters.

Two handwritten letters (with 1 typed German-language translation) written by Rodchenko to Tschichold, dated 28 October 1931 and 20 November 1931. Rodchenko informs Tschichold about various publications they were exchanging, including the journal *Lef.* (See no. 436.)

676. ———. Memoir of Vladimir Mayakovsky. 1936. 5 pp.

Includes a brief account of Rodchenko's work with Mayakovsky on posters, a characterization of Mayakovsky's manner and appearance, and transcriptions of dedications from books that Mayakovsky presented to Rodchenko, Rodchenko's wife, Varvara Stepanova, and their daughter, Mul'ka.

Typescript.

677. **Rodov, Semen.** *Stal'noi stroi: Stikhi, 1921–1922* (Стальной строй: Стихи, 1921–1922 / Ranks of steel: Verse, 1921–1922). Tver: Oktiabr', 1923. 82 pp. 17 cm.

Cover by Noskov.

678. **Roginskaia, Frida.** *Sovetskii tekstil'* (Советский текстиль / Soviet textiles). Moscow: AKhR, 1930. 96 pp., [47] plates. 17 cm.

679. **Roizman, Matvei.** *Khevronskoe vino* (Хевронское вино / Wine of Hebron). Moscow: Vseros. soiuz poetov, 1923. 46 pp. 19 cm.

Cover by Georgii Echeistov.

Poems.

680. **Roizman, Matvei, and Vadim Shershenevich.** *Krasnyi alkogol'* (Красный алкоголь / Red alcohol). [Moscow]: Imazhinisty, 1922. 22 pp. 24 cm.

Cover by Boris Erdman.

Poems.

Contains Roizman's dedicatory inscription on p. [5] in purple ink, dated

Saturday, 10 December 1921: "Serditomu Vasiliiu Pavlovichu ot blagodarnago za stroguiu kritiku pervykh moikh stikhov" (To an angry Vasilii Pavlovich from one who is grateful for exacting criticism of his first verses). "Vasilii Pavlovich" may be Vasilii Pavlovich Bobrov.

681. **Rok, Riurik.** *Ot Riurika Roka chteniia: Nichevoka poema* (От Рюрика Рока чтения: Ничевока поэма / Readings from Riurik Rok: Poem of a Nothingist). Moscow: Khobo, 1921. 15 pp. 18 cm.

Cover by Grigorii Miller.

Copy 355, signed and numbered by Rok and with a dedicatory inscription by him dated 1 January 1921: "Milomu Borisu v znak krepkoi druzhby i v pozhelan'e skorogo vyzdorovlen'ia ot ekspressionizma" (Fondly to Boris in firm friendship and in hopes of a speedy recovery from Expressionism). "Boris" may be Boris Zemenkov.

682. ———. *Sorok sorokov: Dialekticheskie poemy, nichevokom sodeiannye* (Сорок сороков: Диалектические поэмы, ничевоком содеянные / Forty forties: Dialectical poems committed by a Nothingist). Moscow: Khobo, 1923. 32 pp. 22 cm.

Cover by Boris Zemenkov.

Includes illustrations by Zemenkov.

683. ***Roman-gazeta*** (Роман-газета / Novel-Gazette). Moscow: "Moskovskii rabochii," 1927–?. 30 cm.

Bimonthly publication. No. 21 (1930), "Poeziia revoliutsii" (Poetry of revolution), compiled by M. Svetlov, features verses by the most famous poets of the time, including Nikolai Aseev, Aleksandr Bezymenskii, Valerii Briusov, Sergei Esenin, Vladimir Mayakovsky, and Boris Pasternak. Their poetry is separated into groups such as "Krest'ianskie poety" (Peasant poets), "Proletarskie poety" (Proletarian poets), and "Konstruktivisty" (Constructivists).

Publisher varies.

Research Institute's holdings: scattered issues.

684. **Rozanova, Ol'ga.** *Pervaia gosudarstvennaia vystavka, 1918–1919 g.: Katalog posmertnoi vystavki kartin, etiudov, eskizov, i risunkov O. V. Rozanovoi* (Первая государственная выставка, 1918–1919 г.: Каталог посмертной выставки картин, этюдов, эскизов, и рисунков О. В. Розановой / First state exhibition, 1918–1919: Catalog of the posthumous exhibition of paintings, studies, sketches, and drawings by O. V. Rozanova). Moscow: V.Ts.V.B. Otdela izobrazitel'nykh iskusstv Narkomprosa, 1919. vi, 5 pp. 15 cm.

Includes an introduction by Ivan Kliun.

685. **Rozental', Mark.** *Protiv vul'garnoi sotsiologii v literaturnoi teorii* (Против вульгарной социологии в литературной теории / Against vulgar sociol-

ogy in literary theory). Moscow: Khudozhestvennaia lit-ra, 1936. 157 pp. 18 cm.

686. **Rubakin, Aleksandr.** *Gorod: Stikhi* (Город: Стихи / The city: Verse). Paris: AR, 1920. 54 pp., [9] plates. 26 cm.
Cover by Nataliia Goncharova.
Includes illustrations and vignettes by Goncharova.
The French title appears on the back cover: *La cité* (The city). Copy 311 of 325. Text is written in longhand by the author, primarily on folded double leaves (some of which are unopened). Entire volume is reproduced by lithography.

687. ***Der Russische Revolutionsfilm.*** Schaubücher, 2. Zurich and Leipzig: Orell Füssli, 1929. 16 pp., [72] plates. 19 cm.
Includes an introduction by Anatoly Lunacharsky.

688. **Russkaia Akademiia Khudozhestvennykh Nauk** (Russian Academy of Artistic Sciences). Papers. 1921.
Includes 4 pp. of the statutes of the academy that were officially approved at the meetings of the Artistic Committee on 30 September and 5 October 1921, signed by the academy's president, P. Kogan. The statutes are divided into the following sections: general principles, scientific organization, members, organs of the academy, and administration. Also includes a list of the academy's 71 active members, minutes from 4 sessions of the academy (25 and 30 August and 1 and 20 September 1921), and a detailed list of papers read at 26 of the plenary session meetings held between June and September in 1921. The minutes from the 20 September session also include a lecture delivered by P. P. Lazar'ev entitled "O vospriiatii tsveta" (On color perception). The list of papers includes an outline of "Osnovnye elementy zhivopisi" (The basic elements of painting), read by Wassily Kandinsky on 1 September 1921, and the text of "Organizatsionnaia rol' iskusstva" (The organizational role of art), read by Aleksandr Bogdanov on 29 October 1921.

689. ***Russkii khudozhestvennyi farfor: Sbornik statei o Gosudarstvennom farforovom zavode*** (Русский художественный фарфор: Сборник статей о Государственном фарфоровом заводе / Russian art porcelain: A collection of essays on the State Porcelain Factory). Edited by Erikh Gollerbakh and Mstislav Farmakovskii. Leningrad: Gos. izd-vo, 1924. 162 pp., [33] plates. 31 cm.
Essays emphasizing production of the preceding 5 years, including revolutionary porcelain, with some attention to the factory's earlier history. Includes relief halftones, partly in color, and a few collotypes.

690. ***Russkoe iskusstvo*** (Русское искусство / Russian art). Moscow: Tvorchestvo, 1923. 30 cm.

Edited by S. A. Abramov.

Journal dedicated to painting, graphic art, sculpture, folk art, literature, theater, music, and dance. The publisher's symbol on the title page was designed by Lev Bakst, and the lettering for the cover title was designed by Sergei Chekhonin. No. 1 includes an article by Marietta Shaginian on Kuz'ma Petrov-Vodkin; an article by Nikolai Punin on Vladimir Tatlin's stage design for Velimir Khlebnikov's play *Zangezi* (see no. 315); a review of *Erste Russische Kunstausstellung* (First Russian art exhibition) in 1922 in Berlin's Galerie Van Diemen (see no. 167); and reviews of the exhibition *5 × 5 = 25* (see no. 637) and shows by the Society of Young Artists (OBMOKhU), the World of Art group, and the New Society of Painters (NOZh). The cover illustration is a photograph of a work by Petr Konchalovskii. The double issue no. 2/3 contains an article by Abram Efros on Pavel Kuznetsov; an essay by David Arkin on Robert Fal'k; a feature discussing the history and activities of the Institute of Artistic Culture (INKhUK); an article by Erik Gollerbakh on the State Porcelain Factory in Petrograd that discusses Suprematist porcelain produced by Il'ia Chashnik, Kazimir Malevich, and Nikolai Suetin; and an essay on the State Museum of New Western Art, which contains the famous Sergei Shchukin and Ivan Morozov collections. Editions also published in English, French, and German.

A total of 3 issues published.

691. ***Rykaiushchii Parnas: Futuristy*** (Рыкающий Парнас: Футуристы / Roaring Parnassus: The Futurists). St. Petersburg: Zhuravl', [1914]. 119 pp. 22 cm.

Cover illustration by Ivan Puni.

Includes illustrations by David and Vladimir Burliuk, Pavel Filonov, Puni, and Ol'ga Rozanova and poems by David and Nikolai Burliuk, Elena Guro, Vasilii Kamenskii, Velimir Khlebnikov, Aleksei Kruchenykh, Benedikt Livshits, Vladimir Mayakovsky, and Igor' Severianin. Also contains "Tonal'nosti glasnykh" (Tonalities of vowels), 18 scales composed of the vowels of the Russian alphabet by "Elachich." Mikhail Matiushin, who published *Rykaiushchii Parnas* together with Puni, managed to distribute only a few hundred copies before the police confiscated the rest of the edition on the grounds that the illustrations by Filonov and David Burliuk were indecent (Khardzhiev 1976, 155).

692. ***Rzhanoe slovo: Revoliutsionnaia khrestomatiia futuristov*** (Ржаное слово: Революционная хрестоматия футуристов / Rye word: The Futurists' revolutionary reader). [Petrograd]: IMO, 1918. 58 pp. 27 cm.

Cover by Vladimir Mayakovsky (Katanian 1985, 153).

Previously published poems on the theme of revolution. Includes a foreword by Anatoly Lunacharsky, a prose passage by Boris Kushner, and poems by Nikolai Aseev, David Burliuk, Vasilii Kamenskii, Velimir Khlebnikov, and Mayakovsky.

693. ***Sadok sudei*** (Садок судей / A trap for judges). 2 vols. [St. Petersburg]: Zhuravl', [1910–1913]. Vol. 1: 131 leaves, 13 cm. Vol. 2: 107 pp., 20 cm.

Vol. 1 contains 9 illustrations by Vladimir Burliuk, including portraits of all of the literary contributors (except Ekaterina Nizen and A. M. Gei) and literary works by David Burliuk, Nikolai Burliuk, Gei, Elena Guro, Vasilii Kamenskii, Velimir Khlebnikov, S. Miasoedov, and Elena's sister, Ekaterina Guro (under the pseudonym Nizen). Vol. 2 includes illustrations by David Burliuk, Vladimir Burliuk, Nataliia Goncharova, Mikhail Larionov, and Guro and literary works by David Burliuk, Nikolai Burliuk, Guro, Khlebnikov, Aleksei Kruchenykh, Benedikt Livshits, Vladimir Mayakovsky, Nizen, and the 13-year-old "Militsa." An essay by Khlebnikov is wrongly credited to David Burliuk (Markov 1968, 54), and there are 7 illustrations by Guro, not 6 as given in the contents.

Vol. 1 is said to be from an edition of 300 (*Knizhnaia letopis'* 1910, no. 11495), although most copies may never have been released because the printing bill was not paid (Markov 1968, 22). Vol. 2 is from an edition of 800 (*Knizhnaia letopis'* 1913, no. 6267). Vol. 1 is printed on paste side of sheets of wallpaper in 2 striped patterns and is covered in a third wallpaper patterned with small circles and diamonds. Vol. 2 is printed on heavy, light-green paper and is covered in a flowered wallpaper. In Research Institute's copy, the caption mistakenly crediting the illustration on p. [91] to Guro has been blacked out and replaced by one crediting David Burliuk, the actual artist.

694. ***Satirikon*** (Сатирикон / Satyricon). St. Petersburg: R. Golike i A. Vil'borg, 1908–1914. 38 cm.

Research Institute's holdings: scattered issues.

695. ***Satirikon*** (Сатирикон / Satyricon). Paris: Mikhail Kornfel'd, 1931. 35 cm.

Edited by Mikhail Kornfel'd.

Covers by Iurii Annenkov (under the pseudonym A. Sharago).

Weekly publication of literary and artistic satire and humor for Russian émigrés in Paris. (Kornfel'd had published a prerevolutionary Russian periodical of the same name from 1908 to 1914.) Illustration was overseen by Annenkov. Contains numerous illustrations, some colored, by Aleksandr Benua, Ivan Bilibin, Mstislav Dobuzhinskii, Ivan Iakovlev, and Konstantin Korovin and literary contributions by M. Aldanov, Nina Berberova, Ivan Bunin, Valentina Khodasevich, Aleksandr Kuprin, and Aleksei Remizov.

696. **Sel'vinskii, Il'ia.** *Komandarm 2* (Командарм 2 / Commander of the Second Army). Moscow and Leningrad: Gos. izd-vo, 1930. 159 pp., 1 plate. 21 cm.
Cover by A. Surikov (*Knizhnaia letopis'* 1930, no. 30257).
Verse drama.

697. ———. *Pushtorg: Roman* (Пушторг: Роман / Fur-trading company: A novel). 2nd ed. Moscow: Khudozhestvennaia lit-ra, 1931. 192 pp. 20 cm.
Dust jacket signed "A. S.," for A. Surikov.
In verse.

698. ———. *Rannii Sel'vinskii* (Ранний Сельвинский / Early Sel'vinskii). Moscow and Leningrad: Gos. izd-vo, 1929. 255 pp. 18 cm.
Poems.

699. ———. *Ulialaevshchina: Epopeia* (Улялаевщина: Эпопея / The Ulialaev uprising: An epic). [4th ed.] Moscow: Khudozhestvennaia lit-ra, 1935. 126 pp. 18 cm.
Poem.

700. ———. *Zapiski poeta: Povest'* (Записки поэта: Повесть / Notes of a poet: A tale). Moscow and Leningrad: Gos. izd-vo, 1928. 91 pp., 1 folded sheet. 17 cm.
Cover by El Lissitzky.
In verse. The cover incorporates Lissitzky's double-exposure portrait of Hans Arp made in 1924, with Arp's head in 2 positions against the background of a page from the Dadaist periodical *391*.
Signed on the title page by I. Al'pin.

701. **Semenko, Mykhail', Mikola Bazhan, and Heo Shkurupii.** *Zustrich na perekhresnii stantsii* (Зустріч на перехресній станції / Meeting at a transfer station). Kiev: Bumerang, 1927. 48 pp. 18 cm.
Cover by Vladimir Tatlin.
Poems by each of the 3 authors and *Rozmova tr'okh* (Three-way conversation), a short sketch written by them jointly.

702. **Severianin, Igor'.** *Prolog "Ego-futurizm": Poeza-grandioz; apofeoznaia tetrad' tret'ego toma* (Пролог «Эго-футуризм»: Поэза-грандиоз; апофеозная тетрадь третьего тома / The prologue "Ego-Futurism": A grand poeza, the apotheosis of the third volume). Broshiura 32. St. Petersburg: Ego, 1911. 3 pp. 22 cm.
Poeza is an invented term suggesting an especially grand poem.
Inscribed on p. 1 by Severianin to Kornei Chukovskii and dated 13 November 1911. Also with the later signature of Pavel Chaikin.

703. **Severianin, Igor', and Aleksei Masainov.** *Ostrova ocharovanii: Al'manakh 2-kh* (Острова очарований: Альманах 2-х / Islands of enchantment: A miscellany with two contributors). Petrograd: Ariel, 1917. 79 pp. 24 cm.
Poems.

704. **Shaginian, Marietta.** *Kak ia pisala "Mess-Mend": K postanovke "Miss-Mend" Mezhrabpom–Rus'* (Как я писала «Месс-Менд»: К постановке «Мисс-Менд» Межрабпом-Русь / How I wrote *Mess-Mend:* On the occasion of the production of *Miss Mend* by International Workers' Aid–Russia). Moscow: Kinopechat', 1926. 16 pp. 17 cm.

The film *Miss Mend* appeared in 1926. Shaginian maintained that the 2 words of the novel's title *Mess-Mend* were chosen at random by her cat from an English dictionary and were not to be construed as "Miss Mend."

705. ———. *Lori Len metallist* (Лори Лен металлист / Laurie Lane, metal worker). 9 vols. Moscow and Leningrad: Gos. izd-vo, 1925. 18 cm.

Covers by Aleksandr Rodchenko.

Serialized detective novel written under the pen name Jim Dollar, supposedly an American worker in Moscow. The photomontage front covers feature Constructivist color typography.

Inscribed by Shaginian.

706. ———. *Mess mend; ili, Ianki v Petrograde* (Месс менд; или, Янки в Петрограде / Mess mend; or, A Yankee in Petrograd). 10 vols. Moscow and Leningrad: Gos. izd-vo, 1924. 18 cm.

Front covers and most back covers by Aleksandr Rodchenko.

Serialized detective novel written under the pen name Jim Dollar. The story blends adventure plot and revolutionary ideology and contains Soviet satire targeted at American capitalism and the bourgeois lifestyle. The photomontage front covers feature Constructivist color typography.

Inscribed by Shaginian.

707. ———. *Novyi byt i iskusstvo* (Новый быт и искусство / The new everyday life and art). [Tbilisi]: Zakkniga, [1926]. 93 pp. 17 cm.

Cover by Aleksandr Rodchenko.

Essay.

708. **Shershenevich, Vadim.** *Bystr': Monologicheskaia drama* (Быстрь: Монологическая драма / Rapids: A monological drama). Moscow: Izd-vo "Pleiady," 1916. 40 pp. 22 cm.

In verse.

Copy 363 of 500.

709. ———. *2 × 2 = 5: Listy imazhinista* (2 × 2 = 5: Листы имажиниста / 2 × 2 = 5: Leaves of an Imagist). Moscow: Imazhinisty, 1920. 48 pp. 18 cm.

Cover by Boris Erdman.

Essays on Imagism.

710. ———. *Futurizm bez maski: Kompiliativnaia introduktsiia* (Футуризм без маски: Компилятивная интродукция / Futurism unmasked: A compilational introduction). Moscow: Iskusstvo, [1913] (cover date 1914). 105 pp. 18 cm.

711. ———. *Komu ia zhmu ruku* (Кому я жму руку / Who I shake hands with). [Moscow]: Imazhinisty, [1924]. 48 pp. 24 cm.

Essay.

712. ———. *Kooperativy vesel'ia: Poemy* (Кооперативы веселья: Поэмы / Cooperatives of merriment: Poems). [Moscow]: Imazhinisty, 1921. 32 pp. 23 cm.
Cover by Boris Erdman.
Inscribed by Shershenevich to Boris Zemenkov with the saying "V obshchem rusle bystree tech'" (Water flows faster in one common channel).

713. ———. *Odna sploshnaia nelepost'* (Одна сплошная нелепость / Pure nonsense). Moscow: Imazhinisty, 1922. 51 pp. 22 cm.
Verse drama.

714. ———. *Smeshno o kino* (Смешно о кино / A laughing look at the movies). Moscow: Tea-kino-pechat', 1928. 32 pp. 16 cm.
Eleven short sketches.
Supplement to the journal *Sovetskii ekran.* (See no. 745.)

715. ———. *Vechnyi zhid: Tragediia velikolepnogo otchaianiia* (Вечный жид: Трагедия великолепного отчаяния / The eternal Jew: A tragedy of magnificent despair). 3rd ed. Moscow: Chikhi-Pikhi, [1916]. [32] pp. 21 cm.
In verse.

716. [———]. Georges Duhamel and Charles Vildrac. *Teoriia svobodnogo stikha: Zametki o poeticheskoi tekhnike* (Теория свободного стиха: Заметки о поэтической технике / Theory of free verse: Notes on poetic technique). Translated by Vadim Shershenevich. Moscow: Imazhinisty, 1920. 48 pp. 18 cm.
Translation of *Notes sur la technique poétique.*

717. **Shevchenko, Aleksandr.** *Neo-primitivizm: Ego teoriia, ego vozmozhnosti, ego dostizheniia* (Нео-примитивизм: Его теория, его возможности, его достижения / Neoprimitivism: Its theory, its possibilities, its accomplishments). Moscow: [n.p.], 1913. 31 pp., 12 plates. 22 cm.

718. ———. *Printsipy kubizma i drugikh sovremennykh techenii v zhivopisi vsekh vremen i narodov* (Принципы кубизма и других современных течений в живописи всех времен и народов / The principles of Cubism and other contemporary trends in the painting of all times and peoples). Moscow: A. Shevchenko, 1913. 24 leaves, [9] plates. 17 cm.
Cover by Shevchenko.
Includes 2 lithographs by Victor Barthe, 1 by Nataliia Goncharova, 1 by Mikhail Larionov, 2 by Shevchenko, 2 by Illarion Skuie, and "a drawing by a child."

719. [———]. Aleksei Grishchenko and N. Lavrskii. *A. Shevchenko: Poiski i dostizheniia v oblasti stankovoi zhivopisi* (А. Шевченко: Поиски и достижения в области станковой живописи / A. Shevchenko: Experiment and accomplishment in easel painting). Moscow: Otdel izobrazitel'nykh iskusstv Narkomprosa, 1919. 34 pp., 22 plates. 30 cm.
Cover by Shevchenko.
Plates 18 and 21 are missing.

720. **Shklovskii, Viktor.** *Tret'ia fabrika* (Третья фабрика / Third factory). Novosti russkoi literatury. Moscow: Krug, 1926. 139 pp. 17 cm.
Cover signed "IR" in roman characters, for Ivan Rerberg (*Knizhnaia letopis'* 1926, no. 18298).
Reminiscences.

721. ———. *"Tristram Shendi" Sterna i teoriia romana* («Тристрам Шенди» Стерна и теория романа / Sterne's *Tristram Shandy* and the theory of the novel). Sborniki po teorii poeticheskogo iazyka. [St. Petersburg]: OPOIaZ, 1921. 38 pp. 20 cm.

722. ———. *Turksib* (Турксиб / Turkestan-Siberian Railway). 2nd ed. Moscow and Leningrad: Gos. izd-vo, 1930. 32 pp. 21 cm.
Design and cover by V. Lantsetti and M. Seregin.
Children's book.

723. ———. *Voskreshenie slova* (Воскрешение слова / Resurrection of the word). [Petrograd]: EUY, 1914. 16 pp. 21 cm.
Originally delivered as a lecture at the *Brodiachaia sobaka* (Stray Dog Cabaret) in St. Petersburg.

724. ———. *Zoo; ili, Pis'ma ne o liubvi* (Зоо; или, Письма не о любви / Zoo; or, Letters not about love). Berlin: Gelikon, 1923. 109 pp. 21 cm.
Epistolary novel.

725. **Shtorm, Georgii.** *Karma ioga: Poema* (Карма иога: Поэма / Karma yoga: A poem). Rostov-na-Donu: Vseros. soiuz poetov, Rostovskoe-na-Donu otd-nie, 1921. 31 pp., [1] plate. 23 cm.
Cover by Grigorii Miller.
Includes an illustration by Miller.

726. **Sidorov, Aleksei.** *Russkaia grafika za gody revoliutsii, 1917–1922* (Русская графика за годы революции, 1917–1922 / Russian graphics in the years of revolution, 1917–1922). Moscow: Dom pechati, 1923. 113 pp. 24 cm.
Cover by Aleksei Kravchenko.

727. ***Sobachii iashchik; ili, Trudy Tvorcheskogo biuro Nichevokov vtechenie 1920–1921 g.g.*** (Собачий ящик; или, Труды Творческого бюро Ничевоков втечение 1920–1921 г.г. / Dog's box; or, Works by the Creative Office of the Nothingists during 1920–1921). Edited by Sergei Sadikov. Moscow: Khobo, 1921 (cover date 1922). 14 pp. 25 cm.
This "first issue" consists of parodistic literary declarations and manifestos. Sadikov was the chief secretary of the "Tvornichbiuro" (Creative Office of the Nothingists). Other members signing the organizational protocol of 20 August 1920 at Rostov-on-Don are Oleg Erberg, Susanna Mar, Elena Nikolaeva, Aleksandr Ranov, Riurik Rok, and Devis Umanskii. Boris Zemenkov contributed a "Dekret o zhivopisi" (Decree on painting).
From an edition of 500.

728. ***Sofii Georgievne Mel'nikovoi: Fantasticheskii kabachek, Tiflis 1917, 1918, 1919*** (Софии Георгиевне Мельниковой: Фантастический кабачек, Тифлис 1917, 1918, 1919 / To Sofiia Georgievna Mel'nikova: Fantastic tavern, Tbilisi 1917, 1918, 1919). Tbilisi: 41°, 1919. 190 pp., [2] folded plates. 18 cm.

Cover illustration by Kirill Zdanevich.

Miscellany with tipped-in illustrations by Aleksandr Bazhbeuk-Melikov, Nataliia Goncharova, Lado Gudiashvili, Iliazd, Mikhail Kalashnikov, Igor' Terent'ev, Sigizmund Valishevskii, and Zdanevich; literary contributions (some of them in Georgian or Armenian) by Aleksandr Chachikov, Nikolai Cherniavskii, Dmitrii Gordeev, Paolo Iashvili, Iliazd, Kara-Darvish, Vasilii Katanian, Aleksei Kruchenykh, Grigol Robakidze, Grigorii Shaikevich, Titsian Tabidze, Terent'ev, Nina Vasil'eva, and Tat'iana Vechorka; and a chronology of activity by the 41° group in Tbilisi from 1917 to 1919, including lectures and publications by Iliazd, Kruchenykh, and Terent'ev. Iliazd's contribution is *Asel naprakat* (Donkey for rent), the second play in his pentalogy *Aslaablich'ia* (Aspects of a donkey). The 2 folded plates are typographical fantasies by Iliazd, 1 of them in color.

Copy 154 of 180.

729. ***Soiuz molodezhi*** (Союз молодежи / Union of Youth). St. Petersburg: Soiuz molodezhi, 1912–1913. 24 cm.

Organ of the Union of Youth group, which was founded in 1910 and consisted of Hylaea poets and artists such as Pavel Filonov and Ol'ga Rozanova.

Magazine published in editions of 500 and 1,000 copies. No. 1 (1912) includes Persian miniatures, the first part of Vladimir Markov's article "Printsipy novogo iskusstva" (The principles of new art), Ivan Shkol'nik's article "Muzei sovremennoi russkoi zhivopisi" (The museum of modern Russian painting), Eduard Spandikov's article "Po povodu referata S. Bobrova 'Russkii purizm'" (Regarding S. Bobrov's paper "Russian purism"), and translations of Chinese poetry. No. 2 (1912) includes works by Filonov, P. Poipava, Rozanova, Shkol'nik, Ts. Ia. Shleifer, and Spandikov; the conclusion of Markov's article "Printsipy novogo iskusstva"; 2 Futurist manifestos signed by Giacomo Balla, Umberto Boccioni, Cario Carra, Luigi Russolo, and Gino Severini (translated from *Les peintres Futuristes Italiens—Exposition du lundi 5 au samedi 24 fevrier 1912 chez M. M. Bernheim-Jeune et Cie*); Henri Le Fauconnier's essay "Proizvedenie iskusstva" (The work of art), originally published as an introduction to the second exhibition of *Neue Künstler-Vereinigung* (New union of artists), held in Munich from 1910 to 1911; an article by Elie Faure on Kees van Dongen; and letters by van Dongen. No. 3 (1913) includes maxims about art by Spandikov, "Labirint iskusstva" (The labyrinth of art); Rozanova's article "Osnovy novogo tvorchestva i prichiny ego neponimaniia" (The foundations of new creativity and the reasons for misunderstanding it); Nikolai Burliuk's article "Vladimir Davidovich Burliuk:

Ego tvorchestvo" (Vladimir Davidovich Burliuk: His art); Velimir Khlebnikov's essay "Uchitel' i uchenik. O slovakh, gorodakh i narodakh. Razgovory" (The teacher and his pupil. About words, cities, and people. Conversations); a prose poem by Elena Guro; and poems by David Burliuk, Nikolai Burliuk, Khlebnikov, Aleksei Kruchenykh, and Benedikt Livshits.

Irregularly published. A total of 4 issues published.

Research Institute's holdings: scattered issues.

730. **Soiuz molodezhi** (Union of Youth). *Katalog vystavki kartin obshchestva khudozhnikov "Soiuz molodezhi"* (Каталог выставки картин общества художников «Союз молодежи» / Catalog of an exhibition of paintings by the society of artists "Union of Youth"). [St. Petersburg: n.p.], 1912. 29 pp. 15 cm.

Cover by M. Iasenskii.

731. **Sokolov, Ippolit.** *Bedeker po ekspressionizmu* (Бедекер по экспрессионизму / A Baedeker for Expressionism). [Moscow: n.p.], 1920. 8 pp. 20 cm.

Essay.

732. ———. *Bunt ekspressionista* (Бунт экспрессиониста / Revolt of an Expressionist). Moscow: Izd., konechno, avtora, 1919. 16 pp. 12 cm.

Poems and a manifesto.

733. ———. *Ekspressionizm* (Экспрессионизм / Expressionism). [Moscow?: n.p.], 1920. 7 pp. 21 cm.

Essay.

734. ———. *Imazhinistika* (Имажинистика / Imagistics). [Moscow]: Ordnas, 1921. 14 pp. 26 cm.

Essay.

735. ———. *Polnoe sobranie sochinenii: Tom I, ne stikhi* (Полное собрание сочинений: Том I, не стихи / Complete works: Volume 1, not poetry). Nonposthumous ed. Moscow: [n.p., 1919]. [13] pp. 12 cm.

Poems.

736. ———. *Renessans XX veka: Manifest* (Ренессанс XX века: Манифест / The Renaissance of the twentieth century: A manifesto). Moscow: [n.p.], 1920. 8 pp. 21 cm.

737. ———. *Sistema trudovoi gimnastiki* (Система трудовой гимнастики / System of calisthenics in the workplace). Moscow: [n.p.], 1922. 19 pp. 18 cm.

Essay.

738. **Sokolov-Mikitov, Ivan.** *Zasuponia* (Засупоня). Petrograd: Segodnia, [1918]. [4] pp. 20 cm.

Cover by N. I. Liubavina.

Children's story. Includes illustrations by Liubavina. *Zasuponia* is the name of a pine cone, a character in the story.

Copy 89 of 125 that were colored by hand, from a total edition of 1,000 (*Knizhnaia letopis'* 1918, no. 2900).

739. **Sologub, Fedor.** *Charodeinaia chasha: Stikhi* (Чародейная чаша: Стихи / Magic chalice: Verse). St. Petersburg: Epokha, 1922. 46 pp. 23 cm.
Signed on p. [1] by Lev Tarasov in black ink.

740. ———. *Fimiamy* (Фимиамы / Incense). St. Petersburg: Stranstvuiushchii entuziast, [1921] (cover date 1920). 105 pp. 14 cm.
Cover by Vladimir Konashevich (Sidorov 1923, 95).
Poems. Includes 83 vignettes by Konashevich (Sidorov 1923, 95).

741. ———. *Koster dorozhnyi* (Костер дорожный / Roadside campfire). Moscow and Petrograd: Tvorchestvo, 1922. 45 pp. 18 cm.
Poems.

742. ———. *Svirel': Russkie berzherety* (Свирель: Русские бержереты / Pan pipes: Russian bergerettes). St. Petersburg: Petropolis, 1922. 61 pp. 13 cm.
Poems. Bergerettes are eighteenth-century French songs, pastoral in form.

743. ***Sovetskaia arkhitektura*** (Советская архитектура / Soviet architecture). Moscow: Gos. nauchno-tekhnicheskoe izd-vo, 1931–1934. 31 cm.
Cover and design by Varvara Stepanova.
Nos. 1 and 2/3 (1931) contain articles on the Bauhaus, Le Corbusier, and designs by various Russian architectural organizations such as the Society of Urban Architects (ARU), the Association of New Architects (ASNOVA), the Society of Proletarian Architects of Armenia (OPRA), the Division of Architects for Socialist Construction (SASS), and the All-Union Association of Proletarian Architects (VOPRA).
A total of 6 issues published.
Research Institute's holdings: scattered issues.

744. ***Sovetskie subtropiki*** (Советские субтропики / The Soviet subtropics). Moscow: Zhurnal'no-gazetnoe ob"edinenie, 1934. 216 pp. (1 folded). 30 cm.
Design by El and Es (Sophie) Lissitzky.
Special issue of the journal *Ogonek* (Little fire [1923–]).

745. ***Sovetskii ekran*** (Советский экран / Soviet screen). Moscow: Kino-izd. RSFSR, 1925–1929. 29 cm.
Illustrated weekly dedicated to Russian and foreign cinematography.
Publisher varies. Continuation of *Ekran kino-gazety*. (See no. 148.) Continued by *Kino i zhizn'*. (See no. 325.)
Research Institute's holdings: scattered issues.

746. ***Sovetskii farfor*** (Советский фарфор / Soviet porcelain). Moscow: Moskovskoe khudozhestvennoe izd-vo, 1927. 21 pp., [16] plates. 26 cm.

Cover by Sergei Chekhonin.
Includes articles by Anatoly Lunacharsky.

747. ***Sovetskoe foto*** (Советское фото / Soviet photo). Moscow: Ogonek, 1926–1931. 26 cm.
Edited by Mikhail Kol'tsov and V. Mikulin.
Organ of the Committee in Charge of Cinematography at the Council of People's Commissars USSR (SNK USSR).
Monthly journal dedicated to questions of amateur photography and photojournalism. Includes Aleksandr Rodchenko's photographs.
Continued by *Proletarskoe foto*. (See no. 648.)
Research Institute's holdings: scattered issues.

748. ***Sovetskoe kino*** (Советское кино / Soviet cinema). Moscow: Zhurnal'no-gazetnoe ob"edinenie, 1933–1935. 25 cm.
Monthly organ of the Russian Association of the Workers of Revolutionary Cinematography.
Continuation of *Proletarskoe kino: Organ Assotsiatsii rabotnikov revolitsionnoi kinematografii.* (See no. 650.) Continued by *Iskusstvo kino* (Cinema art [1936–]).
Research Institute's holdings: scattered issues.

749. ***Sovetskoe kino: Ezhemesiachnyi organ Khudozhestvennogo soveta po delam kino pri Glavpolitprosvete*** (Советское кино: Ежемесячный орган художественного совета по делам кино при Главполитпросвете / Soviet cinema: The monthly organ of the Artistic Council in Charge of Cinema Under Glavpolitprosvet). Moscow: Knigoizd. RSFSR, 1925–1928. 35 cm.
Edited by Osip Beskin and K. A. Mal'tsev.
Cover and layout by Varvara Stepanova.
No. 4 (1927), which focuses on Soviet movies for children and reviews of American achievements in children's films, contains 2 photographs by Aleksandr Rodchenko, including a double-exposure photograph of the painter Aleksandr Shevchenko in 1924 and a still from the movie *Moskva* (Moscow), directed by Mikhail Kaufman and Il'ia Kopalin.
Publisher varies.
Research Institute's holdings: scattered issues.

750. ***Soviet Cinema.*** Edited by Aleksandr Arosev. Moscow: VOKS, 1935. 312 pp. 27 cm.
Design by Aleksandr Rodchenko and Varvara Stepanova.
Includes a photomontage by Rodchenko and Stepanova.
Research Institute also has a copy of the French-language edition published in Moscow by VOKS in 1936 under the title *Le cinéma en l'URSS.*

751. ***Sovremennaia arkhitektura*** (Современная архитектура / Contemporary architecture). Moscow: Glavnoe upravlenie nauchnymi uchrezhdeniiami, 1926–1930. 29 cm.

Editorial committee included Aleksei Gan, Moisei Ginzburg, and Aleksandr Vesnin.

Covers by Aleksei Gan, E. Nekrasov, Varvara Stepanova, and Solomon Telingater.

Organ of the Union of Contemporary Architects (OSA), which was founded in Moscow in 1925.

Focuses on ideas about new Soviet architecture and the current theory and practice of architects such as Walter Gropius, Le Corbusier, Erich Mendelsohn, and Frank Lloyd Wright. Covers feature Gan's Constructivist designs. Titles of articles are in German as well as Russian.

Publisher varies.

Research Institute's holdings: scattered issues.

752. ***SSSR na stroike*** (СССР на стройке / USSR in construction). Moscow: Ogiz-Izogiz, 1930–1949. 42 cm.

Edited by G. Piatakov. Associate editing by Maxim Gorky.

Covers by El Lissitzky, Aleksandr Rodchenko, and Varvara Stepanova.

Design and layout by Lissitzky.

Monthly illustrated propaganda journal produced for export and concerned with the construction of various Soviet industries, Soviet civil aviation, and Soviet achievements in agriculture, sports, theater, and culture. Includes photomontages by Lissitzky. Rodchenko and Stepanova together produced photomontages for 10 thematic issues, including the construction of the White Sea Canal (1933), the culture of Kazakhstan (1935), Soviet parachuting (1935), the Soviet production of gold (1937), elections to the Supreme Soviet (1938), the twentieth anniversary of the State Commission for the Electrification of Russia (GOERLO [1941]). Lissitzky produced the cover and layout for the issues dedicated to the fifteenth anniversary of the Red Army (1933), the fifteenth anniversary of the industry of Azerbaijan (1935), the Russian navy (1937), the Stalinist constitution (1937), and the Stalin Grand Canal of Fergama (1940). Editions also published in English, French, and German. In 1937 a Spanish-language edition was launched.

Continued by *Sovetskii soiuz* (Soviet Union [1950–1992]).

Research Institute's holdings: scattered issues.

753. ***SSSR stroit sotsializm*** (СССР строит социализм / The USSR builds socialism). Moscow: Izogiz, 1933. xxv, 282 pp., 2 plates. 35 cm.

Design by El Lissitzky.

754. **[Strakhov, Adol'f].** S. E. Raevskii. *Plakat A. Strakhova* (Плакат А. Страхова / A. Strakhov's posters). Kharkov: Mystetstvo, 1936. 39 pp., [18] plates. 30 cm.

755. ***Strakh: P'esa v 4 deistviiakh A. Afinogenova*** (Страх: Пьеса в 4 действиях А. Афиногенова / Fear: A play in four acts by A. Afinogenov). Leningrad: Leningradskii gos. teatr dramy, 1931. 48 pp. 14 cm.

Discussion of Nikolai Petrov's staging of *Fear* and the theater's program in general. The cover reproduces the production's poster by Nikolai Akimov, who was also the stage designer. Other illustrations are by T. E. Vizel'.

756. ***Strelets*** (Стрелец / The archer). St. Petersburg: Izd. Strelets, 1915–1922. 26–29 cm.

Edited by Aleksandr Belenson.

Covers by David Burliuk and Nikolai Kul'bin.

The miscellany includes illustrations by Aleksei Remizov for his prose sketches "Rebiatishkam kartinki" (Drawings for kids), Futurist drawings by David Burliuk, Kul'bin (of which 1 is a portrait of Filippo Marinetti), Ol'ga Rozanova, and Mariia Siniakova, and additional illustrations by Natan Al'tman, Marc Chagall, Mstislav Dobuzhinskii, Vladimir Lebedev, and Ivan Puni.

Irregularly published. A total of 3 issues published.

Research Institute's copy of issue 3 is no. 201 of 300.

757. **Stroitel'naia komissiia EKOSO RSFSR** (Building Commission of the Economic Conference of the RSFSR). *Tipovye proekty i konstruktsii zhilishchnogo stroitel'stva, rekommenduemye na 1930 g.* (Типовые проекты и конструкции жилищного строительства, рекомендуемые на 1930 г. / Model projects and housing designs recommended for 1930). Moscow: Gos. tekhnicheskoe izd-vo, 1929. 155 pp. 36 cm.

The projects and text in the book were developed by Mikhail Barshch, Moisei Ginzburg, Iosif Gurevich, Nikolai Krasil'nikov, El Lissitzky, S. V. Orlovskii, Aleksandr Pasternak, Vladimir Vel'man, I. I. Verezubov, and Viacheslav Vladimirov.

758. ***Stroitel'stvo Moskvy*** (Строительство Москвы / Construction of Moscow). Moscow: Moskovskii sovet rabochikh, krest'ianskikh i krasnoarmeiskikh deputatov, 1924–1941. 30 cm.

Design by Vladimir and Gregorii Stenberg.

Organ of the Moscow District Executive Committee (Mosoblispolkom).

Monthly journal dedicated to industrial building, municipal building, planning of the so-called social towns (such as Great Moscow and the Green City), collective farm building, and the industrialization of construction.

Vol. 6, no. 5 (May 1929) features a cover by El Lissitzky.
Research Institute's holdings: scattered issues.

759. **Struve, Aleksandr.** *Plasticheskie etiudy: Stikhotvoreniia dlia "Tantsev pod slovo"* (Пластические этюды: Стихотворения для «Танцев под слово» / Eurythmic studies: Poems for "Dances to verbal accompaniment"). Moscow: B. V. Reshke, [1913]. 32 pp. 28 cm.
Cover by Iwerm.

760. ***Studiia impressionistov: Kniga 1-aia*** (Студия импрессионистов: Книга 1-я / The Impressionists' studio: First book). Edited by Nikolai Kul'bin. St. Petersburg: N. I. Butkovskaia, [1910]. 127 pp. 28 cm.
Cover by Liudmilla Shmit-Ryzhova.
Includes illustrations and vignettes by A. A. Andreev, Kul'bin, A. A. Nikolaev, Shmit-Ryzhova, N. M. Siniagin, and Evgenii Vashchenko and literary contributions by David Burliuk, Nikolai Burliuk, Nikolai Evreinov, Velimir Khlebnikov, and Kul'bin.
Bears the ownership stamp of K. Ia. Goleizovskii.

761. **Tairov, Aleksandr.** *Zapiski rezhissera* (Записки режиссера / Notes of a director). [Moscow]: Kamernyi teatr, 1921. 189 pp. 23 cm.
Cover by Alexandra Exter.
Includes illustrations and initials by Exter.
Inscribed by Tairov. Research Institute also has copies of 2 editions of the German-language translation published in Potsdam by G. Kniepenheuer in 1923 and 1927 under the title *Das entfesselte Theater* (The unfettered theater). These editions feature covers by El Lissitzky.

762. ***Tamare Platonovne Karsavinoi: Brodiachaia sobaka, 26 marta 1914 g.*** (Тамаре Платоновне Карсавиной: Бродячая собака, 26 марта 1914 г. / To Tamara Platonovna Karsavina: The Stray Dog Cabaret, 26 March 1914). [St. Petersburg]: Brodiachaia sobaka, [1914]. [24] pp. 21 cm.
Tributes to the ballerina Karsavina in prose, verse, and music. Includes portraits of Karsavina by Ludwig Kainer, John Singer Sargent, Valentin Serov, Savelii Sorin, and Sergei Sudeikin and literary contributions by Anna Akhmatova, Nikolai Evreinov, Nikolai Gumilev, and Mikhail Kuzmin. The Stray Dog Cabaret was in Petrograd.
On violet coated paper. The literary and musical contributions are reproduced in the authors' handwriting, some in gold ink.

763. **Tarabukin, Nikolai.** *Opyt teorii zhivopisi* (Опыт теории живописи / Essay on the theory of painting). Moscow: Vseros. proletkul't, 1923. 69 pp. 22 cm.
Cover by Mikhail Sokolov.

764. ———. *Ot mol'berta k mashine* (От мольберта к машине / From easel to machine). Moscow: Rabotnik prosveshcheniia, 1923. 44 pp. 23 cm.
Cover by Antonina Sofronova.
Essay on artistic theory.

765. **Tcheng, Soumé.** *Kitaianka Sume-Cheng* (Китаянка Суме-Ченг / The Chinese girl Soumé Cheng). Moscow and Leningrad: Gos. izd-vo, 1929. 148 pp. 20 cm.
Design by Aleksandr Rodchenko.
Translation of *Souvenirs d'enfance et de révolution* (Recollections of childhood and revolution).

766. **Te, M.** *Bauta*. Teodor Levit. *Siuzemy dnei* (Сюземы дней / Forests of days). [S. l.]: Sodruzhestvo "Fleity Vagrama," [1921?]. [14], 14 pp. 27 cm.
Mimeographed poems. A *bauta* is a monolith often placed upright at the summit of prehistoric burial mounds or memorial sites.
Inscribed by Levit in pencil.

767. **Terent'ev, Igor'.** *A. Kruchenykh grandiozar'* (А. Крученых грандиозарь / A. Kruchenykh the magnificent). [Tbilisi: 41°, 1919.] 16 pp. 21 cm.
Cover linoleum cut by Dmitrii Gordeev of a drawing by Kirill Zdanevich.
Essay on Kruchenykh as a Futurist poet.
Inscribed by Kruchenykh to Boris Zemenkov on p. 1 in red pencil.

768. ———. *Fakt* (Факт / Fact). [Tbilisi]: 41°, [1919]. 30 pp. 17 cm.
Cover by Iliazd (Chapon 1978, 109).
Poems.

769. ———. *Rekord nezhnosti: Zhitie Il'i Zdanevicha* (Рекорд нежности: Житие Ильи Зданевича / The record for tenderness: A life of Il'ia Zdanevich [Iliazd]). [Tbilisi]: 41°, 1919. 22 pp. 14 × 15 cm.
Cover by Iliazd (Chapon 1978, 109).
Includes illustrations by Kirill Zdanevich.

770. ———. *17 erundovykh orudii* (17 ерундовых орудий / Seventeen nonsensical tools). Tbilisi: 41°, 1919. 32 pp. 17 cm.
Cover by Iliazd (Chapon 1978, 109).
A discussion of contemporary poetry followed by 18 typographically inventive absurdist pronouncements, each occupying single page. Includes 2 linoleum cuts by Dmitrii Gordeev of drawings by Kirill Zdanevich.

771. ———. *Traktat o sploshnom neprilichii* (Трактат о сплошном неприличии / A treatise on total indecency). [Tbilisi]: 41°, [1919]. 15 pp. 22 cm.
Cover by Iliazd (Chapon 1978, 110).
Essay on literature and culture.

772. ***Tetrad' pervaia kruzhka "Adskaia mostovaia"*** (Тетрадь первая кружка «Адская мостовая» / First notebook of the circle "Road to Hell"). Moscow: Most, 1922. 53 pp. 17 cm.

Cover by V. K. Likum.

Poems. The contributors are N. Brzhevskii, Ts. Kron, Nataliia Li, N. N., K. Nikol'skii, and T. Shoven.

773. ***Théâtre des petits comédiens de bois de Julie Sazonowa: Représenté pour la première fois en Hollande par le Grand Bazar Royal, La Haye, 1926.*** [The Hague: Le Grand Bazar Royal, 1926.] [36] pp. 33 cm.

Cover illustration, headpiece, and tailpiece by Nataliia Goncharova.

Includes costume and scenery sketches by Goncharova, Mikhail Larionov, and Nicolas Milliotti; photographs of puppets designed by them; self-portraits by Larionov and Marcel Mihalovici; and portraits of Goncharova by Milliotti, of Milliotti by Goncharova, and of Frank Martin by V. Rodionov.

774. **Toporkov, A. K.** *Tekhnicheskii byt i sovremennoe iskusstvo* (Технический быт и современное искусство / Technical culture and modern art). Moscow: Gos. izd-vo, 1928 (cover date 1929). 257 pp. 22 cm.

775. ***Trebnik troikh: Sbornik stikhov i risunkov*** (Требник троих: Сборник стихов и рисунков / Missal of the three: Collection of verse and drawings). Moscow: G. L. Kuz'min i S. D. Dolinskii, 1913. 86 pp., [15] plates. 21 cm.

Includes drawings by David, Nadezhda, and Vladimir Burliuk, Vladimir Mayakovsky, and Vladimir Tatlin, and poetry by David and Nikolai Burliuk, Velimir Khlebnikov, and Mayakovsky.

The second of 2 portraits after p. [34] is not listed in the index, but is apparently a self-portrait by Mayakovsky (Bowlt and Hernad 1993, 67).

776. **Tret'iakov, Sergei.** *Chzhungo* (Чжунго). Moscow and Leningrad: Gos. izd-vo, 1927. 259 pp. 20 cm.

Cover by Aleksandr Rodchenko.

Reportage dealing with China, based on Tret'iakov's extended stay there in 1924.

777. ———. *Den Shi-khua: Bio-interv'iu* (Ден Ши-хуа: Био-интервью / Têng Hsi-hua: Bio-interview). Moscow: Molodaia gvardiia, 1930. 391 pp. 22 cm.

Design and cover by Aleksandr Rodchenko.

An account of the life of a typical Chinese student based on extensive interviews with him.

Research Institute also has a copy of a German translation with a cover by John Heartfield (Berlin: Malik-Verlag, [1932]).

778. ———. *Den Shi-khua: Bio-interv'iu* (Den Shi-khua: Bio-interview). 2nd ed. Moscow: Molodaia gvardiia, 1931. 399 pp. 23 cm.

Design and cover by Aleksandr Rodchenko.

An account of the life of a typical Chinese student based on extensive interviews with him.

779. ———. *Itogo: Stikhi* (Итого: Стихи / In sum: Verse). Moscow: Gos. izd-vo, 1924. 93 pp. 23 cm.

Cover and title page by Aleksandr Rodchenko.

780. ———. *Rechevik: Stikhi* (Речевик: Стихи / Speecher: Verse). Moscow and Leningrad: Gos. izd-vo, 1929. 191 pp. 17 cm.

Cover by Aleksandr Rodchenko.

781. **Tret'iakov, Sergei, and Nikolai Aseev.** *Khudozhnik V. Pal'mov* (Художник В. Пальмов / The artist V. Pal'mov). [Chita]: Ptach, 1922. 26 pp. 19 cm.

782. **Tret'iakovskaia galereia** (Tretyakov Gallery). *Vystavka "Okna satiry ROSTA"* (Выставка «Окна сатиры РОСТА» / The exhibition *ROSTA Windows for Satire*). Moscow: Izd. Gos. Tret'iakovskoi gallerei, 1929. 23 pp. 18 cm.

Exhibition catalog.

783. ***Treugol'nik; Gruppa Venok—stéfanos*** (Треугольник; Группа Венок-стефанос / Triangle; the group Wreath—stephanos). [St. Petersburg: n.p., 1910.] 39 pp. 19 cm.

Catalog of an exhibition held in St. Petersburg in 1910 (Severiukhin and Leikind 1992, 314). Includes text by Nikolai Kul'bin, the leader of Treugol'nik.

784. ***Tridtsat' dnei*** (Тридцать дней / Thirty days). Moscow: "Gudok," 1925–1941. 26 cm.

Covers designed by Vladimir Kozlinskii, B. Nechaev, Aleksandr Rodchenko, Georgii and Vladimir Stenberg, and Boris Titov.

Illustrated literary and artistic monthly. Features photomontages by Gustav Klutsis, photographic illustrations by Rodchenko, and stories by Iurii Olesha, Konstantin Paustovskii, and Andrei Platonov.

Publisher varies.

Research Institute's holdings: scattered issues.

785. ***Truba marsian*** (Труба марсиан / The Martians' trumpet). Moscow: Liren', [1916]. 1 sheet. 64 × 41 cm, folded to 21 × 16 cm.

Broadside manifesto. The first section includes contributions by Nikolai Aseev, Bozhidar, Velimir Khlebnikov, Grigorii Petnikov, and Mariia Siniakova. The second section is by Khlebnikov alone, as is the first of 2 "Prikazy" (Orders); in the latter cases he calls himself "Korol' vremeni Velemir [sic] 1-yi" (Velimir the first, king of time).

786. **Tsentral'noe izdatel'stvo narodov SSSR** (Central Publishing House of the Peoples of the USSR). *Piat' let Tsentral'nogo izdatel'stva narodov SSSR, 1924 13/VI 1929* (Пять лет Центрального издательства народов СССР, 1924 13/VI 1929 / Five years of the Central Publishing House of the Peoples of the USSR, 13 June 1924–1929). Moscow: Tsentrizdat, [1929]. 84 pp., [12] plates. 26 cm.

Cover by Vladimir Akhmet'ev.

Commemorative volume of a publishing house whose output was directed at the Soviet Union's non-Russian readers. The last section consists of single-page summaries of the text arranged alphabetically by language, from Armenian to Shortzy. Each of these pages has a decorative initial designed by Akhmet'ev and Vera Mukhina.

787. **Tsentrifuga** (Centrifuge). *Vtoroi sbornik Tsentrifugi* (Второй сборник Центрифуги / Second Centrifuge collection). Piatoe turboizdanie. Moscow: Tsentrifuga, tretii turbogod [1916]. 112 columns. 29 cm.

Cover by Nataliia Goncharova.

Includes contributions by Sergei Bobrov, Konstantin Bol'shakov, Bozhidar, Riurik Ivnev, Velimir Khlebnikov, Boris Kushner, Konstantin Olimpov, Boris Pasternak, Grigorii Petnikov, Fedor Platov, and Evgenii Shilling.

From an edition of 200.

788. ***Tsentrostil': Deklaratsiia, raboty*** (Центростиль: Декларация, работы / Style central: Declaration, works). Kiev: Tsentrostil', 1925. 16 pp. 21 cm.

Cover by Vladimir Sokol-Chernilovskii.

Includes the "Deklaratsiia" (Declaration) and poems by Nikolai Barabasenko, Vladimir Kovalevskii, Evgenii Nezhintsev, Iurii Nol'den, Boris Turganov, and Nikolai Ushakov.

Inscribed by Ushakov.

789. **Tsetlin, Mikhail.** *Prozrachnye teni: Obrazy* (Прозрачные тени: Образы / Transparent shadows: Images). Paris and Moscow: Zërna, 1920. 69 pp. 23 cm.

Cover by Nataliia Goncharova.

Poems. Includes illustrations by Goncharova.

790. **Tsvetaeva, Marina.** *Tsar'-devitsa: Poema-skazka* (Царь-девица: Поэма-сказка / The maiden tsar: A fairy tale in verse). Moscow: Gos. izd-vo, 1922. 159 pp. 19 cm.

Includes illustrations by Dmitrii Mitrokhin.

791. ———. *Versty: Stikhi* (Версты: Стихи / Miles: Verse). 2nd ed. Moscow: Kostry, [1922] (cover date 1921). 53 pp. 16 cm.

Cover by Pavel Pavlinov.

792. **Tufanov, Aleksandr.** *Eolova arfa: Stikhi i proza, kniga pervaia* (Эолова арфа: Стихи и проза, книга первая / Aeolian harp: Verse and prose, book one). Petrograd: Izd. individual'noe, 1917. 91 pp. 26 cm.
Cover by Ivan Nefedov.
Includes a portrait of the author by Nefedov.

793. ———. *K zaumni: Fonicheskaia muzyka i funktsii soglasnykh fonem* (К заумни: Фоническая музыка и функции согласных фонем / On transrational language: Phonic music and the functions of consonantal phonemes). St. Petersburg: Izd. avtora, 1924. 48 pp., [2] plates. 21 cm.
Cover by Boris Ender.
Poetic theory with examples by the author. Includes a table by Ender of the graphic correlatives of speech sounds, as Tufanov visualized them.

794. **Tugendkhol'd, Iakov.** *Aleksandra Ekster kak zhivopisets i khudozhnik stseny* (Александра Экстер как живописец и художник сцены / Alexandra Exter as painter and stage designer). Berlin: Zaria, 1922. 31 pp., [43] plates. 22 cm.
Research Institute also has a copy of the German-language edition published in Berlin by Zarja in 1922 under the title *Alexandra Exter.*

795. ———. *Edgar Dega i ego iskusstvo* (Эдгар Дега и его искусство / Edgar Degas and his art). Moscow: Z. I. Grzhebin, 1922. 89 pp. 30 cm.
Cover by Alexandra Exter.

796. ———. *Zhizn' i tvorchestvo Polia Gogena* (Жизнь и творчество Поля Гогена / The life and works of Paul Gauguin). 2nd ed., corr. Moscow: D. Ia. Makovskii i Sn., 1918. 168 pp. 31 cm.
Cover by Vera Mukhina. Title page by El Lissitzky.
Includes Russian-language translation of Gauguin's *Noa Noa.*

797. **Tukai, Gabdulla.** *Shurale: Skazka* (Шурале: Сказка / Shurale: A fairy tale). Kazan: Gos. izd-vo, Kazanskoe otd-nie, 1921. 15 pp., [2] plates. 20 cm.
Cover by Illarion Pleshchinskii.
Poem. Translation of the Tartar text first published in 1907. Includes illustrations by Pleshchinskii.

798. **Turgenev, Ivan.** *Das Lied der triumphierenden Liebe* (The song of exultant love). Stuttgart: J. Hoffmann, [1923]. 72 pp. 16 cm.
Translation of *Pesn' torzhestvuiushchei liubvi.* Includes illustrations by Vasilii Masiutin.

799. ***Turnir poetov*** (Турнир поэтов / Tournament of poets). Moscow: Izd. Gruppy lefovtsev, 1929. 18 leaves. 18 × 22 cm.
Cover by Kirill Zdanevich.
Humorous and improvisational verse. Includes notes by Aleksei

Kruchenykh, an illustration on leaf 12 by Ivan Kliun, a portrait of Kruchenykh by Igor' Terent'ev, and contributions by Nikolai Aseev, Vera Inber, Valentin Kataev, Velimir Khlebnikov, Semen Kirsanov, Vladimir Mayakovsky, Boris Pasternak, Nina Sakonskaia, Il'ia Sel'vinskii, Terent'ev, Sergei Tret'iakov, and Tat'iana Vechorka.

Copies 24 and 81 of 150. The first edition of the first of 3 miscellanies with this name, all of them edited by Kruchenykh. (The second miscellany appeared in 1932, the third in 1934.) Text is written in longhand, in some cases by the authors, and is reproduced by lithography on glass primarily in black, but with the cover, the title page, and the portrait by Terent'ev in red.

800. ***Turnir poetov*** (Турнир поэтов / Tournament of poets). 2nd ed. Moscow: Izd. Gruppy lefovtsev, 1930. 18 leaves. 18 × 22 cm.

In this revision, Igor' Terent'ev's portrait of Aleksei Kruchenykh was redrawn and placed at leaf 7 rather than 6, Kirill Zdanevich's cover was redrawn and reproduced in black rather than red, the illustration by Ivan Kliun was replaced with a poem by A. Ostrovskii, and the text was recopied without substantial change.

Copies of the second edition unnumbered, but it is also of 150 copies.

801. ***Udarniki*** (Ударники / Shock workers). Moscow: Izogiz, [1931?]. 196 pp. 21 cm.

Design by Andrei Diderikhs and Valentina Khodasevich.

Volume celebrating in words and pictures the contributions of shock workers to the first Five-Year Plan.

802. ***UdSSR Export 1932.*** [Berlin]: Handelsvertretung der UdSSR in Deutschland, [1932]. [148] pp. 30 cm.

Design by John Heartfield.

In 26 separately paged sections, each of which is the catalog of a Soviet organization engaged in export.

803. ***Ugolok bezbozhnika, n. 1*** (Уголок безбожника, н. 1 / The atheist's corner, number one). Moscow: Bezbozhnik, [ca. 1929]. 11 plates. In folder. 52 cm.

Cover by Mikhail Cheremnykh.

Cut-and-paste projects offered to readers of the newspaper *Bezbozhnik* (The atheist [1922–1941, suspended 1935–1938]) in time for an anti-Easter campaign.

804. **Ukrainska khudozhnia vystavka** (Exhibition of Ukrainian art). *Kataloh druhoi vseukrains'koi khudozhn'oi vystavky NKO USRR: Maliarstvo, hrafika, skul'ptura, foto-kino, teatral'ne oform.* (Каталог другої всеукраїнської художньої виставки НКО УСРР: Малярство, графіка,

скульптура, фото-кіно, театральне оформ. / Catalog of the second all-Ukrainian art exhibition of the People's Commissariat of Culture of the USRR: Painting, graphics, sculpture, photography and film, set design). [Kiev]: Vyd. Narkomosu USRR, 1929. 45 pp., 47 plates. 18 cm.

Cover by M. A. Pavliuk.

805. **Ukrainska khudozhnia vystavka** (Exhibition of Ukrainian art). *Kataloh tret'oi vseukrains'koi khudozhn'oi vystavky NKO USRR: Maliarstvo, hrafika, skul'ptura, teatral'ne oform., oformlennia pobutu, studiini roboty khudozhnikh vyshiv USRR* (Каталог третьої всеукраїнської художньої виставки НКО УСРР: Малярство, графіка, скульптура, театральне оформ., оформлення побуту, студійні роботи художніх вишів УСРР / Catalog of the third all-Ukrainian art exhibition of the People's Commissariat of Culture of the USRR: Painting, graphics, sculpture, set design, applied art, studio works by art students of the USRR). [Kiev]: Vyd. Narkomosu USRR, 1930. 50 pp., 31 plates. 17 cm.

Cover by M. Azovs'kyi.

806. **Umanskij, Konstantin.** *Neue Kunst in Russland, 1914–1919* (New art in Russia, 1914–1919). Potsdam: Gustav Kiepenheuer; Munich: Hans Goltz, 1920. vi, 72 pp., 31 plates. 27 cm.

807. **Union des artistes russes** (Union of Russian Artists). Ephemera from the *Bal banal* (Banal ball).

Ball held 14 March 1924 at the Salle Bullier in Paris, one of a series of charity balls organized by the Union of Russian Artists during the 1920s. Research Institute has the program (a single sheet printed on both sides, 76 × 58 cm folded twice to 38 × 29 cm) and 3 tickets (maximum height 31 cm). Program includes vignettes by Abraham Berline, Constantin Brancusi, Georges Braque, Claire Fargue, Adolphe Feder, Léon Indenbaum, Vladimir Izdebsky, Pinchus Krémègne, Mikhail Larionov, Jean Lebedeff, André Lhote, Pablo Picasso, Constantin Terechkovitch, and Lazar Volovick. The tickets, printed in brown and gray, were designed by Nataliia Goncharova. No. 182, on tan paper, has a printed price of 10 francs, and no. 2970, on cream paper, has a price of 25 francs. Both were perforated near the top and bottom, allowing stubs to be torn off (no. 2970 retains its lower stub), and they are stamped at the perforations in purple ink with the seal of the Union of Russian Artists. The third ticket, on gray paper, may be a proof as it lacks price, perforations, and stamps.

808. ———. Ephemera from the *Bal de la grande ourse* (Ball of the great bear).

Ball held 8 May 1925 at the Salle Bullier in Paris. Research Institute has the program (32 pp., 25 cm), the flyer (1 sheet printed on both sides, 50 cm), and the handbill (1 sheet, 31 cm). Program is signed "M. Larionov" in black ink on the cover and includes illustrations by Serge Fotinsky, Alexandre Frenkel, Nataliia Goncharova, Mikhail Larionov, Henri Laurens, Fernand Léger, Konstantin Mel'nikov, Pablo Picasso, Isaak Rabinovitch, Aleksandr Rodchenko, David Shterenberg, Marc Sterling, Marie Vassilieff, and Lazar Volovick. At the top of the flyer is a drawing by Laurens.

809. ———. Ephemera from the *Bal olympique* (Olympic ball).

Ball held 11 July 1924 at the Taverne de l'Olympia in Paris. Research Institute has the program (30 cm), illustrated by Victor Barthe, Boris Chatzman, Serge Fotinsky, Naum Granovskii, "Manet" (for a drawing after his *Olympia*), Pablo Picasso, and Marie Vassilieff, and the flyer (66 cm folded to 26 cm), illustrated by Barthe and Nataliia Goncharova and printed in black on blue paper.

810. ———. Ephemera from the *Bal transmental* (Transrational ball).

Ball held 23 February 1923 at the Salle Bullier in Paris. Research Institute has copies of the program (8 pp., 33 cm), the flyer (22 cm), and the invitation (50 cm), all of which have linoleum cuts by Mikhail Larionov. The typographic design of the program cover is in blue on tan paper. The program itself includes illustrations by André Derain, Adolphe Feder, Nataliia Goncharova, Juan Gris, and Pablo Picasso and poems in facsimile handwriting and typescript. That by Ramón Gómez de la Serna is a shaped poem in the form of a fan, and that by Tristan Tzara incorporates printed images of various objects along its right margin. The flyer has an abstract dancing figure and is printed in black on green paper. The invitation, in brown and orange on cream paper, repeats the figure. Research Institute's copy is no. 463. It is stamped in brown with Larionov's signature and is also stamped on the front and back in black with the signature of S. Gourévitch, treasurer of the Union of Russian Artists.

811. **Urazov, Izmail.** *Shestaia chast' mira* (Шестая часть мира / One-sixth of the world). Moscow: Kinopechat', 1926. [12] pp. 24 × 27 cm.

Layout and cover by Aleksandr Rodchenko.

Discussion of Dziga Vertov's film.

812. **Ushakov, M.** *Bor'ba: Roman* (Борьба: Роман / Struggle: A novel). Moscow and Leningrad: Zemlia i fabrika, 1929. 289 pp. 21 cm.

Cover by Boris Titov.

813. ***USSR: An Album Illustrating the State Organization and National Economy of the USSR.*** Edited by Ivan Sautin and Ivan Ivanitskii. [Moscow]: Scientific Publishing Institute of Pictorial Statistics, [1939]. 140, [9] pp. 24 × 35 cm.

Design by Aleksandr Grigorovich, El Lissitzky, and Mikhail Nikolaev.

Album produced for distribution at the New York World's Fair of 1939 (Lissitzky 1987, 200). Includes 31 wood-engraved vignettes illustrating the subjects of the graphs; 2 are signed "WF," for Vladimir Favorskii, and 2 are signed "KG." Also contains supplementary 4-page leaflet, *Basic Indices of the Economic and Cultural Growth of the USSR According to the Third Five-Year Plan, 1938–1942,* and a 13-page booklet in Russian, *Perechen' tablits i poiasneniia k nim* (List of graphs and their explanations).

In a pasteboard slipcase. Research Institute's copy signed on title page by F. H. Pritchard.

814. ***USSR Periodica.*** Moscow: Mezhdunarodnaia kniga, [1930–?]. 25 cm.

Covers and design by Nikolai Sedel'nikov (1931) and Solomon Telingater (1932).

Issued by Mezhdunarodnaia kniga, the central publishing organ of the USSR in charge of the export of all periodicals and books produced in the USSR.

Research Institute's holdings: scattered issues.

815. **Vermel', Samuil.** *Tanki: Lirika* (Танки: Лирика / Tankas: Lyrics). Moscow: Studiia, 1915. 48 pp. 20 cm.

Cover by V. Ul'ianishchev.

Includes drawings by David Burliuk.

From an edition of 500 (*Knizhnaia letopis'* 1915, no. 19814).

816. ***Vesennee kontragenstvo muz: Sbornik*** (Весеннее контрагенство муз: Сборник / Vernal forwarding agency of the muses: A collection). Edited by David Burliuk and Samuil Vermel'. Moscow: [Studiia D. Burliuk i S. Vermel'], 1915. 107 pp., [1] plate. 27 cm.

Cover by Aristarkh Lentulov.

Collection containing drawings by David and Vladimir Burliuk and Lentulov, a composition for violin and piano by Nikolai Roslavets, Velimir Khlebnikov's play *Snezini,* 2 short stories by Nikolai Burliuk, a critical essay by David Burliuk, and verse by Nikolai Aseev, Aleksandr Belenson, Konstantin Bol'shakov, David Burliuk, Nikolai Burliuk, Vasilii Kamenskii, Vladimir Kanev, Vladimir Mayakovsky, Boris Pasternak, Dmitrii Varavvin, and Vermel'. Also includes a color relief halftone of a set design by Lentulov for an unrealized production of the tragedy Vladimir Mayakovsky, planned for Moscow in 1914 (Compton 1978, 57).

From an edition of 500 (*Knizhnaia letopis'* 1915, no. 12545). Research Institute's copy has several impressions of the ownership stamp "K. K-K." in purple ink and the signature "Kuz'min-Karavaev" (?) in red pencil on the title page, dated September 1915, Petrograd.

817. ***Vesennii salon poetov*** (Весенний салон поэтов / Spring salon for poets). Moscow: Zërna, 1918. 177 pp. 18 cm.

Cover by Georgii Iakulov.

818. ***Veshch', Gegenstand, Objet*** (Вещь— / Object—). Berlin: Skythen, 1922. 31 cm.

Edited by Il'ia Erenburg and El Lissitzky.

Covers designed by Lissitzky.

Journal is divided into 6 sections, including publications, exhibitions, projects, performances, biographical notes, and actual works of art. Includes an article by Nikolai Punin on Vladimir Tatlin's *Pamiatnik III Internationala* (Monument to the third international), a translation of an article by Le Corbusier on contemporary architecture, a review of Russian art exhibitions that contains 1 of 2 known photographs of the Moscow exhibition of the Society of Young Artists (OBMOKhU) in 1921, and works by Theo van Doesburg, Albert Gleizes, Fernand Léger, Jacques Lipchitz, and Kazimir Malevich. Contains text in French, German, and Russian.

A total of 3 issues published.

819. ***Vestnik inostrannoi literatury: Organ Mezhdunarodnogo biuro revoliutsionnoi literatury*** (Вестник иностранной литературы: Орган Международного бюро революционной литературы / Herald of foreign literature: Organ of the International Bureau for Revolutionary Literature). Moscow: Gos. izd-vo, 1928–1930. 26 cm.

Edited by Anatoly Lunacharsky.

Journal dedicated to the cultural and literary life of both the West and the East. Cover title in Russian and French. Editions also published in Chinese, English, French, German, and Spanish.

Research Institute's holdings: scattered issues.

820. ***Vestnik Ispolkoma Moskovsk. Vysshikh Gosudarstvennykh Masterskikh*** (Вестник Исполкома Московск. Высших Государственных Мастерских / Bulletin of the Executive Committee of the Moscow Higher State Studios). Moscow: VTsIKUCHA, 1920–? 25 cm.

Published by the All-Union Central Executive Committee of the Students at the Department of Visual Arts of the Narkompros.

No. 1 (1920), called "Tretii oktiabr" (Third October), includes an untitled article by Kazimir Malevich; an essay by Sergei Sen'kin, "Pochemu my stoim za organizatsiiu partii" (Why do we stand for the organization of the party?); an article by A. Naumov, "Revoliutsiia i iskusstvo" (Revolution and art); an excerpt from a poem by Konstantin Medunetskii, "Oktiabr'" (October); a short notice by Sen'kin, "UNOVIS. Pasternak i Repin"; a prose composition by Nikolai Prusakov, "Mesto i vremia" (Place and time); and a section "Khronika" (Chronicle). The cover of no. 1 (1920) features a black square and a Suprematist composition in black and white.

Research Institute's holdings: scattered issues.

821. ***Vestnik kinematografii*** (Вестник кинематографии / Herald of cinematography). Moscow: Aleksandr Khanzhonkov i K., 1911–? 30 cm.

Edited by A. O. Donetskii.

Biweekly published by Aleksandr Khanzhonkov, one of the leading Russian movie producers. Includes reviews of contemporary Russian movies produced and shown in Moscow, St. Petersburg, and the provinces. The advertisement section informs the Russian audience about new foreign movies, the production of which was financed by Khanzhonkov's company.

Research Institute's holdings: scattered issues.

822. ***Vestnik Narodnogo prosveshcheniia Soiuza kommun Severnoi oblasti*** (Вестник Народного просвещения Союза коммун Северной области / Popular culture bulletin of the Union of Communes for the Northern Region). Petrograd: Kommissariat Narodnogo prosveshcheniia Soiuza kommun Severnoi oblasti, 1918. 30 cm.

Covers by Petr Miturich.

A journal sponsored by an organization that, under the leadership of Anatoly Lunacharsky, soon became the People's Commissiariat for Education (Narkompros).

Dedicated to educational and cultural matters during the early period of Soviet power. Each issue lists decrees and directives of the Ministry of Education. Contributors include Lunacharsky, Miturich, and Nikolai Punin.

A total of eight issues published from August to November.

823. ***V'iuzhnye dni: Sbornik sibirskikh poetov revoliutsii*** (Вьюжные дни: Сборник сибирских поэтов революции / Stormy days: A collection of Siberian poets of the revolution). Edited by Vivian Itin. Novonikolaevsk: Sibkraiizdat, 1925. 93 pp. 18 cm.

Cover by Veniamin Romanov (under the psuedonym V. Romov).

824. ***V kibitke vdokhnoven'ia*** (В кибитке вдохновенья / In the kibitka of inspiration). [Petrograd]: Imazhinisty, [1923]. [7] pp. 20 cm.

Poems by I. Afanas'ev-Solov'ev, Semen Polotskii, Vladimir Richiotti, and Grigorii Shmerel'son. A *kibitka* is a Russian wagon or carriage with a rounded cover, or a Kirghiz tent of latticework and felt.

From an edition of 500.

825. **VKhUTEMAS.** Archive. Faculty and student work in various media.

Works by professors and students produced as independent experiments or class assignments in various departments of the school, including graphic arts, sculpture, furniture, painting, and textiles. The majority of items (well over 400) are visual images executed in various media, such as prints, posters, lithographs, watercolors, etchings, pencil. The subject matter ranges from still life, cityscapes, landscapes, and the human figure to typographical and furniture designs.

The collection also includes Aleksandr Lushin's workbook with class assignments and an explication of the principles of color theory taught at the school; 4 color plates by Ismail Akhundov; approximately 30 cover designs for unrealized publications; a book published in 1929, *VKhUTEIN* (Higher State Art-Technical Institute); the first issue of 1930 of the *Gazeta poligraficheskogo instituta* (Gazette of the Polygraphic Institute); 5 copies of a collection of poems by Ivan Guzinov, *Bychia kazn'* (Bull's execution [Moscow: Imazhinisty, 1921]); 3 woodcut blocks (2 by Mikhail Tarkhanov and 1 by Georgii Echeistov); 2 ceramic cups by Tarkhanov; 13 textile samples by Sergei Burylin, Zinaida Markina, Raissa Matveeva, Mariia Nazarevskaia, Daria Preobrazhenskaia, and an anonymous artist; furniture designs by Aleksandr Toporkov and Grigorii Zimin; and 2 portfolios of drawings by Zimin (*Skriabin v tantse Lukina* [Skriabin in Lukin's dance] and *Sodom. 10 risunkov is tsikla "Narcotique"* [Sodom. Ten drawings from the circle "Narcotique"], Moscow: [n.p.], 1924). The second portfolio was published in an edition of 25 copies.

826. ———. Archive. Personal and institutional documents.

Personal and institutional documents, including 3 published flyers with detailed descriptions of the school's basic course, its program in advanced mathematics, and its program in physics; an invitation to a discussion group organized at VKhUTEMAS; an art club membership ticket for Grigorii Zimin; a permission slip allowing Zimin to depict the historical buildings and monuments of Moscow and its environs; a diploma issued to Zinaida Markina; a student grade-book issued to Klavdiia Kozlova with a list of the courses she took, grades, and instructors' signatures; a 4-page typewritten list of Aleksandr Rodchenko's personal exhibitions; and 71 photographs, most of which document sculptures by Boris Korolev.

827. **Vladimirskii, Nikolai.** *Pesnia o Tane: Poema* (Песня о Тане: Поэма / Song about Tania: A poem). Biblioteka raboche-krest'ianskoi molodezhi. Moscow: Novaia Moskva (Iunosheskii sektor), 1926. 32 pp. 22 cm.

Cover by Sergei Sen'kin.

828. **Volkovyskii, Arnol'd.** *Solntsa potselui* (Солнца поцелуи / Kisses of the sun). St. Petersburg: [n.p.], 1914. 69 pp. 26 cm.

Cover by Natan Al'tman.

Poems. Includes relief halftone illustrations by Al'tman.

Bears the property stamp of K. A. Shimkevich on inside back cover.

829. ***Voprosy arkhitektury*** (Вопросы архитектуры / Architectural issues). [Moscow]: Ogiz, 1935. 207 pp. 30 cm.

Four articles on historical subjects and 3 on contemporary ones. The latter are Moisei Ginzburg's "Arkhitekturnoe oformlenie magistrali Moskva-Donbass" (The architectural design of the Moscow-Donbass highway), Roman Khiger's "Problema zhil'ia v sovetskoi arkhitekture" (The problem of housing in Soviet architecture), and Vladimir Semenov's "Arkhitekturnaia rekonstruktsiia Moskvy" (The architectural reconstruction of Moscow).

830. **Voronca, Ilarie.** *Ulise.* [Bucharest]: Colecţiunea Integral, 1928. [39] pp. 33 cm.

Poem. Includes a portrait by Marc Chagall of Voronca in the form of the Eiffel Tower.

Copy 5 of 200 ordinary copies from a total edition of 206. Inscribed by Voronca to Tristan Tzara, "le premier parmi les élus de mon admiration. Malheureux hommage, Ilarie Voronca" (the first among the elect of my admiration. With sad respect, Ilarie Voronca).

831. **Vot—In. Krasheninnikov, Il'ia Berezark, Konstantin Roslavlev, M. K. Gol'denberg, Elena Iuvada, Mariia Avenirg, Vladimir Filov, Nina Gratsianskaia, Boris Levin, Boris Virganskii, Georgii Shtorm** (Вот — Ин. Крашенинников— / Here are— Innokentii Krasheninnikov—). Rostov na Donu: Vseros. soiuz poetov (Rostovskoe na Donu otd-nie), 1921. 62 pp. 17 cm.

Poems. Inscribed by Krasheninnikov.

Copy 245 of 500. Inscribed by Krasheninnikov to Glafira Kapustianskaia and dated 19 April 1921.

832. ***Vremia*** (Время / Time). Moscow: Krasnaia nov', 1923–1924. 26 cm.

Covers designed by Gustav Klutsis and Sergei Sen'kin.

Monthly publication by the "Time" League, one of the official groups concerned with the scientific organization of labor during the 1920s.

A total of 11 issues published.

833. ***Vsegdai*** (Всегдай / The alwayser). Edited by Ivan Ignat'ev. Ego-Futuristy 7. St. Petersburg: Peterburgskii glashatai, 1913. 32 pp. 24 cm.

A miscellany with poems and short essays by Ignat'ev, Riurik Ivnev, Pavel Korotkov, Dmitrii Kriuchkov, Konstantin Olimpov, Amfian Reshetov, and Vadim Shershenevich.

834. **Vserossiiskii kooperativnyi soiuz rabotnikov izobrazitel'nykh iskusstv** (All-Russia Cooperative Union of Workers in the Visual Arts). *Khudozhniki RSFSR za XV let (1917–1932): Zhivopis', skul'ptura, plakat, i karikatura* (Художники РСФСР за XV лет (1917–1932): Живопись, скульптура, плакат, и карикатура / Fifteen years' work by artists of the Russian federa-

tion (1917–1932): Painting, sculpture, poster, and caricature). Vols. 1 and 2 of 4. Moscow: Vsekokhudozhnik, 1933–1934. 18 cm.

Catalog of an exhibition that opened 27 June 1933 in Moscow. The complete set contains 4 volumes. Vol. 1 is devoted to painting, vol. 2 to sculpture, and vol. 3 to poster and caricature. An additional exhibit section devoted to graphics opened on 10 December 1933 and the catalog for it, vol. 4, appeared the following year (Azarkovich 1965–, 2:9–17).

835. ***Vserossiiskii soiuz poetov*** (All-Russia Poets Union). *Novye stikhi: Sbornik vtoroi* (Новые стихи: Сборник второй / New verse: Second collection). Moscow: Vseros. soiuz poetov, 1927. 126 pp. 17 cm.

Cover by I. P. Feofilaktov.

Poems by 51 contributors in addition to Aleksei Chicherin's "Zvonok k dvorniku: Poema" (A call to the janitor: Poem), which consists of 6 relief halftone illustrations by Boris Zemenkov, carried out at Chicherin's direction.

836. ———. *Poety nashikh dnei: Antologiia* (Поэты наших дней: Антология / Poets of our time: An anthology). Moscow: Vseros. soiuz poetov, 1924. 107 pp. 18 cm.

837. ———. *Soiuz poetov: Vtoroi sbornik stikhov* (Союз поэтов: Второй сборник стихов / Poets Union: Second collection of verse). Moscow: SOPO, 1922. [30] pp. 18–23 cm.

Contributors are listed on p. [3] by literary affiliation: Acmeist—Osip Mandel'shtam; Abstractionist—N. Khabias-Komarova; Imagist—Matvei Roizman; Neoromantic—Argo; Symbolist—Semen Rubanovich; Futurists—Teodor Levit and M. Zlotopol'skii; Centrifugists—Boris Pasternak and Evgenii Shilling; Expressionists—Boris Lapin and Sergei Spasskii; and Unaffiliated—Nikolai Aduev, Iakov Apushkin, Nikolai Bogoslovskii, Georgii Deshkin, Nikolai Minaev, Aleksandr Olenin, Iakov Polonskii, Il'ia Sel'vinskii, and Marina Tsvetaeva.

Inscribed by Nikolai Apushkin to Nina Manukhina in red ink on the title page and dated 1 January 1922. Aduev's signature in pencil is on p. [20] and is accompanied by the words *vsegda volk* (always a wolf), a reference to his poem printed on that page.

838. ———. *SOPO: Pervyi sbornik stikhov* (СОПО: Первый сборник стихов / Poets Union: First collection of verse). [Moscow]: Vserossiiskii soiuz poetov, chetvertyi god pervogo veka, [1921]. 30 pp. 23 cm.

Contributors are listed on p. [3] by literary affiliation: Imagists—Ivan Gruzinov and Riurik Ivnev; Futurists—Sergei Budantsev and Georgii Echeistov; Acmeist—Oleg Erberg; Centrifugists—Ivan Aksenov and Sergei Bobrov; Eclectics—Nataliia Benar and Viacheslav Kovalevskii; Neoromantic—Valentin Stenich; Parnassian—Vasilii Fedorov; Symbolists—Andrey Bely, Valerii Briusov, and Fedor Sologub; and Classic—Afanasii Fet. Unlisted contributors are Nataliia Kugusheva, Taras Machtet, and Varvara Monina.

839. **Vsesoiuznaia poligraficheskaia vystavka** (All-Union Exhibition of the Printing Trades). *Biulleten'* (Бюллетень / Bulletin). Moscow: Komitet Vses. poligraficheskoi vystavki, 1927. 12 pp. 30 cm.

Cover by El Lissitzky.

The *Biulleten'* was produced as a preliminary catalog because the main publication, the *Putevoditel'* (Guidebook), was delayed. (See no. 840.)

840. ———. *Putevoditel'* (Путеводитель / Guidebook). Moscow: Komitet Vses. poligraficheskoi vystavki, 1927. 27, 23, 25, 32, 10, 25, 11, 12, 4 pp. and many unpaged advertisements. 18 cm.

Design by El Lissitzky. Typography by Solomon Telingater.

Guidebook to the *All-Union Exhibition of the Printing Trades.* (See no. 839.)

841. ***Vse, vse, vse: 7 noiabria 1917–7 noiabria 1924*** (Все, все, все: 7 ноября 1917–7 ноября 1924 / All, all, all: 7 November 1917–7 November 1924). Leningrad: Gubpolitprosvet; Kul'totdel Gubprofsoveta, [1924]. 30 pp. 13 cm.

Constructivist design supervised by Eduard Krimmer.

Pamphlet consisting chiefly of brief descriptions of books suitable for political self-education, with additional advice on how to read for maximum comprehension and a list of public libraries in Leningrad by area.

842. ***Vystavka khudozhestvennykh proizvedenii k desiatiletnemu iubileiu Oktiabr'skoi revoliutsii*** (Выставка художественных произведений к десятилетнему юбилею Октябрьской революции / Exhibition of works of art on the occasion of the tenth anniversary of the October Revolution). Moscow: Vystavochnyi komitet, 1928. 18 pp. 18 cm.

843. ***Vzial: Baraban futuristov*** (Взял: Барабан футуристов / Took: The drum of the Futurists). St. Petersburg: [n.p.], 1915. 16 pp. 34 cm.

Futurist miscellany organized by David Burliuk and Vladimir Mayakovsky. Includes 2 illustrations by Burliuk; an essay by Velimir Khlebnikov, "Predlozheniia" (Proposals); essays by Viktor Shklovskii on Mayakovsky's poem "Oblako v shtanakh" (A cloud in trousers); and poetry by Nikolai Aseev, Vasilii Kamenskii, Khlebnikov, Mayakovsky, and Boris Pasternak.

From an edition of 640. Cover bears the single word *Vzial* (Took) in bold type on dark paper.

844. **Whitman, Walt.** *Pionery* (Пионеры / Pioneers). Translated by M. S. Petrograd: Segodnia, [1918]. [4] pp. 20 cm.

Cover by Vera Ermolaeva.

Translation of "O Pioneers! O Pioneers!" Includes illustrations by Ermolaeva.

845. ***XIX vystavka V.Ts.V.B. Otdela IZO Narkomprosa*** (XIX выставка В.Ц.В.Б. Отдела ИЗО Наркомпроса / Nineteenth exhibition of the All-Russian Central Exhibition Bureau of the Arts Division of the People's Commissariat for Education). Moscow: [Narkompros], 1920. 21 pp. 16 cm.

846. **Zaikov, A. M.** *Izobrazitel'noe iskusstvo v klube* (Изобразительное искусство в клубе / Art in the club). Moscow: Kn-vo VTsSPS, 1929. 82 pp. 23 cm.

Cover signed "Sh."

Practical advice on organizing art circles in workers' clubs.

847. **Zamiatin, Evgenii.** *Vereshki* (Верешки / Slivers). [Petrograd]: Segodnia, [1919?]. [4] pp. 20 cm.

Cover by N. Liubavina.

Four prose sketches. Includes illustrations by Liubavina.

848. **Zamoshkin, Aleksandr** [artist, art historian, and director of the Tretyakov Gallery in Moscow from 1941 to 1951]. Archive. Artists' petitions. 1926–1927.

Bound in a portfolio with the handwritten title *Zhiuri* (The jury) are 24 handwritten sheets consisting of handwritten artists' petitions to be accepted into the Society of Easel Artists (OST); the list of the jury for 1925–1926, including Aleksandr Deineka, Aleksei Fedorov-Davydov, Kostin, Labas, Iurii Pimenov, David Shterenberg (who served as the president of OST from its inception), Konstantin Vialov, and Petr Vil'iams; typewritten minutes from the jury's first meeting, dated 21 March 1926, and from the second meeting, dated 28 March 1926; a handwritten list of the jury for 1926–1927, which included Deineka, Pimenov, Shterenberg, Aleksandr Tyshler, and Vil'iams; and a typed official document dated 4 October 1926 stating that the Self-Taught Artists Society (OKhS) presented the Tretyakov Gallery in Moscow with 73 works of art by 14 artists. OST was officially established in 1925 by Iurii Annenkov, Deineka, Pimenov, Shterenberg, and Vil'iams. It was closed in 1931.

849. ———. Archive. *Biulleten'* (Бюллетень / Bulletin). [N.p.]: International Bureau of Revolutionary Artists, 25 April 1934.

The second issue of *Biulleten'*. Contains articles on artistic activity in Moscow, Leningrad, the Ukraine, Kigiziia, and Georgia. The issue opens with an article by Zamoshkin on the activity of the Moscow Regional Union of Soviet Artists (MOSSKh), organized by a decree of the Central Committee of the Communist Party in July of 1932.

850. ———. Archive. Debate record. 152 pp.

Stenographic record of a debate, "Disput na temu o khudozhestvennykh gruppirovkakh" (Discussion regarding artistic groups), held in Moscow 8 and 16 February 1930 at the Higher State Art-Technical Institute (VKhUTEIN).

The debate took place 4 months before the still relatively independent groups of artists were joined in a Federation of Soviet Workers in the Spatial Arts (FOSKh). Some 20 participants gave speeches, including Nikolai Maslenikov (who became secretary of the federation when it formed in June of 1930), David Shterenberg, and Solomon Telingater.

Hectograph and carbon typescript.

851. ———. Archive. Government orders.

Copies of 4 government orders on cultural matters. Order no. 286—written by the People's Commissariat for Education (Narkompros), dated 28 June 1933, and issued in an edition of 120—praises the organizers of the exhibition *Khudozhniki RSFSR za 15 Let* (Artists of the RSFSR over the last fifteen years). Order no. 672, initiated by Stalin and dated 6 March 1948, concerns the closing of the Museum of New Western European Art, which consisted of the collections of Pavel Morosov and Sergei Shchukin. Both collections were nationalized in 1918. By the time of this decree, all of the museum's holdings were distributed between the Hermitage in Saint Petersburg and the Pushkin Museum in Moscow.

852. ***Za proletarskoe iskusstvo*** (За пролетарское искусство / For proletarian art). Moscow and Leningrad: Ogiz-Izogiz, 1931–1932. 30 cm.

Organ of the Association of Artists of the Revolution (AKhR).

No. 2 (1931) contains several articles on propaganda posters, an article about Soviet textile design featuring propaganda motifs, and an article on Hannes Meyer and his furniture design for a Moscow apartment.

Continues *Iskusstvo v massy.* (See no. 266.)

Research Institute's holdings: scattered issues.

853. ***Za sotsialisticheskii park: Obzor proektov general'nogo plana Tsentral'nogo parka kul'tury i otdykha Mossoveta*** (За социалистический парк: Обзор проектов генерального плана Центрального парка культуры и отдыха Моссовета / In support of the socialist park: A survey of proposals for the general plan of the Central Park of Culture and Leisure of the Moscow Soviet). Moscow: Izd-vo Mosoblispolkoma, 1932. 31 pp., [7] folded plates. 28 cm.

Cover by Boris Iordanskii and Georgii Rublev.

The text consists of 2 parts, the first a general discussion by B. N. Glan concerning plans to extend the Central Park of Culture and Leisure upstream along the right bank of the Moscow River and across the river to the left bank. The second part is a presentation by Leonid Lunts of 10 submissions to a competition held in 1931 to design the extension. Among those who submitted proposals are Moisei Ginzburg and Konstantin Mel'nikov. None of the proposals presented here was adopted and starting in 1935 the park was developed within its original boundaries under the architect Aleksandr Vlasov

(Bakhin 1975, 2:493). Inserted is a folded map showing the site of the existing park and its proposed extension.

854. ***Zateinik*** (Затейник / Entertainer). Moscow: Izd-vo TsKVLKSM "Molodaia gvardiia," 1929–. 25 cm.

Children's periodical published by the Central Committee of the All-Union Young Communist League (TsKVLKSM).

Publication suspended 1941–1946.

Research Institute's holdings: scattered issues.

855. ***Zatychka, sbornik: Risunki, stikhi*** (Затычка, сборник: Рисунки, стихи / The bung, a collection: Drawings, verse). Kherson: Futuristy "Gileia," [1913]. 13 leaves, [2] double plates tipped in at centerfold. 23 cm.

Includes 4 illustrations by Vladimir Burliuk and poems by David and Nikolai Burliuk and Velimir Khlebnikov.

From an edition of 450 (*Knizhnaia letopis'* 1913, no. 27804). None of the illustrations is hand colored (cf. the hand-colored illustration in the copy reproduced in Compton 1977).

856. ***Zavtra*** (Завтра / Tomorrow). Berlin: Petropolis, 1923. 137 pp., including 5 pp. of publisher's listings. 22 cm.

Edited by Mikhail Kuzmin, Mikhail Lozinskii, and Evgenii Zamiatin.

Cover by Natan Al'tman.

Literary and critical miscellany. Includes poems by Anna Akhmatova and Kuzmin and critical essays by Vsevolod Ivanov, Kuzmin, and Mikhail Slominskii. Inscribed "Paris, 1934."

A total of 1 issue published.

857. **[Zdanevich, Kirill].** *Vystavka kartin Kirilla Zdanevicha* (Выставка картин Кирилла Зданевича / Exhibition of pictures by Kirill Zdanevich). [Tbilisi: n.p., 1917]. 8 pp. 18 cm.

858. **Zelinskii, Kornelii, Aleksei Chicherin, and Il'ia Sel'vinskii.** *Mena vsekh* (Мена всех / All are changed). Moscow: Konstruktivisty poety, 1924. 83 pp. 24 cm.

Cover by Nikolai Kupreianov.

Design by Chicherin.

Includes a photomontage portrait of Zelinski by Boris Zemenkov and poems by Chicherin and Sel'vinskii and an essay on literary theory by Zelinskii. The illustration on p. [63] is from Chicherin's "Zvonok k dvorniku" (A call to the janitor), the "poem" in 6 illustrations that appeared in its full form 3 years later in *Novye stikhi: Sbornik vtoroi* (New verse: Second collection).

859. **Zemenkov, Boris.** *Grafika v bytu* (Графика в быту / Graphics in everyday life). Moscow: Khudozhestvennoe izdatel'skoe akts. o-vo AKhR, 1930. 82 pp. 18 cm.

Discussion of applied graphics and its role in the Soviet Union.

Research Institute's copy has a Dutch translation of the title inscribed in black ink on the front cover and bears the property stamp of P. Alma ("Jozef Israëlskade 98, Amsterdam") on the inside front cover.

860. **Zemenkov, Boris, Aleksandr Kraevskii, and Vadim Shershenevich.** *Ot mamy na piat' minut* (От мамы на пять минут / Away from mommy for five minutes). [Moscow]: Farshirovannye manzhety, [1920]. 32 pp. 23 cm.

Poems. Includes 2 illustrations by Zemenkov.

The place of publication printed on the piece is Kholodno, and the date is "XX-yi vek" (twentieth century). Imprint identification is from Tarasenkov (1966, 150).

861. **Zemenkov, Boris, Gurii Sidorov, and Ippolit Sokolov.** *Vozzvanie ekspressionistov o sozyve Pervogo Vserossiiskogo kongressa poetov* (Воззвание экспрессионистов о созыве Первого Всероссийского конгресса поэтов / An appeal by Expressionists to convene a first All-Russian Congress of Poets). [Moscow: Poety], 1920. 7 pp. 21 cm.

862. ***Zhar-ptitsa*** (Жар-птица / Firebird). Berlin: Verlag "Russische Kunst," 1921–1926. 31 cm.

Edited by Aleksandr Kogan.

A publication featuring works by major Russian émigré writers and artists. Contains reviews of important Russian exhibitions in the West such as the World of Art group exhibition in Paris and *Erste Russische Kunstausstellung* (First Russian art exhibition) at the Galerie Van Diemen in Berlin in 1922 (see no. 167); artworks by Lev Bakst, Marc Chagall, Boris Kustodiev, Nikolai Rerikh, Konstantin Somov, and Mikhail Vrubel'; and stories and poetry by Konstantin Bal'mont, Ivan Bunin, and Vladimir Nabokov (under the pseudonym Vladimir Sirin). Cover illustrations include works by Ivan Bilibin, Sergei Chekhonin, and Kustodiev. No. 10 (1922) features a cover designed by Nataliia Goncharova, and no. 12 of the same year has a cover designed by Mikhail Larionov.

A total of 14 issues published.

863. **Zivel'chinskaia, Liia.** *Ekspressionizm* (Экспрессионизм / Expressionism). Moscow and Leningrad: Ogiz-Izogiz, 1931. 139 pp. 19 cm.

Cover by "M. I." (*Knizhnaia letopis'* 1931, no. 15747).

Art criticism.

864. ***Zolotaia kumirnia, chast' 1*** (Золотая кумирня, часть 1 / Golden temple, part one). Kiev: Kn-vo Zolotaia kumirnia, [1921?]. 14 pp. 16 cm.
Poems by Ivan Gruzinov, Antonii Sluchanovskii, Galina Vladychina, and Sergei Zarov.
Title page of Research Institute's copy signed by V. Kovalevskii.

865. ***Zrelishcha*** (Зрелища / Spectacles). Moscow: Izd.-red. L. Kolpakchi, 1922–1924. 26 cm.
Edited by Lev Kolpakchi.
Covers by Petr Galadzhev.
Weekly magazine published by Kolpakchi and dedicated to theater, the music hall, the circus, mass action, theatrical acrobatics, Punch and Judy, and cinema. Contains reviews of Russian exhibitions in the West and articles on jazz music, Constructivist theater, and current trends in Western theater. Galadzhev was its chief illustrator and also produced many photomontages for the publication's cover. Includes work by Boris Arvatov, Osip Brik, Galadzhev, Aleksei Gan, Vsevolod Meyerhold, and Liubov' Popova.
A total of 89 issues published. Publisher varies. Continuation of *Ermitazh* (Hermitage [1922]).

866. ***Zvuchashchaia rakovina: Sbornik stikhov*** (Звучащая раковина: Сборник стихов / Sounding seashell: A collection of verse). St. Petersburg: [n.p.], 1922. 96 pp. 25 cm.
Cover by Elizaveta Dorfman.
Poems by members of Sounding Seashell, the poetry circle organized by Nikolai Gumilev, to whose memory the collection is dedicated.
From an edition of 1,000, of which 18 are personal copies reserved for close associates of Gumilev; Research Institute's copy is identified on the verso of the title page as that of Anna Nikolaevna Gumileva, the poet's second wife.

List of Cited Works

Akimov, V. M. et al. 1959–1972. *Russkie sovetskie pisateli-prozaiki: Biobibliograficheskii ukazatel'*. 7 vols. Leningrad: Gos. publichnaia biblioteka (vols. 1–3); Moscow: Kniga (vols. 4–7).

Azarkovich, V. G. et al., eds. 1965–. *Vystavki sovetskogo izobrazitel'nogo iskusstva: Spravochnik*. 4 vols. Moscow: Sovetskii khudozhnik.

Bakhin, M. G. et al., eds. 1975. *Mastera sovetskoi arkhitektury ob arkhitekture.* 2 vols. Moscow: Iskusstvo.

Biletskyi, Platon. 1985. *Georgii Ivanovich Narbut.* Leningrad: Iskusstvo.

Bowlt, John E., and Béatrice Hernad. 1993. *Aus vollem Halse: Russische Buchillustration und Typographie 1900–1930.* Munich: Prestel.

Chapon, François. 1978. "Bibliographie des livres imprimés édités par Iliazd." In *Iliazd: Centre Georges Pompidou, Musée national d'art moderne, 10 mai–25 juin 1978.* Exh. cat. Paris: Musée national d'art moderne.

Compton, Susan P. 1992. *Russian Avant-Garde Books, 1917–34.* London: British Library.

———. 1978. *The World Backwards: Russian Futurist Books, 1912–1916.* London: British Museum Publications.

Compton, Susan P., ed. 1977. *Russian Futurism, 1910–1916: Poetry and Manifestoes.* Cambridge: Chadwyck-Healey. Microfiche.

Ex Libris. 1977. *Constructivism and Futurism: Russian and Other.* Ex Libris, no. 6. New York: Ex Libris.

Golubeva, Ol'ga Dmitrievna et al., eds. 1977–. *Russkie sovetskie pisateli-poety: Biobibliograficheskii ukazatel'.* Vol. 1–. Moscow: Kniga.

Hellyer, Peter, ed. 1994. *A Catalogue of Russian Avant-Garde Books, 1912–1934.* London: The British Library.

Iatsunok, E. I. 1980. "Iz istorii prizhiznennykh izdanni A. A. Bloka." *Kniga* 41: 73–95.

Janecek, Gerald. 1984. *The Look of Russian Literature: Avant-Garde Visual Experiments, 1900–1930.* Princeton, N.J.: Princeton Univ. Press.

Jangfeldt, Bengt. 1976. *Majakovskij and Futurism, 1917–1921.* Stockholm: Almqvist & Wiksell International.

Karshan, Donald. 1975. *Malevich, the Graphic Work, 1913–1930: A Print Catalogue Raisonné.* Jerusalem: Israel Museum.

Katanian, Vasilii. 1985. *Maiakovskii: Khronika zhizni i deiatel'nosti.* 5th ed., enl. Moscow: Sov. pisatel'.

Khan-Magomedov, Selim Omarovich. 1986. *Rodchenko: The Complete Work.* London: Thames & Hudson.

———. 1990. *Vhutemas: Moscou, 1920–1930.* 2 vols. Paris: Editions du Regard.

Khardzhiev, Nikolai. 1968. "*Pamiati Natalii Goncharovoi (1881–1962) i Mikhaila Larionova (1881–1964).*" In *Iskusstvo knigi.* Moscow: Kniga.

Khardzhiev, Nikolai, Kazimir Malevich, and Mikhail Matiushin. 1976. *K istorii russkogo avangarda.* Stockholm: Gileia Prints; distributed by Almqvist & Wiksell International.

Knizhnaia letopis'. 1907–1977. 70 vols. Moscow: Glavnoe upravlenie po delam pechati.

Kovtun, Evgenii. 1987. "Experiments in Book Design by Russian Artists." *The Journal of Decorative and Propaganda Arts*, no. 5: 46–59.

———. 1989. *Russkaia futuristicheskaia kniga.* Moscow: Kniga.

Lavrent'ev, A. N. 1989. *A. M. Rodchenko, V. F. Stepanova.* Moscow: Kniga.

Le Gris-Bergmann, Françoise. 1987. *Kirill Zdanevich and Cubo-Futurism, Tiflis 1918–1920.* Exh. cat. New York: Rachel Adler Gallery.

Lissitzky, El. 1987. *El Lissitzky, 1890–1941: Catalogue for an Exhibition of Selected Works from North American Collections, the Sprengel Museum Hanover, and the Staatliche Galerie Moritzburg Halle.* Cambridge, Mass.: Harvard Univ. Art Museums, Busch-Reisinger Museum.

Lodder, Christina. 1983. *Russian Constructivism.* New Haven, Conn.: Yale Univ. Press.

Markov, Vladimir. 1968. *Russian Futurism: A History.* Berkeley: Univ. of California Press.

Parnis, Aleksandr. 1985. "100 let so dnia rozhdeniia [Velimira Khlebnikova]." *Pamiatnye knizhnye daty:* 165–69.

Roethel, Hans Konrad. 1970. *Kandinsky, das graphische Werk.* Cologne: DuMont Schauberg.

Rozanov, I. N. 1975. *Biblioteka russkoi poezii I. N. Rozanova.* Moscow: Kniga.

Severiukhin, D. Ia., and O. L. Leikind. 1992. *Zolotoi vek khudozhestvennykh ob"edinenii v Rossii i SSSR, 1820–1932.* Peterburg: Izd-vo Chernysheva.

Sidorov, A. A. 1923. *Russkaia grafika za gody revoliutsii, 1917–1922.* Moscow: Dom pechati.

Sillov, V. A. 1926. "Bibliografiia Velimira Khlebnikova, 1908–1925." In "*Nastoiashchee*": *Poema. Al'vek: Stikhi,* by Velimir Khlebnikov. Moscow: Izd. V. V. Khlebnikovoi.

Tarasenkov, Anatolii. 1966. *Russkie poety XX veka, 1900–1955: Bibliografiia.* Moscow: Sovetskii pisatel'.

Vroon, Ronald. 1993. Personal communication with David Woodruff.

List of Soviet Organizations and Acronyms

Adskaia mostovaia
Road to Hell

AKhR
Assotsiatsiia khudozhnikov revoliutsii / Association of Artists of the Revolution

AKhRR
Assotsiatsiia khudozhnikov revoliutsionnoi Rossii / Association of Artists of Revolutionary Russia

ARU
Ob"edinenie arkhitektorov urbanistov / Society of Urban Architects

ASIS
Assotsiatsiia sotsialisticheskogo iskusstva / Association of Socialist Art

ASNOVA
Assotsiatsiia novykh arkhitektorov / Association of New Architects

Assotsiatsiia rabotnikov revoliutsionnoi kinematografii
Association of Workers of Revolutionary Cinematography

Brigada gorkoma izo
City Council Art Brigade

Cheka
Chrezvychainaia komissiia po bor'be s kontr-revoliutsiei i sabotazhem / Extraordinary Commission to Combat Counterrevolution and Sabotage [predecessor of the KGB]

Chempionat poetov
Championship of Poets

Dekorativnyi institut
Decorative Arts Institute

DPR / Dom prinuditel'nykh rabot
Forced Labor House

EKOSO RSFSR
Ekonomicheskoe soveshchanie RSFSR
Economic Conference of the RSFSR

Federatsiia ob"edinenii rabotnikov prostranstvennykh iskusstv
Federation of Associations of Workers in the Spatial Arts

Federatsiia ob"edinenii sovetskikh pisatelei
Federation of Soviet Writers' Organizations

FOSKh
Federatsiia ob"edinenii sovetskikh khudozhnikov /
Federation of Soviet Artists' Associations

FOSKh
Federatsiia ob"edinenii sovetskikh rabotnikov prostranstvennykh iskusstv /
Federation of Soviet Workers in the Spatial Arts

Glavpolitprosvet
Glavnyi politiko-prosvetitel'nyi komitet narkomprosa RSFSR /
Main Political and Educational Committee of the Narkompros RSFSR

GOERLO
Gosudarstvennaia komissiia po elektrifikatsii Rossii / State Commission for the Electrification of Russia

Gosizdat
Gosudarstvennae izdatel'stvo / State Publishing House

INKhUK
Institut khudozhestvennoi kul'tury / Institute of Artistic Culture

Izogiz
Gosudarstvennoe izdatel'stvo izobrazitel'nogo iskusstva / State Publishing House for the Fine Arts

IZO Narkompros
Otdel izobrazitel'nykh iskusstv pri narodnom komissariate prosveshcheniia / Department of Visual Arts of the People's Commissariat for Education

IZORAM
Izobrazitel'noe iskusstvo rabochei molodezhi / Young Workers' Art Movement

Khudozhestvennyi sovet po delam kino pri Glavpolitprosvete
Artistic Council in Charge of Cinema Under Glavpolitprosvet

Komsomol
Kommunisticheskii soiuz molodezhi / Communist Youth League

LEF
Levyi front iskusstv / Left Front of the Arts

Liga "vremia"
"Time" League

LTsK
Literaturnyi tsentr konstruktivistov / Literary Center of the Constructivists

MAF
Moskovskaia assotsiatsiia futuristov / Moscow Association of Futurists

MAO
Moskovskoe arkhitekturnoe obshchestvo / Moscow Architectural Society

Mezhdunarodnoe biuro revoliutsionnoi literatury
International Bureau for Revolutionary Literature

Mezhdunarodnoe ob"edinenie revoliutsionnykh pisatelei
International Union of Revolutionary Writers

Mezhrabpom–Rus'
International Workers' Aid–Russia

Mir iskusstva
World of Art

Mishen'
Target

MIuD
Mezhdunarodnyi iunosheskii den' / International Youth Day

MONO
Moskovskii otdel narodnogo obrazovaniia / Moscow Department of Public Education

Moskovskaia assotsiatsiia khudozhnikov dekoratorov
Moscow Association of Scene Designers

Mosoblispolkom
Moskovskii oblastnoi ispolnitel'nyi komitet / Moscow District Executive Committee

MOSSKh
Moskovskii oblastnoi soiuz sovetskikh khudozhnikov / Moscow Regional Union of Soviet Artists

Narkompros
Narodnyi komissariat prosveshcheniia / People's Commissariat for Education

NKO USRR
People's Commissariat of Culture of the USRR

NKTP
Narodnyi komissariat tiazhëloi promyshlennosti / People's Commissariat for Heavy Industry

NOZh
Novoe obshchestvo zhivopistsev / New Society of Painters

Oblpolitprosvet
Oblastnoe politiko-prosvetitel'noe upravlenie /
Regional Political Education Administration

OBMOKhU
Obshchestvo molodykh khudozhnikov / Society of Young Artists

Obshchestvo arkhitektorov-khudozhnikov
Society of Artist-Architects

Obshchestvo khudozhnikov moskovskoi shkoly
Society of Artists of the Moscow School

Obshchestvo kinodeiatelei
Society of Cinema Workers

Obshchestvo liubitelei iskusstv
Society of Lovers of the Arts

Obshchestvo moskovskikh khudozhnikov
Society of Moscow Artists

ODSFK
Obshchestvo druzei sovetskoi fotografii i kinematografii /
Society of Friends of Soviet Photography and Cinematography

ODSK
Obshchestvo druzei sovetskogo kino i foto / Society of Friends of Soviet
Cinema and Photography

OKhS
Obshchestvo khudozhnikov samouchek / Self-Taught Artists Society

Oktiabr'
October

OPRA
Society of Proletarian Architects of Armenia

ORS
Obshchestvo russkikh skul'ptorov / Society of Russian Sculptors (the acronym for the English-language translation is SRS)

OSA
Ob"edinenie sovremennykh arkhitektorov / Union of Contemporary Architects

Oslinyi khvost
Donkey's Tail

OST
Obshchestvo khudozhnikov-stankovistov / Society of Easel Artists

Otdel tekhpropagandy stroitel'stva Dvortsa sovetov
Technical Propaganda Department of the Palace of Soviets Construction Project

Proletkul't
Proletarian Culture

RAKhN
Rossiiskaia Akademiia Khudozhestvennykh Nauk / Russian Academy of Artistic Sciences

RAPP
Rossiiskaia assotsiatsiia proletarskikh pisatelei / Russian Association of Proletarian Writers)

RGALI
Rossiiskii Gosudarstvennyi Arkhiv Literatury i Iskusstva / Russian State Archive for Literature and Art

ROSFIL
Rossiiskaia filarmoniia / Russian Philharmony

ROSTA
Rossiiskoe telegrafnoe agenstvo / Russian Telegraph Agency

RSFSR
Rossiiskaia Sovetskaia Federativnaia Sotsialisticheskaia Respublika / Russian Soviet Federative Socialist Republic

SASS
Sektor arkhitektorov sotsialisticheskogo stroitel'stva / Division of Architects for Socialist Construction

SNK
Sovet narodnykh komissarov / Council of People's Commissars

Soiuz arkhitektorov SSSR
Union of Architects of the USSR

Soiuz molodezhi
Union of Youth

Soiuz Sovetskikh arkhitektorov
Union of Soviet Architects

SOPO
Soiuz poetov / Poets Union

Sorabis
Soiuz rabotnikov iskusstv / Union of Art Workers

Spilka prolietars'kykh pys'mennykiv
Proletarian Writers' Union

SSKh
Soiuz Sovetskikh khudozhnikov / Union of Soviet Artists

Stroitel'naia komissiia ekonomicheskogo soveshchaniia RSFSR
Building Commission of the Economic Conference of the RSFSR

Suprematisty (Vitebsk)
Suprematists, from Vitebsk

Tiflisskoe obshchestvo iziashchnykh iskusstv
Tiflis Society of Fine Arts

TsIK SSSR
Tsentral'nyi ispolnitel'nyi komitet SSSR / Central Executive Committee of the USSR

TsKVLKSM
Tsentral'nyi Komitet Vsesoiuznogo Leninskogo Kommunisticheskogo Soiuza molodezhi / Central Committee of the All-Union Young Communist League

Union des artistes russes
Union of Russian Artists

UNOVIS
Utverditeli novogo iskusstva / Affirmers of the New Art

USRR
Ukrains'ka sotsialistychna radians'ka respublika / Ukrainian Socialist Soviet Republic

Venok
Wreath

VKhUTEIN
Vysshii gosudarstvennyi khudozhestvenno-tekhnicheskii institut / Higher State Art-Technical Institute

VKhUTEMAS
Vysshie Gosudarstvennye Khudozhestvennye Tekhnicheskie Masterskie / Higher State Artistic and Technical Workshops

VOPRA
Vsesoiuznoe ob"edinenie proletarskikh arkhitektorov / All-Union Association of Proletarian Architects

VPV
Vsesoiuznaia poligraficheskaia vystavka / All-Union Exhibition of the Printing Trades

Vserabis
Vsesoiuznyi soiuz rabotnikov iskusstv / All-Union Art Workers Union

Vserossiiskii kooperativnyi soiuz rabotnikov izobrazitel'nykh iskusstv
All-Russia Cooperative Union of Workers in the Visual Arts

VSP
Vserossiiskii soiuz poetov / All-Russia Poets Union

VUORRK
All-Ukrainian Organization of Cinema Workers

Index

Note: Bold numbers refer to pages of the introduction; all others refer to entry numbers in the bibliography.

Russian Modernism:
The Collections of the Getty Research Institute for the History of Art and the Humanities, 1
Introduction by Jean-Louis Cohen
Compiled by David Woodruff and Ljiljana Grubišić

Jean-Louis Cohen was born in Paris and received a doctorate in art history from the Ecole des Hautes Etudes en Sciences Sociales, Paris. He is a professor at the Université de Paris–VIII and is the Sheldon H. Solow Professor in the History of Architecture at the Institute of Fine Arts, New York University. He has curated exhibitions at the Centre Georges Pompidou and the Pavillon de l'Arsenal, as well as other museums, and has published on André Lurçat, Mies van der Rohe, Paris, and the history of architecture and town planning. His books include *Le Corbusier et la mystique de l'URSS* and *Scenes of the World to Come: European Architecture and the American Challenge, 1893–1960.*

David Woodruff completed his undergraduate studies at Harvard College and received masters degrees in Slavic languages and literatures and in library and information science from the University of California, Los Angeles. He is Special Collections Cataloger in the Resource Collections of the Getty Research Institute for the History of Art and the Humanities.

Ljiljana Grubišić studied at the University of Novi Sad, Yugoslavia, and received a doctorate in Slavic languages and literature from the University of Southern California, Los Angeles. She is a Serials Cataloger for specialized and rare art periodicals at the Getty Research Institute for the History of Art and the Humanities, where she also participates in the collection development of Russian Modernist holdings.

Bibliographies & Dossiers
In Preparation

Michael Roth, Charles Merewether, and Claire Lyons
Irresistible Decay: Ruins Reclaimed
ISBN 0-89236-468-8

Kevin Salatino
Incendiary Art: The Representation of Fireworks in Early Modern Europe
ISBN 0-89236-417-3

Designed by Bruce Mau with Chris Rowat.
Coordinated by Suzanne Watson Petralli.
Type composed by Archetype in Sabon.
Printed and bound by Thomson-Shore, Inc., on Cougar Opaque.
Color signature printed by Typecraft, Inc.

Bibliographies & Dossiers
Series designed by Bruce Mau Design Inc.